'*Rise & Resist* is the ideal handbook for the revolution. Clare Press has produced a thoroughly researched, engaging and exciting book, that will act as a template for the next phase of the current power-shift. From local to global, she interviews the players in the feminist and environmental movements, joining the dots on the biggest social change since the 1960s. This is an important and powerful work.'

Tracey Spicer

'Already known as a change-maker through her work in ethical fashion, Clare now tackles social justice and the climate movement in this elegantly crafted book. A necessary call to action on how we can reshape a more sustainable world.'

Katherine Keating

'The world needs everyday activists and this insightful book helps you navigate the issues from many angles.'

Natalie Isaacs

'These pages offer badassery, wit, courage and humour. A timely reminder to us all that if we don't like something, it's up to each of us to get off our arses and do something about it—this is pure inspiration as to what that little "something" might look like for you.'

Jess Miller

'Climate science can be intimidating but Clare makes it easy to comprehend. Entertaining, educational and absorbing, *Rise & Resist* is a fantastic read.'

Laura Wells

RISE
&
RESIST

RISE
&
RESIST

HOW TO
CHANGE
THE WORLD

CLARE
PRESS

MELBOURNE
UNIVERSITY
PRESS

MELBOURNE UNIVERSITY PRESS
An imprint of Melbourne University Publishing Limited
Level 1, 715 Swanston Street, Carlton, Victoria 3053, Australia
mup-contact@unimelb.edu.au
www.mup.com.au

First published 2018
Reprinted 2019
Text © Clare Press, 2018
Design and typography © Melbourne University Publishing Limited, 2018

Cover design by Sandy Cull, gogoGingko
Cover image courtesy Shutterstock
Typeset in 10/14pt Plantin Light by Cannon Typesetting
Printed in Australia by McPherson's Printing Group

 A catalogue record for this book is available from the National Library of Australia

9780522873733 (paperback)
9780522873740 (ebook)

Contents

'Take up the battle. Take it up. It's yours. This is your life. This is your world.'

—Maya Angelou, on *Oprah's Master Class*, 2011

'The future depends entirely on what each of us does every day. After all, a movement is only people moving.'

—Gloria Steinem, to *TIME* magazine, 1992

'We can change the world, we will change the world. The question is, in what direction?'

—Richard Denniss, on the *Wardrobe Crisis* podcast, 2017

Author's note

rise vb. rising, rose, risen. *1. to get up from a prone position; to revolt: the people rose against their oppressors*
resist vb. *1. to stand firm (against); not yield (to); fight*[1]

'What do we want? Reverse the cuts! When do we want it? Now!' In February 2018, the Country Women's Association of Western Australia staged the first political march in its 94-year history. Four hundred members of the organisation descended on Parliament House in Perth with placards, chanting to the tune of 'Waltzing Matilda', to protest cuts in rural education services. And I thought the CWA was all about baked goods.

This action came less than three weeks after tens of thousands gathered at Invasion Day protests across Australia, which in turn happened just five days after the second coming of the Women's Marches—the first iteration, the day after Donald Trump was sworn in as US president in January 2017, had erupted across the world twelve months previously. In between, there was barely a contentious issue that didn't have us rallying somewhere. In the United States in August 2017 alone, there were 834 different demonstrations, marches, strikes, sit-ins and rallies.[2] It's starting to feel like *not* protesting is the weird thing to do.

Researchers at Columbia University confirm that we are now living through a 'period of rising outrage and discontent', the likes of which we haven't seen since the late 1960s.[3] We are not happy with our lots, politically or socially. Established power structures seem elitist, remote and unfair.

Trump, for example, polled about 2.8 million fewer votes in the 2016 US election than his rival Hillary Clinton, but he still won. Forty-two per cent of the eligible population didn't even cast their ballots.

There are numerous examples of a widening gulf between what governments and big businesses pursue, and what citizens want. In Australia, the majority opposes Adani's Carmichael mega-mine,[4] which, if it goes ahead, will be at least 30 kilometres long and, at peak capacity, dig up 60 million tonnes of coal per annum, when we should be curbing carbon emissions, and yet both state and federal governments are pushing to get it over the line. Globally speaking, it is madness to keep burning fossil fuels, let alone commission new facilities to extract them. The icecaps are melting, the oceans are acidifying and global warming is accelerating, as scientists warn of 'biological annihilation' caused by human overpopulation and overconsumption, and the clearing and poisoning of natural wildlife habitats. Averting this is still just about possible, but 'the window is rapidly closing'.[5]

Meanwhile the gap between the super-rich and everyone else continues to grow. Tax avoidance at the top end of town is rife—more than a third of the 2000 largest companies operating in Australia paid zero corporate income tax here in 2015/16. Underfunded welfare services are showing the strain. There might be more jobs, but they are less secure and more often part-time. Most of those lucky enough to 'own' their own homes have mortgages they've no hope of paying off. We carry record levels of credit card debt. And for what? Our current consumerist model is a rort—we've been trained to unthinkingly buy mountains of stuff we don't need, then throw it away, adding to a gargantuan waste problem that's choking the oceans with plastic. Then there's the creeping suspicion that there's more to life than a new phone or pair of box-fresh sneakers. No wonder we feel cornered and powerless when faced with all this.

Depression, anxiety and loneliness are on the rise. The Red Cross warns that nearly one in four Australians are lonely almost all the time or on a regular basis. It's such a worry in the United Kingdom that the British government has appointed the world's first loneliness minister.[6] Single-person households are increasing in affluent countries, while we are more transient and less likely to know our neighbours than in previous generations. As socialising moves into the virtual space, entire relationships are lived online, with barely a need to meet in person.

In this context, joining marches makes perfect sense. The opportunity to discuss, stand and chant together, shoulder to shoulder with other human beings; to be both emotional and physically present—in person, in real time—around a deeply felt cause, carries a visceral thrill. And to be recorded, to literally be counted for being there, moves us. This way we can begin to take our power back. Marches are on the rise because of the political climate and mounting fears that if we don't start doing right by Mother Nature it will be too late, but also because we yearn to reconnect.

It's not just marches, of course. Activism is growing everywhere, and it's taking increasingly creative forms. Movements are building and linking together. The old silo mentality is falling away to be replaced by a new web of connectivity. The veteran American feminist Gloria Steinem has been talking for years about the need to connect social and climate-justice movements. The young Peruvian activist Maria Alejandra Rodriguez Acha believes it's finally happening, as young women in particular are increasingly making spaces to 'to discuss our roles and experiences in climate advocacy, environmental activism and feminist movements'.[7] The Women's March organisation also brings those threads together. One of its board members, Carmen Perez, calls the marches 'an entry point for a new wave of activism'[8]—it worked for me. It was witnessing the excitement rising all over the world in the run-up to the Women's March on Washington that got me thinking about this book.

I set out to explore what the new activism looks like, not just at the rallies and protests but beyond them. On country, online, off-grid, in yarn shops, at food co-ops, on organic veggie patches, at the beach, in our civic buildings, schools, public spaces and communities, and ultimately in our hearts, where a new counterculture is forming.

I sought out people who are leading and joining these cross-movements, interviewing some by Skype or phone, others in person. I took myself along to as many marches and actions as possible, and even staged one myself. There were a few moments when I felt like the universe was looking out for me, as when May Boeve, the California-based cofounder of climate action group 350.org (whose name was top of my interview wish list) turned up in Sydney to speak at a university event—I booked myself a ticket, then pounced. In Adelaide for work, I drove out to visit the founder of the Grow Free movement. I flew to New Zealand to interview a 'tiny house' builder and stay with a family living off-grid in a yurt. In a few cases, as with the story of the American student gun-control activists behind March for Our Lives, I wrote about events from afar, glued to the international news coverage with my heart in my mouth and my mascara running. How could these kids, who are survivors of the Parkland school shooting, be so brave and so wonderful? I found myself thinking, If the future's in their hands, it is bright. I was not a guest at the Golden Globes when the Time's Up Now campaign launched, but I was at the Stop Adani marches that happened in Australia in October 2017. I've been involved with the Fashion Revolution movement since it began in 2014. I enrolled online in Resistance School at the University of California, Berkeley. I campaign against ocean plastic in real life, every day.

There are lots of different causes and stories in this book. You can't take them all up, but if you find one that resonates, that tugs at you, gets under your skin and inspires you to go out into your own community and make positive change, I've done my job.

Rise & Resist is the title, the beginning of the journey if you like, but where we're headed is a step further—to a world reshaped and reimagined.

A word on language

I have chosen to capitalise Black but not white in this book, in order to centre anti-racism. While we do not have equality, these terms are not equal, and as my friend Kimberly Jenkins, a New York–based lecturer on fashion history, theory and race, advises, 'language plays a crucial role in how we identify ourselves as we navigate society and various spaces'. As a white woman, I take my cue from several inspirational Black writers, including Lori L. Tharps, who notes in *The New York Times*, 'Black should always be written with a capital B. We are indeed a people, a race, a tribe. It's only correct.'

With regards to my use of the terms LGBTQ, LGBTQI, LGBTQIA and queer, I have been guided by those about whom I am writing, and, in each case, used the terms that they prefer.

Last but not least, Nature. I have capitalised the 'N' throughout to show my respect for her. And yes, I see her as feminine. No apologies there.

1

The Pussyhat Project

You will need
Yarn: Malabrigo Worsted (210 yd per 100 grams), in Fuchsia Pink,
1 skein (any shade of pink & any worsted weight yarn will do)
Needles: US 8/5mm, straight

Vital signs

Some of us planned it; others were swept up in the moment. On that greyest of British days, the third Saturday after New Year, when there were no more Quality Street left in the box, I was at London's King's Cross station waiting for the 11.05 to Leeds.

To pass the time I counted the number of people wearing dark colours (everyone), then the ones who looked miserable (same), and it was into this scene of soul-destroying drabness that three young women hurtled in knitted pink beanies, scarves flying, placards at the ready, warning, 'The future is nasty!' and 'Together we rise.' They were obviously on their way to the London Women's March event, which culminated in a peaceful, hundred-thousand-strong gathering at Trafalgar Square. They were wonderful.

One of them dropped a glove, and as she ducked to retrieve it, the orange neon sign she was clutching twisted towards me. It showed civil rights activist and 1970s counterculture icon Angela Y. Davis punching the air, alongside the slogan 'I'm no longer accepting things I cannot change. I'm changing the things I cannot accept.' It took me all of two seconds to decide to run after them. There would be other trains.

I caught them up and asked why they were marching. The event, initially inspired by Trump's election, had quickly gathered momentum and gone global, gathering issues as it went. The reasons tumbled forth. The women talked about 'a line in the sand' and said this was the moment for standing up to the unjust patriarchy, a day they would tell their children about. If they decided to have children. My body, my choice. They'd had enough of casual sexism and rape culture and feeling afraid to walk home in the dark. They were fed up with systemic racism too, and with the glaring disconnect between the powers that be and everyone else. We talked about our fears for the safety of minorities under the new hardline regimes, and the likelihood that we were headed backwards on women's rights. I was the one who brought up Trump.

The previous day, Donald J. Trump had been sworn in as the forty-fifth president of the United States of America. At seventy, he was the oldest in history to assume the office and, after a campaign characterised by bullying, scaremongering and pandering to fears of 'the other', one of its most divisive. Trump campaigned like the reality television star that he was: as outrageously as possible, to boost the ratings, forging a culture of fear fuelled by the lowest sort of anti-immigration rhetoric and misogyny.

One of his tricks was to focus on the looks and sex appeal of his female foes. He called these women 'nasty' and 'unattractive'; he once told a female journalist she had 'the face of a dog!' He tweeted of his presidential rival, 'If Hillary Clinton can't satisfy her husband, what makes her think she can satisfy America?' Time and again, Trump proved himself uncomfortable and inappropriate in female company. He finds the idea of breastfeeding 'disgusting' but thought it was 'natural' for beauty pageant contestants to flirt with him, as the owner of those pageants. He joked about dating his own daughter, and criticised older women for supposedly losing their looks: 'Heidi Klum. Sadly, she's no longer a 10.' Objectifying women became par for the course; sexual assault something to joke about. It may yet be his undoing, but during the campaign the exposure of a 2005 video in which Trump brags, 'When you're a star, they let you do it … Grab 'em by the pussy. You can do anything' did not stop him winning.

And so the placards read, 'Super Callous Fascist Racist Extra Braggadocious.' They read, 'A Woman's Place is in the Resistance' and 'Love Trumps Hate.' They read, 'This pussy grabs back.'

'Yeah, him,' said the woman in the train station who was brandishing Angela Davis like a promise. We were none of us happy about him. 'But let's not give him the credit, eh?' she said. Trump was just the spark that lit the fuse.

There were wide-ranging reasons that people of all genders joined the Women's March protests across the world on 21 January 2017. Here are some, as documented by *The Guardian*: in Florence, Edward marched 'for women's rights and human rights [and] … against climate change'.[1] In Prague, Andreea warned that Trump 'is bad news not only for Muslim, Black, Mexican [and] LGBTQI [people] but for the entire planet'. In Paris, Maggie was concerned about 'climate disaster and human rights violations'. Others raised concerns over Brexit, corporate greed and discrimination in general. They were heeding the Women's March organisation's rallying call: 'To show up and be counted as those who believe in a world that is equitable, tolerant, just and safe for all, one in which the human rights and the dignity of each person is protected and our planet is safe from destruction.'

The marches were about all the unfair bullshit our young people have inherited: entrenched racism, gender and class inequality, and the rich getting richer as they sell us up the river they're polluting; as they deny climate change, trash our wild spaces and gamble on our future, while telling us, 'This is for your own good. It's what the market demands. This is how we safeguard your jobs.' The marches were about the lies we are told (and that we also tell ourselves) to keep the system in place: That the future of work will look anything like it does today. That natural resources aren't finite. That shopping will make us feel better, and it's our duty to spend 'for the good of the economy'. That we're better off than ever before. And happier. That women can have it all!

So we gathered our courage and our indignation, we gathered our sisters, our mothers, our daughters and our allies, we made our placards and banners and donned our slogan T-shirts and badges, and we marched.

Exactly how many people are we talking about? The logistics of counting them are tricky, involving not just satellite images and pictures taken from helicopters and drones, but counting the numbers of heads, one by one, in specific areas of the photographs. American political scientists Erica Chenoweth and Jeremy Pressman started a Google spreadsheet to amalgamate the data. They figure the 'best guess' is that 4.5 million people turned out across the world.[2] Maybe it was closer 5.7 million.

Let's err on the side of caution, so that Trump does not accuse us of fake news. At the main event in Washington, DC, the best guess is that 725,000 protestors thronged the National Mall and filled the Ellipse in front of the White House, where Gloria Steinem and Madonna spoke. In the run-up, sister events were announced from London to Lisbon to Lima, from Kenya's Karura Forest to Kolkata in India. 'Yes! Antarctica will have a march!' promised organisers; they were expecting at least 670 separate marches around the world. But according to Chenoweth and Pressman's data, those projections were conservative. In the end, events took place in 915 towns and cities worldwide.

Nearly half a million turned out in downtown Los Angeles, marching from Pershing Square to City Hall, to hear speakers from Congress, City Council and organisations like Planned Parenthood; at least 400,000 rallied outside Trump Tower in New York. In Australia, 10,000 marched in Melbourne, and another 7000 in Sydney. More than 3000 marchers hit New Zealand's streets. The numbers were much smaller in South America, Africa, Asia and the Middle East, but protests happened there too. Ninety-seven people marched in the Balinese town of Ubud, 300 in the Qatari capital, Doha.

No one counted how many marchers wore pink knitted 'pussyhats', but we know it was plenty. Seen from the air, Washington, DC was a sea of pink.

From little things, big things grow

It didn't look like a hotbed of political activism. The Little Knittery yarn store was on a busy stretch of Glendale Boulevard in LA's gentrified Atwater Village. Next door to an organic café where the salad bowls included massaged kale, and a rustic-chic furniture place that sold old Moroccan grain sacks as wall art and called such things interiors 'accents'. And yet. The Little Knittery was a radical establishment. The Little Knittery changed the fucking world.

On 10 November 2016, two days after Trump's election, friends Krista Suh and Jayna Zweiman joined the store's owner Kat Coyle around her communal table, surrounded by open shelving crammed with squashy balls of coloured yarn and the agreeable creative mess of crafting-in-progress. They planned to knit away their anxiety and frustration over the news. It didn't work.

Zweiman, thirty-seven, found her worldview shaken by the rise of Trump. She'd been raised 'to believe in equality, dignity and respect'; her mother was an attorney who'd sat on the board of a local women's refuge. 'I grew up thinking her generation fought the equality battles for us and if they didn't exactly win, made some serious headway. Like, thanks Mom, thanks suffragettes, you got this.'[3]

After graduating with a Masters in architecture from Harvard, Zweiman realised there was still a way to go, even for her as a privileged, tertiary-educated white woman. 'Construction, you know? It's a boy's club,' she tells me over Skype. 'Women are often relegated more towards interiors.' Blokes erect skyscrapers; women and gay men fuss around with the wall art. Seriously? Seriously.

In 2010 Zweiman and a male architect friend Christian Stayner curated an art show inspired by sexism in their field. Borrowing from the structure of Lucy Lippard's 1973 exhibition about the lack of women celebrated by the conceptual art world, they called the show '13.3% is an exasperated reply to those who say: "there are no women making architecture."' The 13 per cent bit refers to how many women in the United States were registered architects at the time. In 2017, architecture was still a male-dominated profession. 'It takes a while,' says Zweiman, 'but it's changing.' She had retained her fundamental belief that most people support fairness and equality. Trump's misogynistic posturing was upsetting, but it was surely fringe stuff. I mean, come on.

Politically, Zweiman is liberal-leaning. At college, during Bill Clinton's presidency, she interned at the White House's National Economic Council. In the 2016 election, she voted for Hillary. 'I really thought we'd see our first female president.'

Of course, Hillary Clinton was not the perfect candidate (there is no such thing): too white, too 'establishment' and too late to bring intersectionality into the conversation. Political blogger Imani Gandy summed it up for many women of colour when she told *Vox*, 'The election of a white woman to the highest office doesn't say a whole lot about my feminism.'[4] Millennials were similarly lukewarm. In her book *The Destruction of Hillary Clinton*, Susan Bordo argues that 'what was perceived as [Clinton's] membership in the dominant class, all cleaned up and normalised, aligned with establishment power rather than the forces of resistance, and stylistically coded (her tightly coiffed hair; her neat, boring pantsuits; her circumspection)' put the younger generation off.[5] The majority of millennials who voted for Clinton did so grudgingly, as the best of two bad options. She won 55 per cent of the youth vote, but only 18 per cent were excited about their candidate.[6]

Yet, as *Slate* columnist Michelle Goldberg notes, Clinton 'proposed policies that would have increased women's power and autonomy at every level of society: equal pay, paid family leave, subsidized child care, abortion rights ... The arc of history was bending toward women,' but Trump's victory 'obliterated this narrative,' she writes.[7] 'The very idea that women are equal citizens, that barriers to their full human flourishing should be identified and removed, is now up for grabs.' Not good, not good at all.

Krista Suh, then twenty-nine, was gutted. 'I kept thinking about the cultural element of what the White House represents, and it just really saddened me. I imagined a high-school volleyball team. Sometimes, if you win a national championship, you get to visit the White House and meet the president, and I just couldn't imagine being the parent of one of those children. You'd be so proud of them, but do you let them go to the White House? I'm thinking not.'[8] She resolved to do something about it. Maybe with knitting needles. Suh was kind of obsessed with the Little Knittery. 'Krista got the special parking spot, she went so much,' jokes Zweiman.

A screenwriter trying to break into the Hollywood bigtime, Suh combines a love for hot pink and glitter with a sharp wit and a serious brain. She is proof that a taste for sartorially girlish clichés has nothing to do with how strong and capable you are, or how effective a feminist you can be. Krista Suh is a woman of action. The child of a 'classic Asian tiger mom', she is a Mensa member with a degree in art history, who 'wasted years' trying to be 'the exceptional woman' before she figured out that she wasn't interested in competing on the patriarchy's terms. Giving up on that left Suh with a rebellious streak.

She developed a theory inspired by her favourite Disney princess, Cinderella. The story offers a useful analogy for young, career-minded, middle-class feminists like Suh. 'We can't play by the rules of the patriarchy in order to topple it,' Suh tells me. 'When Cinderella wants to go to the ball, her stepmother says, "Well, of course you can go, so long as you find something appropriate to wear and finish all your chores first." And Cinderella, like so many of us, is like, "Yeah, I can totally do that." But it's a trick. First of all, they give her so many chores she can barely finish; then when she does finish with the help of her friends and she gets that dress, they literally tear it off her back.' Suh saw parallels in her own experience. 'It's basically bullshit,' she says. 'Like, "Oh women, you can succeed if you get a degree and have a great social-media presence, and also have a family and do all the chores, and look the part, except that it doesn't really matter what you wear; it will always be too short or too long ... " It's a fake obstacle course to give the appearance of being fair.'

Coming up with creative ways to protest what Trump represented felt like giving that entire system the finger. Elton John and other musicians were making it known that they would decline invitations to perform at Trump's inauguration. Fashion designers including Tom Ford and Marc Jacobs said they'd refuse to dress the First Lady. Suh 'felt really proud' that artists were taking a stand. 'We resist in the different ways we can.'

Resistance spreading

The month before the election, Libby Chamberlain, a 33-year-old working mum from Maine, set up a private Facebook group called Pantsuit Nation in honour of Clinton's signature outfits. 'We talked about how beautifully and stoically Hillary embodies women's fight for equality, and how the pantsuit is an emblem of that struggle,' she told CNN.[9] The group started with thirty members; by election day, there were more than three million. Members shared their experiences, hopes and fears, and memes about the trouser suits; they raised money for the Clinton campaign, and the ire of critics who thought their activism wasn't active enough.

Daily Beast senior editor Erin Gloria Ryan describes it as 'a space for white people to pat each other on the head for acting in a manner most woke'.[10] But whether or not you were mad at Chamberlain for failing to police the tone of every member of the group (or for daring to sign a book deal, which she did two months in, making a lot of pantsuiters very cross indeed), Pantsuit Nation facilitated something big.

It was via this Facebook group, on 9 November, that a retired attorney from Hawaii named Teresa Shook posted her resistance idea. 'I think we should march,' she wrote. The next day, she set up her own event page, which quickly went from forty to 10,000 RSVPs. At the same time, Brooklyn fashion designer Bob Bland was rallying her own following. She had proved herself a swift actor after Trump called Clinton a 'nasty woman' during a debate in October; Bland screen-printed T-shirts with 'Nasty women vote' to raise money for Planned Parenthood. She reached out to Shook, they combined their events, and word spread. After that it snowballed. By 20 November, the movement had four co-chairs and a name: Women's March on Washington (an earlier idea to call it the Million Women March nearly sunk it; it was appropriated. The original Million Woman March was organised by Black women in Philadelphia in 1997.)

Joining Bland as co-chairs were three female activists who'd worked together for years through The Gathering For Justice, an organisation that fights racism in the criminal-justice system: civil rights activist Carmen Perez, Linda Sarsour, then executive director of the Arab American Association of New York, and Tamika Mallory, known for her galvanising speeches on gun control, race and feminism. They were building the movement together, and reaching out to a network of like-minded organisers ready to help. They put out stirring mission statements and press releases defining their positions on issues such as immigrant rights and environmental justice. Buses were organised to bring marchers to Washington, while committees planned sister marches in other cities. It was not until the end of December that Gloria Steinem was announced as an honorary co-chair, and organisers waited until a few days before the event to confirm that Angela Davis would speak, but the buzz was steadily building. Everyone was talking about it, including at the Little Knittery.

Suh resolved to go to Washington, but she wanted to bring something extra. 'Krista was full of ideas,' recalls Zweiman. 'She was talking about stripping naked.'

That summer, photographer Spencer Tunick had staged a demo in Cleveland on a patch of scrubland opposite the Republican National Convention venue. As dawn broke, 100 nude 'women art warriors' held mirrored discs aloft 'reflecting the knowledge and wisdom of progressive women and the concept of "Mother Nature" into and onto the convention center, cityscape and horizon'. According to Tunick's website, over 1800 women signed up for a hundred available spaces 'to bare all in this heightened arena of politics and protest'.

Washington in winter would be less appealing; January temperatures are chilly. Zweiman wouldn't be there anyway, even in clothes. She was recovering from a freak accident. Three years earlier she'd been shopping with her husband when a metal pole fell off a wall and knocked her out. She developed post-concussion syndrome, which lasted longer than expected. She suffered headaches, tired easily and found it tricky to travel. There was a lot of lying around in darkened rooms. 'It was very isolating,' she says.

Knitting offered respite. It was something creative and enjoyable she could do that also helped with her cognitive skills. She'd learned the skill while at Harvard, after winning a grant to study sculptural knitting at the Haystack Mountain School of Crafts. That was knitting intellectualised, an exploration of form. 'It was about looking at the relationship between a line, a surface and an object. I was interested in coding and how knits and purls are like 0s and 1s,' she explains. (It's not as unlikely as it sounds. Two British maths teachers have been using knitting since the mid-1990s to visually express concepts like curvature and how numbers relate to one another; they call themselves 'mathkniticians'.)

But by the autumn of 2016, knitting was about more personal problem-solving for Zweiman. It cheered her up. She persuaded Suh, the ex-girlfriend of one of her friends, to take some crochet classes with her at the Little Knittery, and they both enjoyed the vibe there. 'It's like a clubhouse,' says Zweiman. 'Kat creates this atmosphere where you can stop by and hang out whenever you want. You go at your own pace; you don't have to be good, and you're doing this thing—the act of knitting or crocheting an item—alone, but also together.' Something deep was at play here: Zweiman understood that the Little Knittery was building community.

Historically, some snide critics have dismissed knitting circles as mere forums for female gossip. Others have gone further, belittling female crafters as almost-nutters, teetering on the brink of feminine hysteria, towards which they would surely careen, blushing and sobbing and quivering as their minds unravelled, were it not for the safe, grounding practice of repetitively clicking their wooden needles together. Can you imagine the mayhem we women would cause without domestic tasks to keep us sane?

Naomi Wolf argues in *The Beauty Myth* that crafting, like fashion, is one of the tools that's been used to keep middle-class Western women 'enclosed' in the feminine sphere—via that 'cloying domestic fiction of "togetherness"'—since the Industrial Revolution.[11] Keeping us busy with lace-making, needlepoint or the latest dress styles prevented us from thinking about sex or, god forbid, reading.

In *No Idle Hands: The social history of American knitting*, Anne L. Macdonald quotes from a needlework handbook from the 1880s: 'With some women brain-work is impossible. It produces all sorts of diseases and makes them at once a nervous wreck … The quiet, even, regular motion of the needles quiets the nerves and tranquilizes the mind and lets thought flow freely.'[12]

I can't even. But knitting circles do encourage talking together and sharing stories and confidences over time, while knitting's repetitive hand action does have a meditative effect that can help the practitioner to manage pain, boost memory and, most importantly for our purposes, focus their thoughts. If you're trying to figure out how to change the world, you could do worse than knit while you do so.

Suh points out that knitting takes time and commitment, and 'you see the signs of progress, right in front of you … that's what [a] movement needs'. Zweiman, the architect, reads it 'in terms of projects not objects. How do people connect with each other? How can you create an urban network? How do you harness spaces and change spaces?'

In *Blessed Unrest*, his 2007 exploration of community activism, the American environmentalist Paul Hawken writes, 'We are moving from a world created by privilege to a world created by community.' He offers the work of biologist Mahlon Hoagland as a frame for understanding the role that grass-roots community activities can play in growing momentum for change:

> Life builds from the bottom up. Just as complex organisms are built of cooperating communities of cells, [movements are] built up by small, cooperating groups of people. Just as cell communities in the body attend to different functions, from taste buds to kidneys; groups organize around specific causes, missions, and objectives.[13]

Dismiss a roomful of women knitting at your peril, because they know how to link to other roomfuls of like-minded women, and before you know it: boom!

When Suh came up with the idea for a mass hat-knitting project, Zweiman was reminded of Spencer Tunick. In 2002 she'd been living in Santiago when the photographer staged a happening there in collaboration with the Museo de Arte Contemporáneo. Previous events in São Paolo, Montréal and London had been well received, with laudatory pieces in art magazines, but Chile at that time was conservative after years of military rule (General Augusto Pinochet was commander-in-chief until 1998) and Tunick's naked ambitions caused offence. Lawyers tried to stop the disrobing and Evangelical Christians protested outside Tunick's hotel. Few predicted 5000 people would show up in their birthday suits and transform the event into a freedom rally, singing the Chilean national anthem. 'It changed the conversation,' says Zweiman.

Christo and Jeanne-Claude's 2005 artwork *The Gates* was another inspiration. The duo, famed for wrapping landmarks in fabric, set up more than 7500 saffron-coloured, fabric-draped archways in New York's Central Park. 'The shocking bright colour, in the middle of the winter, had this joyful power,' says Zweiman.

Suh wanted to harness the power of the knitting community to create a visual symbol for the Women's Marches that would bring a similarly impactful pop of colour to Washington, DC. They chose pink, says Suh, 'because today it represents the opposite of any patriarchal ideal,' although 'a few hundred years ago pink represented fire and the blood from war, and kings wore it. Blue was for girls, like the Virgin Mary.'

Hats could be knitted by people who planned to attend a march and wear them, but also by those, like Zweiman, who were unable to attend. Knitters could send hats in their place as proxies. The project would 'provide women's rights supporters a way to come together in a virtual march to represent themselves, connect, and support women's rights, whether or not they are physically marching.'

It was Kat Coyle who came up with the name, and it was not over-thought. Tasked with designing the simplest hat pattern for the greatest take-up by makers of all skill levels, she plumped for a rectangle. When you put your head inside it, the two top corners stick up like little cat ears. Cat hat, pussycat hat, pussyhat. Grab one of these, Mr President.

On 22 November, Suh and Zweiman launched the Pussyhat Project online, with a manifesto illustrated by LA artist Aurora Lady and a free pattern to knit a 'pussyhat', created by Coyle. They called on us to 'Make a hat! Give a hat! Wear your hat! Share a hat!' Makers dispatching hats were encouraged, but not obliged, to include a note to share their story, or thoughts on a motivating issue. Soon, members of the community were adding patterns for crocheting and sewing hats, and translating them into different languages.

'The women's rights movement is not a one-issue thing,' says Zweiman. 'The note template allowed knitters to write about whatever they wanted to share, and reach another person directly. So, "I care about girls' education," or "I care about Planned Parenthood," and here's why.'

'The reason why we're marching, organising, protesting is that we care about each other,' says Suh. It's this community aspect that gave the Pussyhat Project wings. One woman wrote that knitting a hat helped bring her out of depression. Another explained that she couldn't make it to Washington because of post-traumatic stress disorder from being raped;

making the hats allowed her to take part in spirit. 'We got boxes like that day in, day out,' says Suh. In the planning stages, they 'understood the breadth of the project and that it was going to spread, but not its depth.'

An older woman who'd marched passed away shortly afterwards and was buried in her pussyhat. 'That was very moving,' says Suh, who now talks about the project in terms of a baby that grew up and left home. 'Yes, I made this child, but what the child has done since is way beyond what I could have done [as an] individual.' She says she was 'very determined to not be an Asian tiger mom to my child. I would talk to it, like, "I'm going to be proud of you whether you are this small or this big, or whatever."'

Krista Suh is five feet tall. When she arrived at the Washington march, a photographer helped her climb onto the guard rail to get a better look. And there it was: the jubilant, peaceful, rolling swell of pink she'd dreamed about. It wasn't a surprise. 'A lot of people ask me that: did we know it would be big? I think the right answer, the one they want to hear, is, "Oh golly no. It was just a little project I did with my friends and it completely surprised us when it took off." But honestly? I knew.'

It was clear from social media, where knitters shared snaps and videos overflowing with participants and pink wool. It was clear from Ravelry, the seven million–strong online community for knitters, crocheters, designers, spinners, weavers and dyers, which Zweiman describes as 'Facebook for knitters'.[14] After Kat Coyle posted on her Ravelry page, thousands of users shared their progress and pattern tweaks.

Knitting meet-ups spread across America and overseas, and the story went viral. CNN brought a film crew to the Little Knittery. People were making the hats alone in their pyjamas in Nebraska, on the plane to Indiana for the holidays, and in groups in coffee shops and yarn stores from Brooklyn to Belgium. Punk icon Patti Smith was seen wearing a pink pussyhat. Madonna got hold of a black one. In February, the Italian fashion house Missoni, famed for its chic knitwear, closed its Autumn 2017 runway show at Milan Fashion Week with every single model sporting a designer pussyhat.

TIME magazine made the hat a cover star, for a story titled: 'The resistance rises—how a march becomes a movement.' The Victoria and Albert Museum in London acquired a hat, noting its status as an 'immediately recognisable expression of female solidarity'. The Fuller Craft Museum in New England planned an entire exhibition around it. *Revolution in the Making: The Pussyhat Project* opened in January 2018 telling the story of 'the largest example of social activism through craft in US modern history'.

In Sydney, the Museum of Applied Arts and Sciences partnered with the Women's Electoral Lobby (Australia's oldest women's rights organisation) to hold a pussyhat knitting circle for International Women's Day 2017. The museum acquired a pussyhat for its permanent collection, knitted and donated by one of the country's feminist icons, Anne Summers. But if Krista Suh had an inkling that this idea of hers was going to be big, she didn't anticipate the ways in which it might offend.

Anne Summers takes up needles

You can't keep everyone happy. In Tennessee, a church lady who owns a yarn store called The Joy of Knitting told customers seeking pink wool to shop elsewhere. It was her Christian duty, she explained, to oppose 'the vulgarity, vile [sic] and evilness of this [Pussyhat] movement'. That's her prerogative, just as its mine not to name her—a little rebellion, like Tamika Mallory's refusal to say Trump's name. She calls him 'Number-forty-whatever-it-is, the orange man in the White House'.

Some women worried that the hats were a distraction from the more pressing issues that inspired the marches. 'The infantilizing kitten imagery combined with a stereotypically feminine color feels too safe and too reductive to be an answer to the complex issues facing women today,' writes Holly Derr in *Bitch Media*.[15] Others complained that the Pussyhat Project is frivolous or silly, to which Suh says, 'The fact that we have a sense of humour shows we haven't succumbed to the gloom that they are imposing on us. That in itself is an act of resistance: to laugh.'

The odd hater was angry that knitting was even a thing, arguing that anyone struggling to balance work, pay the bills and raise kids has no time to indulge in the luxury of a craft hobby. To which I say, if you've got time to watch *The Bachelorette* ...

The thorniest questions lie with the representation debate: Is the pussy-hat gender essentialist? Does it reduce women to their body parts and exclude those who don't have 'pussies'?

'We're not actually putting vaginas on our heads; we're putting hats shaped like cat ears on our heads,' counters Zweiman. 'I am sorry if anyone felt excluded by it. Our intention was always inclusion. Everyone's welcome, cisgender, the trans community, men. We don't make a distinction. Anyone could put the pussyhat on.'

How about Black freedom fighter and former slave Harriet Tubman? On the first anniversary of the Women's Marches, someone put a pussyhat on Tubman's statue in New York, prompting reactions on Twitter ranging from 'That's the problem w/ identity politics, it's based on symbolic actions that tap into sensory displays while changing nothing at all' to 'Harriet Tubman was a disabled black woman, an enslaved person who risked her life to free other enslaved people. Keep your cutesy symbol of cisnormative, white normative, made-a-supposedly-subversive-joke-about-sexual-assault accessories off her head.'[16]

The problem, as writer Collier Meyerson points out in her insightful essay 'Pulling the wool over their eyes: The blindness of white feminism', is that 'straight, white, middle-class women have long dominated feminism's main stage, and so have their issues.'[17]

I phone up Anne Summers to ask how best to navigate the gender essentialism conversation, admitting I've spent days writing and deleting passages from this chapter for fear of causing offence. She responds, 'Oh boo hoo! It's an absurd argument. I was at an event at the weekend wearing my pink pussyhat and someone in the audience shouted, "Not everybody's got a pussy and not every pussy is pink!" So what? That's got nothing to do with anything. The hat is a symbol. It's a gesture of protest, and it's not meant to match anybody's anatomy.'[18]

Summers is the author of *Damned Whores and God's Police*, published in 1975 and informed by her experiences in the women's liberation movement and helping to set up Australia's first women's refuge in the early 1970s, when 'we had immense faith that we really could change the world.' In the 1980s, Summers ran Australia's Office for the Status of Women, then became editor of *Ms* magazine in New York (which Steinem, Dorothy Pitman Hughes and others founded in 1971). In her 2013 book *The Misogyny Factor*, Summers argues that what she dubs 'the Equality Project' has not yet succeeded because women are still not included in all areas of our society, or treated equally and with respect once they are there.

Anne Summers knitted thirteen pink pussyhats. She says that movements benefit from visual symbols. 'We used to screen-print T-shirts to wear at demonstrations. We embroidered banners. The history of protest has always had an element of creativity to it, whether it's silk screening or painting or embroidering or knitting or crocheting. We put our skills to use in order to make comment, to make symbols and to display our feelings via these symbols.'

The pussyhat, she writes in *The Sydney Morning Herald*, 'has the potential to become as potent an international symbol of protest and resistance as the iconic 1960 Alberto Korda photograph of Che Guevara that has for decades adorned millions of T-shirts, or the early emblem of the women's liberation movement: the clenched fist inside the symbol for women.'[19]

Which leaves us with the word. Can we really reclaim it? Since Trump let the cat out of the bag, we have no choice. Before the Pussyhat Project was born, *The Washington Post* was reporting that children as young as six were asking their parents what it means to grab someone by the pussy. In their manifesto, Suh and Zweiman say they chose the word because they wanted to reclaim it as a means of empowerment. 'A woman's body is her own. We are honouring this truth and standing up for our rights.'

Before Trump's locker-room talk was exposed, '*pussy* was a word women didn't use,' Summers tells me, 'a word that was meant to demean us'. She describes the hats and their adoption by 'so many women and such a range of women' in 2017 as 'an incredible act of defiance and reclamation', drawing parallels with how the suffragettes embraced the name they were given by detractors in 1906.

The first Australian women won the right to vote in 1895 (in South Australia, including Indigenous women. It went downhill from there though for Indigenous suffrage; the *Commonwealth Franchise Act 1902*, while extending votes for women to New South Wales, Tasmania, Queensland and Victoria, denied the vote to Indigenous people who were not already on state rolls. This injustice was not fully rectified until 1965).

In America, while Susan B. Anthony and Elizabeth Cady Stanton were campaigning for women's rights in the 1850s and '60s, progress was glacial. Suffragists protested Woodrow Wilson's inauguration in 1913, when in scenes foreshadowing those described at the beginning of this book, thousands of women marched on the White House led by Alice Paul's National American Woman Suffrage Association. These early marchers were not, however, accorded the same respect: harassed and attacked by male onlookers, at least a hundred women ended up in hospital. And there was something else: Alice Paul purposefully excluded Black women. It was not until 1920 that the Nineteenth Amendment outlawed the denial of the

1st womens march

15

right to vote on the basis of sex. But even then, there were ways round it, and many Black American women were also effectively disenfranchised until 1965.

In the early twentieth century, the campaign gathered pace in Britain after the National Union of Women's Suffrage Societies brought together various groups in 1897. Emmeline Pankhurst and her daughters Christabel and Sylvia formed the more radical Women's Social and Political Union (WSPU) in 1903. While the former was in favour of leafleting and signing petitions, the Pankhursts and their followers engaged in disruptive direct action: 'deeds not words'.

'*The Daily Mail* began to call us "suffragettes" in order to distinguish between us and the members of the older Suffrage Society, who had always been called "suffragists" and who strongly objected to our tactics,' explained Sylvia Pankhurst in her memoir.[20] Those tactics included women chaining themselves to railings, smashing windows with hammers and bombing postboxes. In 1913, suffragette Emily Wilding Davison threw herself in front of a horse at the Epsom Derby in protest, and died as a result.

The *Daily Mail* meant 'suffragette' as an insult, '–ette' being diminutive, belittling; it meant 'slip of a thing'—worse still it was French—and in this case, went the tabloid line, the 'little' troublemakers were a disgrace to their class. The popular press painted the suffragettes as posh female hooligans, a rowdy, criminal, unfeminine rabble. The Pankhurst crew responded, as Summers notes, the same way the pussyhat-knitters did: 'by reclaiming the word, turning a pejorative into a badge of pride.'

They also had their sartorial symbols. At a major Votes for Women march on 21 June 1908, when 300,000 people amassed in London's Hyde Park, many protestors adopted a military-style sash in purple, white and green. Purple stood for dignity, white for purity and green for hope. The suffragettes sold badges, banners and other accessories in these colours, many handcrafted, which became a symbol of rebellion. Wearing a green and purple dress or hat trim during this period spoke of your progressive politics.

The suffragettes had a clear goal: votes for women at a time when the right belonged to male property-owners. And they had plans to achieve it, through protests, marches, direct action, lobbying MPs and rallying public support. More than a thousand women were imprisoned for their troubles, where some went on hunger strike and were violently force-fed. Many more indulged in quieter acts of rebellion. In advance of the 1911 census, for example, a campaign by the Women's Freedom League encouraged women not to fill out the forms, instead writing: 'I don't count so I won't be counted' or 'No persons here, only women.'

The *Representation of the People Act 1918* abolished practically all property qualifiers for men over twenty-one and enfranchised women over the age of thirty who met the minimum property qualifications. (The age barrier was to ensure that with so many men killed in the First World War, women didn't become the majority of the British electorate.) The Suffragettes were helped in their battle by their singular purpose and concrete goal.

Summers believes the women's movement needs clearer goals today. She says the Women's Marches were a good start—'a very important mobilisation; they definitely energised and inspired women of all ages, and I think young girls are now interested in feminism in a way that they wouldn't have been before'—but warns against complacency. 'We don't want this just to be a feel-good moment; that we march, we get headlines, we go home. I want us to marshal that energy and our numbers into achieving real, lasting change for all women: of all ages, backgrounds, ethnicities, and income levels. It has to be about political power, freedom from violence and the ability to control our economic destinies, our reproduction and our bodies, on the part of all women everywhere, in every country in the world. It is within our grasp, but first we have to understand that's what we want. Then we have to find the focus and determination to fight for it. Then we have to make it happen.'

On 7 March 2017, the eve of International Women's Day, while Summers was in Melbourne to give a speech about her experiences as an activist, she nailed a manifesto for change to the door of the Australian Education Union in Victoria. 'I've been saying these things for decades, but I thought it needed to be written down now in an easily accessible form: if women want to be equal, how do we do it?' She decided to act, she says, because after the marches, 'there were all these rallying calls, particularly to young women to get engaged, but what do we want? Everyone's getting angry but no one's laying down what we need to do to make change.'

The Woman's Manifesto: A blueprint for how to get equality in Australia begins:

What we want is very simple:
1   financial self-sufficiency
2   reproductive freedom

3　freedom from violence
4　the right to participate fully and equally in all areas of public life.

And yet the gender pay gap still exists; sexual and family violence rates are high; at the time of writing, abortion is still on the criminal statutes in two Australian states (Queensland and New South Wales). 'We are constantly on the defensive about our right to determine when, and if, we have children,' says Summers. 'We are under-represented in the key decision-making organisations of our society.' Our voices still count for less. She writes:

> For too long now, we have been promised equality but we are not there. We will not be satisfied until all of us—no matter what our age, our colour, our ethnic or religious origin, our sexual preference or our ability—are able to lead the lives we choose, free from discrimination and repression.

In the manifesto, which Summers has made available online and hopes a new generation of activists will take up and make their own, she quotes the English philosopher John Stuart Mill's treatise from 1869, *The Subjection of Women*: '[The] legal subordination of one sex to another is wrong in itself, and now one of the chief hindrances to human improvement.' Eighteen-sixty-nine. I can't believe I still have to protest this shit, I tell her, or words to that effect. Does it make her mad that she must keep on repeating herself?

'Well yeah, sometimes I feel that way,' she says, 'but then I think for how many thousands of years did we have nothing? This battle only started a little over a hundred years ago, so when I do get impatient and frustrated, I try to remember that we have actually done a lot in the last century, and a hell of a lot in a couple of decades. While we are by no means there, many women's lives today, when compared with those of my mother and grandmother, have changed beyond belief.'

2
On craftivism

'I will build a great, great wall on our southern border, and I will have
Mexico pay for that wall. Mark my words.'
—Donald Trump at the speech announcing his candidacy,
June 2015

'I like to fight the establishment by using methods that are so far removed
from establishment-type thinking that the establishment doesn't know how
to fight back.'
—Yoko Ono[1]

Everybody's welcome
After Jayna Zweiman learned to knit at the Haystack Mountain School of
Crafts, she set herself a task: to build an artwork out of knits and purls, her
0s and 1s, a mile long. 'I made a piece called *Hop n' Pop*, which represented
a mile of caution tape. My husband was skydiving at the time, and it really
freaked me out. I asked, "Where is he pulling his 'chute?" and it was a mile
up. It took me a long time to knit that mile, but in doing so, an abstract
distance became tangible.'

Fast forward. Trump is talking his big talk about building a wall along
the Mexican border to keep the bad hombres out of the US of A, and
Zweiman thinks, 'I wonder how long it would take to knit that?' She couldn't
do it alone obviously, not in this lifetime. America's border with Mexico,
from San Diego in California to Brownsville, Texas, stretches some 3145
kilometres (nearly 2000 miles).

Barely a week after the Women's Marches, Trump signed an executive order suspending refugee admissions and blocking people from seven majority-Muslim countries from entering the United States. Although no one was entirely sure what that meant—What if they had valid visas? Would green card holders be prevented from returning to the US after travel? Was this a Muslim ban?—one thing was certain: it marked a new era of inhospitableness, shaming of refugees and unfair generalisations about entire nationalities. There were protests at airports, and challenges were rushed to the courts.

As she watched the story unfold on the news, Zweiman thought of other stories, those she'd heard from her own family. Her grandmother was a Jewish refugee who arrived in New York from Europe after the First World War. 'Her home was caught between the trenches,' she explains. 'My grandfather was not an official refugee, but he spent over eight years in a foreign country waiting for his visa. Imagine how they felt when they saw the Statue of Liberty, this potent symbol that they'd finally gotten here,' says Zweiman. 'You come through LAX and it's just an airport. Where is the symbol? In my mind's eye, I see my grandparents and I see all my relatives who never made it, and I see these people trying to come here now, and it's one long progression.'

As an artist, Zweiman makes work that explores how political activism can be positive, creative and collective; as an organiser, she knew how to engage the knitting community; as a human, she wanted to do something decent to extend a warm welcome to tired travellers entering a new land. She called the project Welcome Blanket and pitched it, as a crowd-sourced platform, to the Smart Museum in Chicago, where the director's response was an immediate 'We want it!'

Zweiman got busy.

Immigration is a complex topic; she wasn't presuming to try to solve it. 'I just wanted to help create a framework for dialogue. To bring in people who don't necessarily think of themselves as liberal ... to take it beyond politics.' Just like in Australia, where if you're not Indigenous, you're an immigrant; any American who is not a Native American has an immigrant history. Yet how easy it is to forget. 'A lot of us have had to move around,' says Zweiman. 'I believe the ideas and experiences of relocation and migration to be very American, and I don't think that's party specific. I wanted to create space for those with different views to talk to each other.'

Launching the project, she explained, 'A welcome blanket is traditionally created to lovingly mark the arrival of a new person into the world.' She invited the public to hand-make blankets to welcome new immigrants, not metaphorically as some lofty art idea to be discussed by gallery-going elites, but practically. A blanket solves a basic human need by providing warmth. If you fancy, think of it as a hug. These embraces-in-yarn would be posted to the Smart Museum, where a team of volunteers would catalogue them, building an exhibition as they went.

Welcome Blanket opened on 18 July 2017 in an empty room. By the show's close six months later, Zweiman had amassed enough blankets to stretch across the Mexican border. With the help of local resettlement organisations, these were dispatched as gifts to new migrants, many with notes sharing makers' own stories of family migration. Zweiman was building community again.

Kat Coyle created another free pattern, this one based on sixteen squares, but because Welcome Blanket 'is about diversity, it's not iconographic in the way the Pussyhat was,' says Zweiman, she encouraged makers to create blankets any way they pleased, which is exactly what they did. A high-school teacher developed a curriculum around the project, and a class of third graders submitted a grin-inducing blanket formed from embroidered self-portraits. Three generations of one family made blankets together. The Little Knittery hosted a knitting circle, and people across the country crocheted blankets, knitted, wove and quilted them.

While Trump and his damn wall were the catalyst, Zweiman didn't design this as an anti-Trump project. It's a pro-inclusion project, a pro-discussion project, pro-tolerance, pro-listening. And fuelled by generosity and slow contemplation—not the first words you think of with traditional activism. 'When you're making a gift, you're volunteering your time to do something for someone else,' says Zweiman. 'I like the idea of that as rebellion.' A craftivist revolution built on empathy, where everyone's welcome. 'Exactly. I'd love this to become a new American tradition.' Does she think Trump might be knitting a blanket as we speak? 'I don't think he is. Maybe Melania is! I don't know, I would love her to, I mean, she's an immigrant. Why not?'

Embroidering the truth

The word *craftivism* was popularised by Betsy Greer in the early 2000s. It was an experiment really. She wanted to see how far it would go. In 2003 Greer, a self-confessed 'social science dork',[2] was about to leave her home-town in North Carolina to study in London. She had long been excited by the change-making possibilities of creative pursuits. Did the 1960s folk singers not change the world with their music? Didn't jazz musicians, rock'n'rollers, punks? Artists through history have changed culture, as well as expressing and documenting it, through paintings, sculpture, plays, dance, film, photography, creative writing—take your pick.

What Greer loved was to cross-stitch. She was also part of a knitting circle, and had begun to notice that something interesting happened at the junction between craft and activism, something that had been going on forever but hadn't been widely written about, at least not by her generation. She tested out her argument on two male friends, who both said it was stupid. 'Then I told a roomful of women and they were like: that's amazing.' One of her friends suggested Greer squeeze the words together to coin a term. 'You could call it craftivism,' she said.

Greer did an internet search and discovered that, as far as she could see, the word had been used just once before to describe a workshop run by a Seattle-based group called the Church of Craft. 'It had four hits,' she tells me. While there are pages and pages of links to craftivism today, I still found Greer easily. Her website was the first to pop up in my search.

In early 2003 she registered craftivism.com and started blogging about her idea that craft could make a difference, whether in 'fighting against useless materialism or making items for charity' or something more overtly political like a peace demonstration. Like Zweiman, Greer is convinced that creative, inviting spaces encourage positive dialogue around difficult subjects. She's an activist, just not the sort that waves placards: 'I have not found that a way to change anyone's mind.' She prefers the winding route. As she writes in her 2008 book *Knitting for Good!*, 'When we make change within ourselves and then apply it to our world, we can become better examples for others via our actions.'[3]

The subversive aspect of craftivism (more on this later) is also appealing to Greer, its wolf in sheep's clothing power. The unlikeliness of politicised cross-stitch, knitting or crochet packs an unexpected punch—it's what sends the work of Australia's Knitting Nannas Against Gas viral, for example, in the campaign against fracking. Their logo is a skein of acid-yellow wool, with two indents to suggest a skull's eye sockets, above crossed knitting needles, and the video for their parody pop song, 'The Nanna Wrap', begins with one of the knitters pushing a Zimmer frame down a graffiti-strewn alley; she's soon joined by her friends and they rap, 'You can't eat coal and you can't drink gas, so you can take your drilling rig and shove it … '

Craftivism as a concept has well and truly taken off, but the community has kept Greer close, which suits her just fine. 'I'm not really someone who needs to be the leader,' she says. 'I just wanted to unleash this idea and see what other people did with it.'

Greer enrolled at Goldsmiths college at the University of London. She started work on her Masters thesis on knitting, punk/DIY culture and community, and moved into a shared house with 'guerilla knitter' Rachael Matthews. Matthews was a bit of a celebrity. With Amy Plant, she ran the Cast Off Knitting Club, which had been written up by the British broadsheets and convened anywhere that would have them: doctors' waiting rooms, London pubs, the American Bar at the Savoy (before, famously, they got kicked out), in tube carriages on the Circle Line. Officially the Cast Off founders aimed to have a laugh while promoting knitting as 'a healthy, contemporary and creative pastime', but there was a political element too. They sold provocative 'knit-kits' through their online store, including woolly joints ('Skin Up in Stocking Stitch—the non-toxic, totally legal way to share a spliff with friends') and penises ('make a knitted willy with realistic head and veins'). Matthews marched against the Iraq War with a knitted banner that read, 'Drop stitches not bombs.' Greer had found her tribe.

She, too, had been thinking a lot about armed conflict. In 2003 it was impossible not to. I remember what it was like when millions tipped onto London's streets that February for 'an epic day of protest by people who didn't usually do that sort of thing'.[4] The numbers were staggering. Between January and April, an estimated thirty-six million people around the world protested over the decision of the United States and Britain to wage war on Iraq, helped by a 'coalition of the willing' that included Australia.

Greer kept thinking about the millions who were against it versus the tiny number of people in charge who made decisions about it. While public opinion initially backed the removal by force of dictator Saddam Hussein (a 2003 poll found 54 per cent of Brits in favour of military action), support slipped as the war dragged on (by 2007, two-thirds thought it unjustified). Opponents argued that the war was certainly immoral and possibly illegal, as doubts about the legitimacy of the invasion spread. There are military men in Greer's family, and she'd once had an army boyfriend. The subject was fraught.

Asked to describe her childhood, she talks about it being 'conservative' with 'this expectation of being polite to everyone and saying "y'all" a lot. We drank a lot of sweet tea.' Her grandmother, a keen knitter, introduced her to crafting, and Greer has fond memories of learning to cross-stitch as a child by making a bookmark as a gift for her mother. But the teenaged Greer was into skateboarding and Riot Grrrl punk bands. She'd read about the band Bikini Kill in a magazine and started buying their records (*Revolution Girl Style Now! Pussy Whipped*). Greer loved how lead singer Kathleen Hanna called 'all girls to the front' at gigs—sometimes wearing just her bra with 'slut' scrawled across her stomach as a fuck-you to photographers; the male gaze.

Kathleen Hanna came of age while mainstream American culture was busy pronouncing second-wave feminism dead. Growing up witnessing domestic violence, and later working in women's refuges and, briefly, as a stripper, Hanna figured, if we're living in a post-feminist world, how come the women's shelters are full? How come the rape crisis lines ring off the hook? And the band scene is dominated by men?[5]

In 1991, in the second edition of the *Bikini Kill* zine, Hanna published a sixteen-point 'Riot Grrrl Manifesto', rejecting sexism, capitalism, the patriarchal power structure and traditional hierarchies in general, not least 'BECAUSE us girls crave records and books and fanzines that speak to US that WE feel included in and can understand in our own ways.' There she writes, 'I believe with my whole heart/mind/body that girls constitute a revolutionary soul force that can, and will change the world for real.'

Greer says punk girl bands like Bikini Kill, Heavens to Betsy and Sleater-Kinney gave her 'permission to not be perfect' and to throw off the clichéd southern American expectations she grew up with: that women and girls should be 'demure, polite, quiet'. She says, 'It was like, wait, I can be loud! I can talk about things that happened to me, and things that matter to me.'

All this led to a few fights around the Greer family dinner table. War, she says, was always 'a flashpoint … It was frustrating because it just got divisive. And it's my family, you know? I want it to be a space where we could talk and disagree and not have all that anger.' Only later did she discover that craft could provide 'a softer landing place' for awkward political conversations, whether with loved ones or strangers.

In 2004 Greer embarked on a cross-stitch project inspired by anonymous anti-war graffiti she'd found on the internet. She stitched a soldier leading a child by the hand, and Lady Liberty holding a bomb instead of her torch, posting the results on craftivism.com and showing them in books and galleries. The work got people talking and crucially, says Greer, gave them space to figure out their own reactions because she wasn't there waving a placard. A similar thing happens with craft group dynamics, she says. 'It's a way people can open up. When you're talking with somebody face to face, it can be confrontational, even if you're not arguing; it can be scary because you're looking into someone's eyes, you're watching to see if they approve or disapprove. [When] you're stitching, you can look down at your hands and no one thinks you're being rude. Sometimes we need that little psychic break [when faced with complex political issues].'

Crafting, making art, volunteering, even mindfulness, all sorts of things can be 'activism' in Greer's opinion, if the intent is to take action to change the world via engaged creativity. Some acts of craftivism are very subtle, affecting a handful of people, or even just one. It's not a numbers game for Greer. 'What is the metric of change?' she says. 'You can't count it. Just like there's no one way to knit something, there is no one standard metric of change.'

Is the most effective craftivist project the one that brings in hundreds of thousands of makers, like Pussyhat did? Thousands, like Welcome Blanket? Or hundreds, as in the case of Wool Against Weapons' seven-mile 'Peace Scarf', which CND campaigners unveiled as the British government prepared to renew its Trident nuclear weapons in 2014. (That scarf was pink too, incidentally, but there were precisely no ranty op-eds about its colour being controversial.) Or is it the one that's the most disturbing and sticks in your brain forever? Like the white headscarves of the 'Mothers of the Plaza de Mayo', embroidered with the names of their missing children, the 'disappeared', *desaparecido.*

On 30 April 1977, fourteen Argentine mothers assembled in a historic Buenos Aires square, the Plaza de Mayo, led by an unassuming looking 53-year-old housewife named Azucena Villaflor de Vicenti. With her carefully set hair and sensible clothes, she didn't look like a troublemaker, but 'she was a born leader, spontaneous, always with ideas, always helping,' recalled her friend. 'She was like the mother hen who watched out for all of us.'[6]

Six months previously, Villaflor's son Néstor and his girlfriend Raquel had been abducted by the authorities. His crime? No one knows. But his father was a union leader, and it seems Néstor, twenty-four, had been helping factory workers to organise. His politics were not in line with those of dictator General Jorge Videla's regime. Villaflor got nowhere pestering the police for information, so she began to round up other women who were experiencing similar stonewalling, and they hatched a plan to express their outrage in public.

Police warned the mothers (later registered as the Asociación Madres de Plaza de Mayo) not to loiter in the square, and so they marched around it, in an extraordinary act of courage at a time when dissent was viciously repressed. Between 1976 and 1983, an estimated 30,000 suspected dissenters were 'disappeared' by the military junta—tortured, imprisoned, killed. As more joined their ranks, more Madres joined the protests. Only once did a government official meet with them, and then merely to ridicule them. The Madres began to march weekly on Thursday afternoons, and their numbers swelled from the initial fourteen to more than a hundred and fifty. Each put herself in danger by attempting to use her cultural power as a mother to shame the junta.

Villaflor was herself 'disappeared' in December 1977. The story of her horrific end was hidden until her remains were exhumed from an unmarked grave in the mid-2000s. She'd been executed by 'death flight': tortured, then thrown from a plane into the sea.

The Madres' white headscarves were initially old cloth diapers, decided upon hurriedly as a cheap and easily accessible symbol, because what mamma did not have a stash of old nappies? And the nappies were poignant, having been worn by the *desaparecido* as babies. The occasion, three months before Villaflor was taken, was the annual Luján pilgrimage. The annual holiday was one of the few that allowed for mass gatherings under junta rule. The scarves would help the Madres recognise each other in the crowds.

'We'd managed to attract attention so we decided to use the scarves at other meetings and then every time we went to the Plaza de Mayo together,' recalled one activist mamma.[7] 'We all made proper white scarves and we embroidered on the names of our children. Afterwards we put on them *'Aparición con Vida'* [reappearance with life] because we were no longer searching for just one child but for all the disappeared. We used to go to the military regiments together to look for other women like us.'

The scarves stood for solidarity among the victims, and for courage. Forty years later, the remaining Madres are still showing up, lest we forget. 'Argentina's new government wants to erase the memory of those terrible years and is putting the brakes on the continuation of trials,' 86-year-old Taty Almeida said in 2017, after president Mauricio Macri downplayed the number of killings under junta rule.[8] Almeida's son Alejandro disappeared aged twenty in 1975.

Greer tells me about another example that brings craftivism into life-and-death territory: that of the Arpilleristas. Argentina was not the only South American country scarred by violent repression in the 1970s. People were also disappearing in neighbouring Chile, where Pinochet was establishing a reign of terror, the aftermath of which made Spencer Tunick's art happening so loaded when Jayna Zweiman lived in Santiago. 'Men and boys were disappearing,' says Greer. 'Women were allowed to go once a week to the local government office and ask, but no one would tell them anything. They couldn't speak out because they were worried about their neighbours spying. Talking against the government was dangerous.' Many of the women, having lost their family breadwinners, were struggling financially, and the Catholic Church, which opposed the regime, stepped in to help.

According to Margaret Snook, an American anthropologist who lives in Chile and interviewed several of the Arpilleristas in later life, the church workshops helped women earn money while still being able to take care of their children, and provided a space for them 'to share information and express their jangled emotions'.[9] Here, the women sewed *arpilleras* (appliquéd quilts or wall hangings) from fabric scraps, some cut from the clothes of their missing loved ones. Through pictures they told the stories they dare not speak in words. 'As these women perfected their craft, their needles and thread, scraps of cloth and bits of yarn became powerful language-independent tools with which to tell their tales.' The Church organised sales of the *arpilleras* abroad, helping spread news of what was happening inside Chile. For years Pinochet and his henchmen were oblivious; they dismissed the tapestries as mere women's hobby work.

Greer is inspired by the historical threads that link crafting across generations and borders. 'It's helped me think about different women's stories and experiences,' she says, 'and all the women around the world doing similar things.' She talks about a kind of alchemy that happens when crafters tap this age-old knowledge, quoting from Barbara Deming's *Revolution and Equilibrium*: 'We reach out our hands to give what extra strength we can to these who have acted; and in the process, we draw more strength from them that we give.'

ways to share messaging given the dismissal from men

The popularity of knitting, crocheting and sewing has surged and retreated over the years. With the dawn of the Machine Age in the early twentieth century, modernists dropped it. In the 1940s, the 'Make Do and Mend' campaign brought it back as a wartime necessity, but the fun was missing. In the 1960s, feminists shunned it, but in the age of globalisation, knitting began to be more broadly framed as rebellion. The hand-made, in all its noble glory, came into focus as the natural antidote to unethically produced fast fashion. Yale students staged a knit-in in protest over sweatshop labour, while groups like the Cast Off Knitting Club provoked write-ups in the mainstream press.

Crafting links us not only to past but also present practitioners, inspiring active networks of people who take up the threads of existing projects and translate them into their own communities. A lovely example is yarn bombing. The Texan artist Magda Sayeg is widely credited with starting this movement around the same time that Greer was getting crafty in London.

Sayeg, bored one day, crocheted a cover for the door handle of her Houston boutique, then swaddled a stop sign pole in the street with a knitted cosy. 'All I wanted to see was something warm and fuzzy and human-like on the cold, steel grey facade that I looked at every day.'[10] She got some mates involved; they called their group Knitta Please and started humanising other drab municipal items around town: bike racks, lampposts, railings. 'I may have started yarn bombing but I certainly don't own it anymore,' she says. The further it spread, the more she began to think about communities. 'It was through this granny hobby that I found commonality with people that I never thought I'd have a connection with.'

In London, 'yarnstorming' collective Knit the City dressed a phone box near the Houses of Parliament in crocheted regalia, and draped the statue of Charles Darwin outside the Natural History Museum in a giant orange squid knitted from plastic bags—dangerous work in a city where it's deemed vandalism or littering.

In Melbourne, a guerilla knitter calling herself Twilight Taggers became a cult figure. The group she started, Yarn Corner, is now one of the biggest in the world. Today there is a global web of guerilla knitters livening up inner-city streetscapes with colourful cladding in various forms, from the simplest crocheted lamppost 'sweater', designed to reclaim public space for a joyful moment (eventually the yarn will fall away), to Grand Guignol performances like Danish knitter Marianne Jørgensen's anti–Iraq War *Tank Blanket*, made in collaboration with the Cast Off Knitting Club. Smothered in hot-pink squares, with a pompom dangling absurdly from the tip of its gun, the hulking piece of green tin, designed to kill, looks chastened. It's brilliant, and perfect for the Instagram age. Share these images on social media or a crafting website and they jump containment lines. Greer has been delighted to watch how her own *You Are So Very Beautiful* project has spread.

After a journaling project that required her to come up with a positive affirmation every day left her stumped, she began stitching tiny encouraging messages ('You are amazing', 'You are enough') onto miniature samplers and leaving them in public places. 'Creating positive messages is a subversive act because we are hit by so many negative messages every day,' she says. Advertising tells us constantly that we don't own enough of the right things; that we aren't thin, young or beautiful enough. Even for those of us with very strong psyches, this has a subliminal effect, whether it makes us feel unconfident and somehow less, or only swivels culture that way to allow others to judge us so.

Craft, says Greer, can help us tell alternative stories. It can offer a new perspective on what activism looks like—bring in new voices and new tones—and by doing so make activism more appealing and inclusive. But is it enough? Can we really change the world with a scrap of embroidery? 'We can change someone's world,' she says.

Guerilla kindness

Australian craftivist Sayraphim Lothian arranged a *You Are So Very Beautiful* drop around Melbourne, so library browsers might come across 'You are in control' on a book shelf, and payphone users, 'You are so amazing' in a callbox.

Lothian has been working on guerilla kindness projects of her own since she began leaving fake cupcakes made from Spakfilla at tram stops for a project she called *For You, Stranger*. Her aim, which she sees as political, was simply to make unknown recipients smile. Lothian achieves these 'random acts of radical kindness' by making small handcrafted artworks and leaving them around the streets for people to find and take. As the Cast Off Knitting Club once did, she sells kits online to help others get involved. No willies for Lothian though; she favours 'Kindness Birds', which are dispatched with felt, thread, wadding and instructions for DIY movement-building. A church group in New Zealand made some birds to raise awareness around modern slavery, but mostly Lothian's message is less issue-specific.

'Some take the view that it's not activism, but I disagree,' she tells me when we speak by phone.[11] 'Waiting for you to call, I was watching *Project Runway*; I enjoy the maker aspect of it, but the strongest takeaway for me was the culture of criticism. Judging and bitching is so pervasive that going out into the world to be nice, anonymously, is an act of resistance.' She also emphasises its novelty factor. 'We can delight and surprise with our craftivism. Don't underestimate the power of that.'

Clive Hamilton, author of *What Do We Want? The story of protest in Australia*, describes how in their 1960s and '70s heyday, street marches were effective means of getting social justice issues on the front pages of the newspapers and changing government policy:

> At the 1970 Vietnam Moratorium rallies around Australia, 200,000 marched against the war. Even the police were afraid. It was seen as a turning point in our history. The game was up. Our troops would have to be withdrawn from Vietnam, and across the nation people came to believe that taking to the streets could change the world.[12]

But by 2003, as we have seen, the authorities felt able to ignore large numbers of people protesting against the Iraq War. Activists had to find new ways of getting their points across.

'My mum was a radical lesbian feminist in the '80s,' says Lothian, 'and we used to go on protests with her and her friends. I was always holding banners. There was a women's refuge near where we lived, and I remember how we used to go there and have chats about how we were going to change the world. Mum was also involved in the teachers' union, so I was raised in traditional activism: marching, door-knocking, letter-writing.'

Lothian was grown-up by the time she decided of her own accord to write to an MP. She was concerned over the treatment of refugees and the reopening of the Manus Island offshore processing centre in 2012 (by Julia Gillard's Labor government; offshore immigration processing was controversially established here by John Howard's Liberal government in 2001 and closed by Kevin Rudd's Labor administration in 2008). 'I remember how I felt all proud of myself, like I'd taken sensible action and it would be rewarded. About three weeks later, I got a form letter back. It didn't even have my name on it; it was like, "Dear Voter" or "Dear Constituent" and simply restated Labor's policies on Manus Island. I was so fricken deflated. I'd done this thing that is supposed to work and, in that moment, it became blindingly obvious to me that it never works. Some intern had selected the correct form response and that was that. I picked up a needle and thread and started stitching my disobedience.'

Lothian says craftivism's time has come, although she acknowledges its rich history (she presents a YouTube series called *Craftivism 101*). 'It's not like it was when my mum was first politically active. I don't need to catch the interest of commercial television to spread my messages; I can reach thousands by Instagram and Twitter. The power of the internet. It's about building a tribe as well as a movement, and its members can be all over the world.'

And it feeds itself. 'I think we get braver when others stand up,' she says. 'Most of society is made up of people waiting for someone else to say, "Hey, we're going this way, are you coming?" They want to move; they just don't know how to start.'

Rebel rebel

Lothian describes craftivism as 'a non-threatening form of activism, mostly', but some craftivists, like another Melburnian, Casey Jenkins, challenge that assumption. We can follow the thread from Zweiman's *Hop n' Pop* scarf via the hot-pink CND Peace Scarf to Jenkins' polarising vaginal knitting project.

In 2013, she performed *Casting Off My Womb* over twenty-eight days at the Darwin Visual Arts Association, sitting quietly on a stool as she knitted a long scarf using wool unravelled from her vagina. She popped a-skein-a-day up there, and during the course of the month, it was dyed red for a period, which appears to be the thing that most upset her critics. 'You have to remember,' she tells me, 'the only "menstrual blood" on television up to this point had been blue.'[13]

'The performance wouldn't be the performance if I cut out my menstrual cycle,' she told SBS television program *The Feed*. Their film of it has been viewed on YouTube more than seven million times. 'The expectation when you show the vulva is that people are going to experience feelings of fear and repulsion, and so by linking the vulva with something that people find warm and fuzzy and benign and even boring—knitting—for a long period of time, I hope that people question their fears,' said Jenkins.

Emma Rees, author of *The Vagina: A literary and cultural history*, follows the yarn back to New York in 1975 and artist Carolee Schneemann's performance piece, *Interior Scroll*. Before an audience comprised mostly of other female artists, Schneemann daubed herself in paint, removed her apron (the only item of clothing she'd been wearing) and slowly extracted a long, concertinaed paper scroll from her vagina, reading it as she went. 'Schneemann was acknowledging the power of the female body both to shock and to produce meaning,' writes Rees, who sees Jenkins's work in similar terms. 'For Jenkins … to stitch is to campaign.'[14]

But how does Jenkins see it? What did she intend? I have a long and fascinating phone conversation with this incisive, intelligent artist about her work. Frustratingly, most of the online commentary is one-dimensional. The *Daily Mail* can't resist the wink, wink headline possibilities of, 'She didn't learn that at the WI!' fnarr fnarr (the Women's Institute is the British equivalent of the Country Women's Association). Critics pull out all the clichés: How is that art? 'She needs psychological help.' Disgusting! She's one of those angry feminists, and probably a lesbian too …

Jenkins laughs, as she has learned to do. She describes the creation of *Casting Off My Womb* as 'almost inevitable. I'd been working with yarn for so long, and also with the taboos around women's body parts. It was just bringing these things together.'

Her first noteworthy activist action had nothing to do with craft or the sacred feminine. In 2007, the twenty-fifth Prime Minister of Australia, John Howard, had been in office for eleven years, and an election was looming. Jenkins and her friends were pissed off. 'We had no money; we felt like we had no power. We kept saying, "Oh no, he's going to get in again. Why aren't people up in arms?"' Tax breaks for the wealthy, Howard's failure to say sorry to the stolen generations, committing troops to Iraq, border control. 'There was a lot I disagreed with,' says Jenkins. 'I could make a very long list, topped by [the] children overboard [scandal].' Ah yes, that. Howard used this untrue story in an interview as a graphic example of supposedly immoral asylum seekers, smuggled by boat and willing to chuck their kids into the sea as a ploy to be rescued—not the sort of people we'd want in this country. Not the sort of people on the boat either, as it turned out. It was a lie. As Mr Howard's advisers knew full well.

Jenkins and a friend challenged each other to come up with the most effective opposition campaign for a budget of ten bucks. 'I listed Howard's integrity on eBay,' says Jenkins. 'Finally eBay removed it, invoking their "no item" rule. They wrote to me saying, "Anything listed must be tangible and of value." So I sent out a press release.'

'John Howard's integrity ruled "Non-Existent"' went out to Australian media on 3 May 2007, detailing that 'the item was listed for 67 hours and generated significant attention, attracting over 1354 visits and 27 bids, with a highest bid of US$51.00 before it was pulled ... The seller, "Capitalideas2007", who described the item in the auction house notes as a "genuine 1950s mindset ... in splendid condition", answered queries from potential buyers during the auction.' An example? 'Will I save on shipping costs if I also take Tony Abbott's dignity when purchasing from you?'

Game, set and match to Jenkins.

Somewhere in Melbourne, a radical crafter named Rayna Fahey saw the coverage and laughed her head off. She got in touch and together the pair formed Craft Cartel, and started organising political craft markets in an inner-city bar. After a while this seemed too tame. Jenkins worried that commerce, even the peanuts they were earning, tarnished the politics. 'Craftivism has this strong tradition of sharing and sanctioned copying, open source patterns,' she says. 'It's the total opposite of the "genius artist" model. When it becomes a commodity, even for a nominal fee, it blunts it.'

The duo staged guerilla craft happenings in alleyways instead, then started running workshops in pubs and parks under the banner Trashbag Rehab. 'We made crocheted explosives and sent them to the Wilderness Society in Tasmania in solidarity with the fight against the Gunns pulp mill.' They made balaclavas to show the love for outlawed Russian punk girl band Pussy Riot. Somewhere along the line it became about cunts.

In Melbourne streets, as in many cities, you often see sneakers dangling from power lines. What does that mean? Gangs or drug dealers marking their turf? Litterers disposing of worn-out kicks? Teenaged mark-makings? Fling-ups are part of the fabric of our streets. What if? thought Jenkins and Fahey. Imagine ... Trashbag Rehab began making 'cunt fling-ups'.

'I wanted to talk about why the word is considered the most terrible swear word in our lexicon,' says Jenkins. 'Why it's censored for the pro-tection of women when in fact its etymology comes from power.' While that's debatable—the c-word has been used as an insult since Shakespeare's time—I agree with Jenkins that it's annoying that a word for a female body part is considered one of the most offensive.

Germaine Greer was arguing for a reclamation of the word in the 1970s, and we've come ... not very far, clearly, when you consider the pussyhat panic. The Australian feminist changed her mind in 2006, explaining her reasoning thus: 'I thought this word for the female genitalia shouldn't be abusive. I believed it should be an ordinary, everyday word ... I tried to take the malice out of it, I wanted women to be able to say it ... It didn't work and now in a way I'm sort of perversely pleased because it meant that it kept that power.'[15]

Jenkins disagrees. She started a Facebook page called 'Cunt Is Not a Dirty Word', which Facebook shut down, so she started a blog. When she was invited to take part in a group art show in Sydney, the gallery censored her bio. She did radio and was asked not to use the c-word, even though the slot was about the very thing. 'Every place you go you are blocked from talking about it so I wanted to take it to the streets.'

She says the cunt fling-up workshops were a lot of fun. They were also educational because they used anatomically correct diagrams—who knew the clitoris extends all that way back into a women's body? But the main thing was to make the resulting craft items visually non-threatening. 'We made them deliberately soft and fluffy and cutesy, something people would laugh at. It was about saying, there's nothing to be afraid of here.'

Casting Off My Womb was partly a response to all that, and partly an artistic expression of Jenkins's personal head space at the time. 'My sexuality, my age, thinking if I would have kids, and how that might happen when at that time I was only sleeping with women. It was a work about what I wanted to do with my body and the pressures I felt.' She wasn't aiming to shock, and she insists that she didn't expect to, at least not very much. 'I don't think shock in and of itself is very productive, do you? It just makes people tense up and reject things,' she says. 'In my activism, I tend to self-censor a bit, shape the works so that they are more palatable.' But did she really think vaginal knitting would go down a treat with the masses? Quite apart from that fact of her doing it in Darwin, hardly Australia's most obviously urbane metropolis. 'I wasn't prepared for such a massive and extended furore,' she says, carefully.

The online commentary, she says, contained 'real vitriol'. I ask her how she felt to read reactions such as, 'I'm going to puke' and 'effing foul,' and she says, 'at first overwhelmed, then mostly disconnected; it felt surreal'. She figured—incorrectly—that the shock would subside and culture would move along a bit. Maybe some of the haters would start to reconsider their initial reactions, once they saw that the end of the world did not ensue because one woman made a statement as an artist using her own body. 'But it lasted a couple of years; every few months more articles would appear in the *Daily Mail* or on *Huffington Post*, basically rehashes of the same stories, and they would elicit more of the same comments.' The story was picked up by New York media blog *Gawker* (since folded), where some bloke called Adam described her work as 'discomforting exhibitionism' and concluded with, 'You've come a long way, baby; now get back to your knitting.'[16]

Men are always telling women to shut up. It's been happening for thousands of years. The first known example of a culture trying to silence women is found in the carved law stones of the ancient Sumerians of Mesopotamia, which date from around 2400 BCE. They decreed that a woman who spoke out of turn may be punished by having her teeth smashed in with a brick.

Women are always refusing to be silenced. In 2016 Jenkins performed a sequel to *Casting off My Womb* at the Festival of Live Art in Melbourne. She titled it *Programmed to Reproduce*. Again, she knitted from her vagina, not a scarf this time but a protective cocoon for herself. As she stitched, two industrial knitting machines hummed busily in the background, programmed to knit banners that spelled out some of the worst abuse she'd received online.

3
Make the change you wish to see

'If we want our world to be a more beautiful, kind and fair place, then shouldn't our activism be more beautiful, kind and fair?'
—Sarah Corbett, *How to Be a Craftivist: The art of gentle protest*

'Where there is love, there is life.'
—Mahatma Gandhi

Forms of protest

In 1973 the American political scientist Gene Sharp published *198 Methods of Nonviolent Action*,[1] a list he'd been compiling since 1960[2] that ran the gamut from letter-writing, speech-giving, marches and 'rude gestures', to seizure of assets and seeking imprisonment. It covers mock funerals, walk-outs and, since this was the tail-end of the '60s, all manner of sit-ins, including the 'stand-in', 'ride-in', 'wade-in' and 'teach-in', plus two methods yours truly is highly experienced in: the 'stay-at-home' and 'sitdown'. More likely to thrill the heart are a plethora of pickets, specific boycotts and strikes. One I had to look up; 'Lysistratic non-action' means the withholding of sex and originates with an ancient Greek play by Aristophanes. So now we can give it a name. To read Sharp's list is to be reminded of just how many protest routes there are to take.

The classic image of the impassioned marcher, waving her banner, has its place. The suffragette chained to the railings has a place too. The student crashing the corporate board meeting plays her part, as do the civil rights and anti-war protestors, the hunger striker, the animal liberator and government overthrower. The hippie occupier singing, 'We shall not be moved/ We shall not be moved/ Just like a tree that's standing by the water/ We shall not be moved.' The greenie on her makeshift platform high up in the forest canopy, blockading the chainsaws and bulldozers. Her friends lying in the road in front of the trucks. The meme-maker has her place. The guerilla knitter. The political poet, playwright, 'artivist'. So too does the craftivist who stitches her demands for change onto a handkerchief and delivers it, tied up with ribbon, to the oppressor. The trick is to find the method that best resonates with you. Partly it comes down to personality.

Sarah Corbett is an introvert. She finds crowds draining. If you can't locate this quirky, impassioned Englishwoman at a party, chances are she's hiding in the toilets. Traditional forms of activism, 'as the default for people who like performing and being loud', are not a natural fit for her.[3] Nevertheless, she persisted.

Corbett was raised on community organising in the 1980s. 'I grew up in a low-income area of Liverpool in an activist family,' she tells me. 'It was quite an unusual background in that my dad is a vicar and my mum now is a politician, and my family was always discussing local issues when I was a kid.' She was taken to protests as a toddler, but what Corbett liked most as a wee one was to be left to her own devices. They used to park her pram by a window and she'd quietly occupy herself for hours watching the world go by. 'I'm a listener,' she says. 'I love thinking, churning it all through in my head, but I also know how difficult activism can be, and how important it is to do it well.'

As an adult, Corbett, who always knew she wanted to change the world, worked in youth advocacy, then as an activism manager for Oxfam. For years, she dutifully encouraged strangers to sign petitions, and attended marches and protests. Once, she even organised one. She did her homework, checked out the legalities, then led a demo at the opening of a Primark store in Liverpool to protest against unfair labour practices. They got some press, collected some signatures, and they made an old lady cry. Corbett felt dreadful. The woman had been shopping for gifts for her grandchildren and explained it was all she could afford. She was visibly distressed to hear that Primark might not be treating workers fairly, and as she trundled off with her now tainted gifts, Corbett questioned the protest's methods. The problem with so much traditional activism is that it tends to oversimplify:

you're either for us or against us. Issues, however, are rarely black and white. Writes Corbett in her book, *How to Be a Craftivist: The art of gentle protest*, the Primark demo 'felt like a battle, not an activity that inspired action from the public'.[4]

In 2008, Corbett was feeling frazzled, exhausted from all the confrontational campaigning that didn't come naturally to her (and seriously questioning whether it worked anyway), when she bought herself a cross-stitch kit to play with on her train commute. She says it immediately clicked that stitching had magic powers; there was something in the act of it that allowed her clarity of thought, plus it was a conversation starter. What she did next was a bit weird, a lot wonderful: she stitched a message, onto a cloth handkerchief, to a local politician who'd been ignoring her. It asked her not to blow her chance of making a positive difference, and Corbett gave it to her as a gift. Did other people do this? Were there unknown armies of cranky hanky embroiderers out there, quietly pressuring pollies to lift their game? Corbett typed 'craft + activism' into Google. What she found was Betsy Greer.

Today Corbett runs the Craftivist Collective, which inspires a community of creative change-makers to make their activism as beautiful, gentle, kind and intentional as they want their world to be. 'My approach says, you could use your powers for good and be part of the solution, and I want to be an encourager and a nurturer to help you to do that. That's really difficult to dismiss.' She talks about things like 'investing hope in the power-holders' and 'intelligent empathy', which she defines as 'when you don't just try to put yourself in someone else's shoes; you also try to understand how they might have come to the decisions that they've made.' Much time is dedicated to careful word selection and persuasive fonts. 'Oh, and never underline,' she says. 'It's aggressive.' She's no fan of capitals either ('too controlling').

The crafting itself is a tool. 'I'm not passionate about craft; I'm passionate about improving our world,' says Corbett, although she obviously enjoys making things. The added bonus is that craftivism offers introverts a pathway into activism that won't leave them burned out, or put them off entirely. 'Did you know one in three people is an introvert?' Most of all she likes that it works. 'If being angry was the most effective way of doing activism, I'd be angry,' she says, but as numerous studies have shown, shouting is rarely the most effective persuader. In the long term, we are less likely to remember the content of a message delivered by someone with a raised, emotional voice than if it were delivered by someone using calm, measured tones. In short, when someone accosts us, rants at us, invades our personal space, it triggers fight or flight.

'Too much of what we accept as activism just feels like kids having a tantrum to me,' says Corbett. 'In any other area of life, you'd be laughed out of the room; you'd be told, "Stop it! Can you please be mature? Then we might listen." It's like when people say, "Trump has tiny hands! Ha ha ha!" Why do we let them get away with that?'

'Because he does have uncommonly small hands,' I say. 'Have you seen that meme of the Trump portrait made from slices of pink ham and yellow cheese? Ha ha ha!'

'It's more harmful than helpful and focuses on personality, not policy,' she says. 'It needs to be strategic; we've got to really hone our craft.' Corbett's tips for craftivists include, 'Virtue requires thought', and 'critical thinking is discipline'.

'It's not very ...'

'Fun?' she laughs. 'It can be, but that's not the main aim, no. As humans, we usually prefer the easy way out, the one thing that's quick and easy in the short term; so, swearing about a politician's personality, rather than thinking carefully about how we'd like to see a policy fixed in the long term, which is less fun and requires greater commitment. It's harder.'

Corbett, incidentally, found the pussyhats 'really frustrating. I just thought, What a wasted opportunity. Okay, it was amazing that crafters got together and people felt empowered, but where was the policy ask? Where was the accountability? I felt like that about the Women's March in general,' she says. 'I was googling madly, what are they demanding? And I couldn't work it out.'

'They stood for women's rights, ending violence, reproductive rights,' I say, rattling off the Women's March 'Unity Principles' and realising, as I do so, that none of this is a policy ask. 'LGBTQIA rights, workers' rights, civil rights, disability rights, immigrant rights, environmental justice ... '

What do we want? All the rights! When do we want them? Now.

'Trump's administration didn't have to reply because no one asked them anything specific,' says Corbett.

I always need an ask - fundamental!

Your mission, should you choose to accept it ...

A parcel has arrived from Sarah Corbett, covered in doodles of Madonna in her Material Girl phase and cartoons of a figure in a banana suit with the slogan 'You are a top banana!' It's my Mini Fashion Statement kit, and it carries a warning: 'Use with courage and care.'

My covert mission is to inscribe tiny paper scrolls with on-point messages, tie them up with ribbons and 'shop-drop' them into the pockets of naughty clothes. Shop-drop is the opposite of shoplift, involving giving rather than taking. Because this project has been designed in partnership with the Fashion Revolution campaign, the issues we are addressing include garment worker conditions, fast fashion's unsustainable pace, clothing waste and pollution caused by the textile industry.

The idea of hiding political messages inside new clothes is not unprecedented. In 2014 Welsh shoppers found labels inside Primark garments that read, 'Forced to work exhausting hours' and, 'Degrading sweat shop conditions' supposedly sewn in by garment workers. Primark investigated and decided it was a stunt. Two years later, an American woman found part of a dead mouse sewn into the seam of her Zara coat, which may or may not have been an accident. And in 2017, Zara shoppers in Istanbul found surprising tags inside their new purchases, which read: 'I made this item you are going to buy, but I didn't get paid for it.'

A supplier in Zara's chain, Bravo Tekstil, had gone bust and failed to pay its workers. Inditex (Zara's parent company) responded with the assurance that they were in talks with unions and the other brands who'd sourced from Bravo (namely, Mango and Next) to 'establish a hardship fund for the workers affected by the fraudulent disappearance of the Bravo factory's owner.' It sounded reasonable. Except Bravo had closed more than a year earlier, when unpaid workers headed to the Turkish courts, which found in their favour. According to the Clean Clothes Campaign, 'After more than a year of negotiation Zara, Next, and Mango have not been able to come up with a settlement to fully compensate all 140 workers in the factory. The brands' offer would cover only about a fourth of the amount agreed upon by the workers.' It's a nonsense for brands to palm this off by arguing that they're only the retailers, they don't own the factories, yada yada yada … The guerilla campaign was a PR headache for Zara, but it didn't result in justice for workers. In April 2018, they accepted partial payments from the hardship fund as better than nothing. As reported by Clean Clothes Campaign, 'Many workers, who were on the brink of losing everything, say they felt like they could no longer take the risk of continuing the campaign.'

My own shop-dropping mission will be a gentler affair. Corbett suggests it is best undertaken in contemplative silence, but I find myself resistant.

I've been writing in my office alone for days. About community. The irony is not lost on me. I don't want to pop my craftivist cherry quietly on my tod, or indeed quietly in company, so I call in some noisy activist friends. Forgive me, Sarah—there is beauty in our high spirits.

Ellen McMahon is an op-shop blogger with a passion for social justice. She volunteers for a community running festival and at a free café. In fact, she volunteers for everything; I've lost count of the times I've asked for help and she's put her hand up first.

Ellen says her shifts at the Early Bird Cafe, which in 2016 served 14,000 free breakfasts to disadvantaged people in Sydney's CBD, remind her that 'homelessness can happen to anyone. At the café, we just try to be friends to people. In some cases talking to us is the only conversation someone will have all day. It's upsetting. Imagine living like that where no one touches you or talks to you?' Ellen looks stricken, then laughs. 'I am hideously empathic. I was like this as a kid.'

I ask her if empathy is where her activism comes from, and she says, 'That and Catholic guilt. That's my formula!' Ellen has never heard the term *craftivism*. 'I like it,' she says.

Embossed paper scrolls, coloured ribbons and pens. I spread them out on the table and read Corbett's instructions. 'Breathe, take it slow. Craftivism is about taking the time to question the way we see world issues.'

All four of us are hyper-aware of ethical fashion. We've read the Ethical Fashion Guide reports put out by Baptist World Aid, and Oxfam's disturbing *What She Makes* exposé of garment-worker conditions in Bangladesh. Maybe if this information were new to us, we'd be more contemplative. Instead, we bat some stats back and forth—'An estimated hundred pairs of hands touch our clothing in the supply chain,' says Daisy; 'Fashion is a $2.4 trillion industry, yet most garment workers aren't paid a living wage,' I say; '80 per cent are women, most aged between eighteen and twenty-four,' says Kirsten.

Kirsten Lee teaches a sustainable fashion course at a Sydney university and sits on Fashion Revolution's Australian working committee. She is generous, with infectious energy, and active in queer arts and culture groups, but if I had to choose one word to describe her, I'd go for 'exuberant'. She's just back from a ten-day Vipassana meditation retreat, the one where you don't talk and they lock up your phones. She says she sat like a statue on a concrete floor and it made her feel centred and present, but I know she fell asleep most lunchtimes. I read it on her Instagram the day she got her phone back.

Now, we scroll through our feeds and look for unethical fashion facts, and I keep forgetting what I'm supposed to be writing. Corbett counsels, 'Throughout the process of writing your scroll, from deciding what to write to where to leave it, you should embrace the most important element of craftivism: peace and quiet.'

'I'm just not good at this,' I say.

Daisy Little is a high-school art teacher who loves yoga so much she trained to be able to teach that too. 'Let's do the Breathe app,' she suggests. 'We can do it together.' She taps on her Apple Watch and the mesmerising animation does its work. We breathe in, breathe out. We think deep thoughts, consider how else we can speak out against fashion injustice. 'You need to stand,' says Daisy, so I jump up, but she's just reading her reminder alert.

'I spent the whole time,' says Ellen, 'thinking, I want an Apple Watch.'

Daisy has crafted before. She has been known to do decoupage. Recently, Kirsten encouraged her to take a sewing class. 'When you do something with your hands, you can be in the moment,' says Daisy. 'I like the mindful aspect of it.' Connecting craft with activism, however, is something new. Does she think it's going to work? 'Define work,' she says. 'I don't know. I think it's better than doing nothing, like the story about throwing the starfish back into the ocean.'

In *The Star Thrower* by the American anthropologist Loren Eiseley, the narrator, a man of science contemplating the vacuum where God once was, walks along a beach after bad weather has washed up thousands of starfish. He sees a man lobbing a few back into the sea. It's impossible to save them all, but this dude is calmly saving some of them 'amidst the wreckage of the shore'. The story ends with the narrator joining him. The subtext? What Betsy Greer said: it starts with one.

That's thinking Daisy applies to her volunteer work with Camp Out, an annual camp for LGBTIQ teens that provides, she says, 'all the usual stuff you do on a school camp, sport, art activities, but also workshops and an opportunity for young queers to meet each other, find their community, stay connected and build resilience.' Daisy got involved four years ago. She saw, repeatedly, what it was like for queer kids to come through the school system feeling isolated, and it was something she'd experienced herself. 'I found my community when I got to university, but it would have made a big difference to me in high school to have been able to come out to even one person, or just interact with another queer person who was not in a book or on TV.'

I ask her if Camp Out isn't more about volunteering and mentoring rather than political activism, and she says they are one and the same thing to her these days. 'The gay marriage debate really brought that home to me, and to the queer community. We have to organise because there are parts of society that are against us. It's really shit that young people are getting those messages. I've never before in my life had to fight so fucking hard just for people to think that I have a right to exist, and a right to have relationships.' If I'd asked her the same question last year, she would have smiled and said, 'Probably a bit of both', but right here, right now—in Australia in the aftermath of the same-sex marriage referendum, which tore a deep, jagged hole in the fabric of our society, then poured something toxic down it— Daisy finds herself and her community under attack.

'Did you guys see the flyers that came in the mail that said if gays can get married there will be typhoons and cyclones?' says Kirsten. 'I almost believed it! Like, can I cause that?' We laugh but it isn't funny.

'There was a lot of vile graffiti on a lot of walls,' I say.

Daisy recounts the story of the Saint George mural commissioned by two Sydney DJs after George Michael died. It shows the singer and gay rights campaigner in rainbow robes with a halo, and was so popular it inspired a float at Mardi Gras. The artist Scott Marsh is a political painter. Another one of his murals depicts Tony Abbott marrying himself. When Prime Minister Malcolm Turnbull inflicted a non-binding postal vote on the Australian public in September 2017, unleashing a two month–long campaign that fast turned ugly, Abbott's was one of the loudest negative voices. Voting no, he claimed, would 'help stop political correctness in its tracks'. Girl, please. 'So far, it's the supporters of change, not the opponents, who've been responsible for bullying and hate speech,' said Abbott, stirring trouble at the start of the campaign. We've all heard what Tony thinks about those ungodly 'good people who deserve our love and respect' threatening society's stability with their deviant desires to get wed.[5]

By the campaign's end, the Saint George mural had been defaced with homophobic slurs. Vote No campaigners were throwing rocks at houses and defacing postboxes. A dog, whose owner had tied a pro-marriage equality scarf around his neck, was threatened by a thug in a Melbourne park. A trans teen reported that a no voter had tried to strangle her in a Hobart shopping mall, while in Melbourne, neo-Nazis put up posters linking same-sex marriage with paedophilia. The digital youth service Reach Out reported a rise in calls from distressed teens, as mental health care professionals voiced concerns, one saying he was 'in no doubt the spike is linked to the divisive debate unleashed by the postal survey campaign.'[6]

'I'm exhausted from the onslaught of homophobic rhetoric spewing into my life,' wrote journalist Sherele Moody in a Queensland newspaper.[7] 'I cannot tell you how badly I wish some Australians would take a step back and think about the damage they are doing. I thought coming out as a teenager in regional Queensland twenty-seven years ago was distressing, but the attacks of the past few weeks are the worst displays of homophobia I've endured. It's almost broken me.' So, yes, volunteering for Camp Out is activism.

Kirsten is writing some kind of essay; it's taking her ages and she's trying very hard to make it neat and legible: 'Beauty is not just in the eye of the beholder. It is woven into the very fabric of the cloth. Our clothes can never be truly beautiful if they hide the ugliness of worker exploitation. Join the #Fashionrevolution and find out if your values are threaded through your clothes.' She signs it with a kiss and the Instagram handle @Fash_Rev.

4
Fashion Revolution

'Fashions have done more harm than revolutions.'
—Victor Hugo, *Notre-Dame de Paris*

'Vain trifles as they seem, clothes have, they say, more important offices than to merely keep us warm. They change our view of the world and the world's view of us.'
—Virginia Wolf, *Orlando*

'For anyone labouring under the misapprehension that their individual decisions are too small to have any influence over the status quo, I want to set you straight.'
—Lucy Siegle, *To Die For: Is fashion wearing out the world?*

Be curious, find out, do something

A few days after the Rana Plaza garment factory complex collapsed in 2013 in the Dhaka suburb of Savar, Bangladesh, Carry Somers was at home in London taking a bath. Ordinarily this, one of her favourite rituals, involved a relaxing soak while listening to *The Archers*. But now she was alone with her thoughts: What the hell was fashion going to do about cleaning up its act?

As riots broke out in Dhaka's garment district, the news swelled uncomfortably with stories of unethical practices and responsibility-shirking. Bangladesh's Prime Minister ordered the arrest of the Rana Plaza owners, but their famous clothing company clients seemed to be getting off lightly.

45

Primark, Joe Fresh (stocked by J.C. Penney) and Benetton labels had been found in the wreckage. Benetton was denying doing business there, although it later emerged they had sourced 266,000 shirts from Rana Plaza makers in the six months prior.[1] That 'campaigners had to physically search through the rubble for clothing labels to prove which brands were producing in there' showed how complex and opaque fashion's supply chains were, said Somers.[2]

The death toll rose daily. On 26 April, it was at least 187. On 30 April, it reached 380. By 9 May it had passed a thousand. 'Each time we moved a slab of concrete, we found a stack of bodies,' Brigadier-General Siddiqul Alam, the man at the helm of the recovery operation, told the BBC.[3]

Bangladesh's High Commissioner to London had just been on the telly, explaining that about 10 per cent of his country's exports ended up in the UK. Buyers, he said, 'go round these manufacturers and they negotiate every cent of it … they place their order with those who give them the most economy in terms of cents.'[4] He called it 'a pity'; what he meant was shame. 'If you are cutting a cent here, you cut a cent across the entire production chain.' He suggested, '[the] middle class here might have to pay a bit more' for their clothes.

Somers didn't need telling. She was a key player on the UK's growing ethical fashion scene, acutely aware of the injustices routinely metered out to garment workers in the global South by fast-fashion and low-price apparel companies—many, household names—based Europe, North America and Australia.

As part of her research for an MA in Native American studies in the early 1990s Somers had visited Ecuador and met some women from local garment-making co-operatives. 'I was not prepared for the inequitable trading patterns I witnessed. Seeing the weighing scales, an international symbol of justice, being loaded with wool on one side and then seeing the producers being charged a price which bore no resemblance to the stated cost per kilo, I felt a sense of outrage at the clear discrimination.'[5] She thought she could make a difference, 'even if it was just a small one, during my holidays. I decided I could probably design something.'[6] She returned the next summer and 'gave two co-operatives the financial resources to buy raw materials in bulk'. The resulting knitwear was so popular it sold out in six weeks. She gave up her studies to focus on improving the lives of more producers in the Andean region, eventually starting a business specialising in panama hats made the traditional way. In 2009, Pachacuti became the

first brand in the world to gain a new World Fair Trade Organisation certi-
fication (which looks at a brand's entire supply chain, rather than assessing
products individually). Somers had proved you could build a thriving business without exploiting people. Fashion needed to wake up to itself. Fashion
needed a revolution.

Somers jumped out of the bath and called her friend Orsola de Castro,
designer of upcycled label From Somewhere and the driving force behind
Estethica, the sustainable fashion hub at London Fashion Week. De Castro
was reinventing the game. She'd gone from crocheting around the holes
in an old jumper to becoming fashion's go-to creative on textile waste,
collaborating with prestigious design school Central Saint Martins and high-
street giants like Topshop and Jigsaw. In the late '90s, she and her partner
Filippo Ricci had launched one of the first attention-grabbing dead-stock
projects, Reclaim To Wear, making collections out of factory surplus cloth
and production offcuts. De Castro was determined to push the conversation
about the conventional fashion industry's profligate wastefulness, and its
impacts on people and planet. She too had been trying to figure out how
best to respond to Rana Plaza.

'We all felt this huge powerlessness,' she tells me.[7] 'We knew something
needed to change. Carry is a good friend, and she was also one of the most
successful designers at Estethica. She'd come up with the name, Fashion
Revolution, and we decided very quickly: we would build this movement.
We got together and started mapping it out, clear that we didn't want it to
be a commemorative event for Rana Plaza; we wanted to build something
that was going to be alive for the rest of the year, galvanising other people.'
Sustained action.

Their mission, they decided, would be to advocate for a more transparent
fashion industry. Long-term, they would aim to work with policymakers.
Although initially they didn't imagine the campaign would be global, within
months they'd been contacted by a Sydney-based activist keen to bring
Fashion Revolution to Australia. Melinda Tually became their first country
co-ordinator outside the UK. The first volunteer to join her was my friend
Kirsten Lee. 'By the time the campaign went live in April 2014, we had fifty
countries wanting to take part,' says de Castro.

In their first four years, they produced fanzines, podcasts and reports,
and even managed to pull off 'fashion question time' in the House of
Commons. They spoke at the European Parliament, and team members met
with officials in South Africa, Malaysia and Cambodia.

Intuitively, they understood that governments and other old-style monolithic power structures, while key to the work of rewriting laws and regulations, would not and could not alone build the movement for change. As campaign strategist Erin Mazursky explains, that requires 'an ongoing process of building leadership, relationships and avenues for getting involved. It catalyzes community involvement and finds localized ways to continuously bring new people into the movement and keep them there through a unified strategy and a broad common purpose.'[8] In Fashion Revolution's case, that purpose was 'radically changing the way our clothes are sourced, produced and consumed',[9] with transparency, fairness and safety in mind.

Not that they consulted Mazursky or indeed any other political experts. They were winging it. De Castro, with characteristic positivity ('I don't do negative standpoints; when I'm told, "no", I want to turn it into a "yes"'), paints that as a plus. 'I think one of the reasons why people believed in us was because we were a little bit haphazard, a bit rough around the edges. Our naivety and innocence allowed us a kind of freedom.'

Take their name. The word *revolution*, meaning the overthrow of an established political system, has violent connotations dating back centuries. In the seventeenth, the Glorious Revolution deposed the Catholic King James II (of England and Ireland) and VII (of Scotland) from the throne, resulting in the bloody Jacobite rebellions. *Vive la révolution!* is still fighting talk; the guillotine remains one of the defining symbols of the French Revolution. In the Russian Revolution, the Bolsheviks murdered five Romanov children, as well as the Tsar and Tsarina, and while we cannot say exactly how many people died during the ensuing civil war, the consensus is around eight million. When we think of revolutions, we think of bloody coups. In China, two million people died during the Cultural Revolution over a terrifying decade from the mid-1960s.[10] Mao Zedong's propaganda warned dissidents, 'Your days are numbered',[11] as his Red Guard attacked people in the street for wearing the wrong clothes, and officials hounded, imprisoned and murdered anyone suspected of being a capitalist or having bourgeois tendencies.

De Castro admits, 'We thought at one point to change to Fashion Evolution, but we trusted the name. Potentially if we'd gone to some kind of branding expert, they would have said, "It's too provoking. How is it going to play in China and in Russia?" Again, out of sheer instinct and ignorance, we went with it and it worked.'

The next step was persuading the right people to join their working committee or assist in other ways. Easy. De Castro and Somers might not have been seasoned campaigners, but they worked in fashion. Fashion is a networked community, and they were well connected. De Castro was prepping an exhibition in a Notting Hill gallery, with an opening night Q&A session with her friend Lucy Siegle, author of a book about unsustainable fashion called *To Die For: Is fashion wearing out the world?* Although she didn't come aboard in a formal role, Siegle's support of Fashion Revolution would be valuable. One of the loudest voices for social justice in British journalism, her *Guardian* columns are widely read. Headlines such as 'How can we get young people to say no to fast fashion?' and 'How ethical are your high street clothes?' could only help the movement.

In the aftermath of Rana Plaza, Siegle was churning out stories full of motivating details. 'The gruesome accounts of rescuers cutting off limbs from trapped workers (sometimes without anaesthesia) surely leaves a stain on brands that no new collection, celebrity endorsement or micro-trend can wash away? Doesn't it?' she wrote on 5 May.[12] Alas no, she concluded, as proven by a long list of less-widely-reported industrial accidents in Bangladesh, which had done precisely nothing to make the apparel industry take serious responsibility. The previous year, a fire in the Tazreen Fashions factory killed 117 people. In 2005 the Spectrum knitwear factory building had collapsed, killing sixty-four. Siegle quoted campaigner Livia Firth: 'The industry is plagued by disposability and sensationalism. Fashion editorial, in my opinion, should be there to teach us about the beauty of craftsmanship, ateliers, seamstresses, to celebrate fashion's heroes. [Without this] we don't give a damn about the people who make the garments. They're incidental.'[13]

Siegle and Firth had worked together on the first Green Carpet Challenge in 2010. Firth is an Italian film producer who at that time ran a little shop in west London that sold eco-friendly fashion and homewares. Her actor husband Colin Firth was up for a string of awards for his performance in the film *A Single Man,* including the Best Actor Oscar, and the plan was for Firth to wear 'only ethical and sustainable dresses' on the red carpet. A stylist friend Jocelyn Whipple was roped in to help. On Oscars night, Firth wore a black, ruffled upcycled gown by de Castro. 'Every scrap of fabric is from end of rolls, discarded silk and organza off-cuts, silk chiffon un-finished petticoats (rescued from the trash) and off-cuts from the cutting room floor,' wrote Firth on her blog.[14]

Having Firth and Siegle in their corner helped, but de Castro and Somers had to build a team. They now invited Whipple to join the committee, along with: Martine Parry, a media whizz from the Fairtrade Foundation; educator and supply-chain expert Ian Cook; Sarah Ditty, formerly of the Ethical Fashion Forum and textile recyclers Worn Again; and Roxanne Houshmand-Howell, who had worked for Katharine Hamnett for years. Hamnett is British design royalty and an outspoken environmental activist. She too became a vocal fan of Fashion Revolution, along with another London-based ethical fashion hero, People Tree's Safia Minney. Their secret weapon was their graphic designer friend Heather Knight, formerly of Futerra, a highly regarded London creative agency that is a B Corp and works with brands selling positive change messages, from environmental groups to big fashion players like Kering and H&M.

They briefed Knight, stressing the idea was 'to start a conversation that connected the whole fashion supply chain, from the cotton farmers, the ginners and spinners to the garment workers, the policymakers, the designers and students right through to the consumers. I think that's what made us unique,' says de Castro: 'that we really wanted to be inclusive rather than shaming.' On the first Fashion Revolution Day, on the anniversary of Rana Plaza, they would encourage people to turn their clothes inside out, show the label, snap a selfie and ask brands, 'Who made my clothes?' thus igniting a massive public, easy-access conversation about transparency. In theory, it would take minimal resources, which was handy, because they had no money.

They recruited student ambassadors. An online 'action kit' explained the inside-out concept, and suggested further ideas for engagement like clothing swaps and film screenings. From 2015 Andrew Morgan's documentary about fast fashion, *The True Cost,* was a staple—Siegle and Firth were executive producers. And anyone could access the Fashion Revolution info graphics and quote tiles.

'When Heather showed us her vision, it was perfect. It looked co-ordinated and designed from the start,' says de Castro. 'Instead of having people scribbling on a piece of paper, "Who made my clothes?", we created branded posters. The result was something that looked like a very organised, very strategised campaign, even though it was total fake-it-till-you-make-it. In hindsight, the cleverest thing we did was allow our assets and content to be downloadable by anyone, with no hoops to jump through. We only realised afterwards that wasn't how it was normally done then. Brands were protective and jealous of their logos, frightened of what would happen in terms of intellectual property or brand misrepresentation. We didn't have that fear. We believed in the goodwill of the people, that they were going to be using it in a positive way.'

In the second year, more than a thousand brands and retailers responded, and over 2600 producers, garment workers and makers used the hashtag #imadeyourclothes on social media. People were screen-printing T-shirts with the 'Who Made My Clothes?' slogan. I painted it in giant black letters on the outside of my house. Full disclosure: I joined Fashion Revolution's Australian advisory committee in 2014, persuaded to donate my journalism skills after a meeting with Siegle.

'In my opinion we managed to put together the best team,' says de Castro. 'We cherry-picked people we trusted, we liked, we loved—this kind of mixture of creative and strategic and policy thinking, but also very free.' It was the only way they knew. They hadn't read the theory; had no well-thumbed copies of Saul Alinsky's *Rules for Radicals* by their beds. But if they weren't familiar with Alinsky's famous quote, 'The organizer becomes a carrier of the contagion of curiosity, for a people asking "why" are beginning to rebel,' it didn't matter: they knew already that curiosity was key. They wrote it in their tag line: 'Be curious, find out, do something.'

'I think the great strength of Fashion Revolution initially was its spontaneity,' says de Castro. 'It was a campaign begun by non-campaigners, so we broke all the rules. We didn't break them because we decided we were going to; we simply didn't know what we were doing, and so our approach was completely instinctive, and very human I think. What we did was what a group of friends would have done: I allow you into my thoughts, I allow you into my home, I let you share my clothes; that's how it was for us.'

In 2018 they published their third Fashion Transparency Index, which ranks 150 of the world's biggest fashion brands and retailers according to how much they disclose about their social and environmental policies, practices and impact. Brands were scored on five key areas, and the scores were converted into percentages. The average score was 21 per cent. An increasing number of brands are disclosing who their suppliers are, but fewer than a quarter have made a commitment to pay a living wage. The practice of disclosing—or even considering—environmental impacts remains in its infancy. Brands are getting better at sharing their policies and commitments, but 'there is still much crucial information about the practices of the fashion industry that remains concealed, particularly when it comes to brands' tangible impact on the lives of workers in their supply chains and on the environment.'[15] A start, then, but there's more campaigning to be done.

Who makes your clothes?

When Rana Plaza collapsed, Kalpona Akter, executive director of the Bangladesh Centre for Worker Solidarity, was touring America with a young garment worker who'd survived the Tazreen fire by jumping out of a third-floor window. 'These tragedies can be prevented by multinational corporations like Walmart and the Gap that operate in Bangladesh,' said Akter in a public statement.[16] 'Because of these companies' negligence and wilful ignorance, garment workers are in danger every day. As we learn more details, we will better understand the brands that were manufactured in these factories, but we already know that the largest retailers in the world hold tremendous power to transform conditions for garment workers— mostly young women—in Bangladesh.'

She sped home. What she found there was even worse than she'd imagined. 'I was there for seventeen days of the rescue operation,' she tells me.[17] 'The air was polluted from people dying and their bodies spoiling in that death trap in the rubble. But at that same time, you can feel the pain, the screaming and the crying in the air, and you can't take it. Just think about those families, who is having a picture in their hand ... and asking everyone, "Did you see my son? Did you see my daughter?" Or kids are coming and they are saying, "Did you see my mum? This is my mum in this picture."' Many of the bodies were in such a bad state that they were unidentifiable by their faces alone. 'So how are they recognising them? By the clothes, or sometimes by a nose pin.'

Kalpona Akter is a short, curvy lady in a blue sari with a kind, open face and twinkling eyes, and when we meet in the offices of Human Rights Watch, she gives me a huge, mama-bear hug. She looks sweet, but only a fool would underestimate this formidable political operator. A former child worker herself, Akter entered the garment industry at twelve years of age. By sixteen she was a union leader. A year later, she'd been fired as a troublemaker. Akter has withstood bullying and intimidation from her opponents, who wish to paint labour rights activists in Bangladesh as harbingers of unrest rather than leaders of a movement. By speaking out, Akter antagonises them. She has been imprisoned for her trouble (a close union colleague was murdered for his), but Akter is stubborn as well as smart. She refuses to give up.

When she tells me that as a consumer, my voice 'is crucial and powerful in the supply chain,' she knows that hers is even more so, because to listen to Akter is to be persuaded of your own power. 'The ethical fashion movement,' she says, 'needs you.'[18] If you wear clothes, you'd better listen. You'd better learn and you'd better start speaking out, she says. 'After Rana Plaza there was a global outcry, and you consumers were phenomenal; you did raise your voices.' Public pressure helped steer more than 200 brands, retailers and exporters to sign the Accord on Fire and Building Safety in Bangladesh. 'You made these brands sign on to this legally binding agreement,' she says.

I ask her if she feels that, globally, we have entered a new phase of consumer activism, a reawakening, and she says, 'I do,' and reminds me that each person who speaks out makes a difference. The star thrower again. 'A small bell can make a huge noise when we are gathered together,' she says. And now we must do more. Child labour, for example, is rife in the sweatshops of old Dhaka.

Ethical fashion is a feminist issue, because it is mostly women who wear fashion, and it is mostly women who sew it. It can be a tool for female emancipation and economic empowerment, says Akter, who stresses that she does not want to see a boycott of 'Made in Bangladesh'—'that means no jobs'—but the business of fashion manufacturing is still too often a context for repression.

I ask her to describe a typical day for a female garment worker in her country. It begins at 4.30 in the morning with queuing. One kitchen might be shared by twenty families. 'It's a hard battle she fights in the queue for cooking, [and for] using [the] toilet, because it's maximum two-to-four toilets they have for almost a hundred people,' says Akter. Work starts at 8 a.m. sharp. Being even slightly late for three days' running means losing a full day's pay. Once at her machine, our worker is so under the pump that 'she [often] forgets she needs to drink.' To use the bathroom, she must ask permission. Talking to her co-workers is discouraged. Usually, she must complete between 100 and 120 pieces an hour, and her job is to monotonously sew the same little bit of a garment, be it a side seam, a pocket, or joining a collar, over and over again. If she misses her targets, she must make them up during unpaid overtime. She gets home at 8 or 9 p.m. to cook, clean and wash clothes. 'Her husband is hanging around with friends in the tea stall; he is not helping her,' says Akter.

'That's a familiar story,' I say.

'And we need to change this,' she says.

The minimum wage for garment workers in 2018 in Bangladesh is about US$68 per month. It is not enough for one person let alone an entire family, says Akter. A third or more goes on rent 'in a semi-slum, a tin-shed house'. Food is very basic and there is no fridge. 'She cannot afford meat more than one time a month, sometimes not at all; fish maybe twice a month. Mostly she lives on rice, vegetables and dal, no fruit. She doesn't have any savings for medical expenses.'

A minimum wage is not a living wage. In October 2017, an Oxfam Australia report titled *What She Makes* revealed that on average just 4 per cent of the retail price of a piece of clothing sold in Australia but made offshore goes to the garment factory worker. 'By not paying a living wage, big brands are keeping the women who make our clothes in poverty. But this can change,' say the report's authors, calling on consumers 'to stand in solidarity with the women who make our clothes' and let the big brands know it.

Soon Target's Facebook page was filled with messages from shoppers politely warning that if the brand didn't step up its commitment to pay a living wage, they would take their business elsewhere. While I can't say for sure, it felt to me like these letters were written by perfectly ordinary women, not career activists or seasoned feminist campaigners. It felt like something wonderful was happening.

5
Three ways to be an activist

'Most people never listen.'
    —Ernest Hemingway, *Across the River and into the Trees*

'Racism should never have happened and so you don't get a cookie for reducing it.'
    —Chimamanda Ngozi Adichie, *Americanah*

'Always remember you have within you the strength, the patience, and the passion to reach for the stars to change the world.'
    —Harriet Tubman

Start looking

Child labour is not confined to Dhaka's sweatshops. According to UNICEF, it's a particular problem in the fashion industry because much of the supply chain requires low-skilled labour and 'some tasks are even better suited to children than adults.' Employers might actually prefer to hire kids to pick cotton because little fingers are less likely to damage the crop. In fields and factories, children can be seen as the easier, more malleable option, less likely to kick up a fuss over deplorable conditions, and less expensive. Free in some cases—one in four victims of modern slavery is a child.

Modern slavery traps an estimated forty million people worldwide, through forced or bonded labour or forced marriage. One in five is a victim of forced sexual exploitation, and there are fifteen million women and girls in forced marriages. This issue is something most of us are vaguely aware of but don't like to examine too closely, because it's too big, too upsetting. Our easier option is to look away.

In her book *With Ash on Their Faces*, Iraq-based British author Cathy Otten describes how the Yezidi women were systematically rounded up, raped, beaten and sold by ISIS in 2014. Three years later, about 2500 women and children had escaped, but more than 3000 remained enslaved. 'Around the world,' writes Otten, 'a broader kind of cold violence continues. It's the violence of indignity, of forgetting, of carelessness and of not listening. It's there in the way politicians talk about refugees, and in the way the stateless are sometimes written about and photographed by the western media. It's there in the fear of outsiders. It's there in the way humans dismiss other humans as less worthy of protection or care.'[1]

But what good is knowing about such atrocities when we can't do anything about them? Sharing a story on social media isn't going to help the Yezidi women, or free children from slave labour in the cotton fields of Uzbekistan. Last time I checked, there were 50,000 posts on Instagram using the hashtag #stophumantrafficking. It hasn't stopped though, has it?

In the middle of writing this chapter, I break to interview the feminist historian Amanda Foreman for *Vogue*, and I ask her what she thinks about all this. 'Give your money, give your time. Go and help in a women's shelter!' she tells me.[2] 'For the past two millennia, women have been conditioned into a state of being, not doing. You're to be silent, to be mothers, to be sexually attractive. Men are meant to do the doing: to make money, or art, to build buildings, to wage wars, whatever it is. That deep conditioning between the being and the doing is so entrenched in the human psyche that even now, it's playing out in the click and the tweet.' She brings up #BringBackOurGirls, the Boko Haram campaign. The year ISIS began their genocide against the Yezidi, the terrorist group Boko Haram kidnapped 276 schoolgirls in Nigeria. 'Being outraged and retweeting something with that hashtag did absolutely nothing to bring back those girls; that was simply being. Whereas the doing … ' That, says Foreman, is what activism means. 'Go volunteer. There are thousands of ways you can be active in advancing the rights of women or oppressed minorities everywhere, and until we can understand the difference between wearing a T-shirt or a particular hat and posting on Instagram, and actually doing something real, nothing is going to change. Just do something.'

I spend a day researching human trafficking and making a list of possible actions I could take, from donating money or time—Stop the Traffik always needs volunteers—to something higher-stakes. On discovering that child labour is rampant in the yarn and spinning stage of the fashion supply chain, I seriously consider launching a fair trade fashion business or social enterprise like Freeset, which provides ethical work opportunities for women and girls keen to leave Kolkata's Sonagachi red-light district, or Outland Denim, which works with forced labour survivors from the Cambodian sex trade.

Stop the Traffik says modern slavery is everywhere. Your neighbour's cleaner might have been trafficked, or the dishwasher in your favourite takeaway shop. Your dinner could have been caught as well as cooked by trafficked workers. Forced labour in the Thai fishing industry is on the rise, in part because of loopholes in the law that prevent migrant workers from forming unions. There's a petition to sign, but they're also asking prawn fans to look more deeply at the issues. It's the not knowing that allows the situation to continue unchecked. They've designed a 'discussion menu' of conversation starters to raise over dinner: 'Pranh from Myanmar was enslaved on a fishing boat in Thailand and did not step on land for 17 years. How do you think that impacts a person?' I think, horrifically. The discussing, thinking and looking are prerequisites for the doing. It has to be all of that combined.

Nicholas Mirzoeff, author of *How to See the World*, echoes Otten's idea of the violence of looking away, but takes it a step further to argue that its opposite—looking at a problem head on—can be a political act in and of itself.

In our hyper-visual world, which has been transformed by the internet and the sheer volume of images we're bombarded with daily, difficult issues such as violence or racism often fall off the agenda. Nothing to see here, move on. When we refuse to be distracted by a new Kardashian hairstyle or cat video, we awaken our inner activist. And it works beyond the individual experience, says Mirzoeff. The collective act of witness can transform culture, readying mindsets for change when grassroots organisers get into position. This happened with the Arab Spring.

In December 2010, a 26-year-old Tunisian street vendor named Mohamed Bouazizi was harassed by the authorities and set himself on fire in protest, prompting his friends to take to the streets. They were quickly joined by people they didn't know, in solidarity—police harassment, it turned out, was a familiar story in the town of Sidi Bouzid, in the country's capital Tunis and throughout the region. Everyone knew that already, but now it was out in the open, being discussed, examined, decoded. The fact that Bouazizi's act was motivated by personal desperation rather than politics was eclipsed by the story of people like him being discriminated against and abused. Citizens grasped the opportunity to look more closely at the instruments of repression.

'Social media enabled people to set aside the unseeing of this crisis required by the [Tunisian] regime,' writes Mirzoeff. 'Facebook did not cause the [Arab Spring] but it allowed for the dissemination of information.' By January the ripples of unrest had spread to Egypt, Yemen, Syria and Morocco. The pictures had told their thousand words.

Change the conversation

Mirzoeff defines visual activism as 'the interaction of pixels and actions to make change', like the 'Hands up, don't shoot!' meme that spread in response to the shooting, by a white policeman, of the unarmed Black teenager Michael Brown in Missouri in 2014. Its creators were challenging the entrenched power structure (the police, traditional media) to reframe the conversation, using democratic social media and the power of visual messaging as their tools.

Changing the conversation changes the way we see the world. 'Communications experts tell us that when facts do not fit with the available frames, people have a difficult time incorporating [them] into their way of thinking about a problem,' says Kimberlé Crenshaw,[3] the critical race theorist who coined the term *intersectionality*.[4] In one of Crenshaw's talks on the subject, she asks the audience to stand up. They should sit down, she says, when she mentions a name they don't recognise. She reads out eight names: 'Eric Garner, Mike Brown, Tamir Rice, Freddie Gray.' By this point, half the audience members are back in their seats. 'Michelle Cusseaux, Tanisha Anderson, Aura Rosser, Meagan Hockaday.' Barely a soul is left standing.

The names belong to African Americans who've been killed by police, she explains. But the 'women's names have slipped through our consciousness because there are no frames for us to see them, no frames for us to remember them, no frames for us to hold them, [and] as a consequence reporters don't lead with them, policymakers don't think about them.' We might be surprised, she says, because the two issues involved in this example—police violence against Black people and violence against women—are often in the news. '[But] without frames that allow us to see how social problems impact all the members of a targeted group, many will fall through the cracks of our movements.'

Crenshaw's work shows how social justice issues can overlap and add up to multiple oppressions. The discrimination experienced by these women does not fit into neat boxes marked 'sexism' or 'racism'; the two things are impossible to disconnect and 'double down on discrimination'. We need to re-examine the system, to restructure it. It's no excuse saying, 'But I don't see race.' The system sees it, and the system is rigged in all kinds of complex ways.

Colour blindness can be another potentially violent act of looking away, albeit one dressed up in the regalia of equality. In her book about structural racism, *Why I'm No Longer Talking to White People About Race*, British journalist Reni Eddo-Lodge describes how 'Racism is woven into the fabric of our world. This demands a collective redefinition of what it means to be racist and what we must do to end it.' The book grew from a blog post that went viral. 'I can no longer engage with the gulf of an emotional disconnect that white people display when a person of colour articulates their experience,' she writes. 'You can see their eyes shut down and harden.' Eddo-Lodge says colour blindness, sold as progressive, forward thinking, is really denial: 'It is that skirt around the issue; don't raise it. And what it does is, essentially, create a situation where if you do start naming the problem, which is race and racism, then you become the problem.'[5] The real problem though, the big one, is not seeing, not hearing, not talking, not evolving.

Part of the art of conversation is knowing when to listen. The Australia Day public holiday is 26 January. On that day in 1788, 'First Fleet' Captain Arthur Phillip raised the Union Flag in Sydney Cove, marking the first colonial settlement of this country. As the holiday approached this year, a friend sent me a flyer for an Invasion Day rally, with a march beginning at the Block in Redfern and ending up at the Yabun Festival, a beautiful coming of together of Aboriginal and Torres Strait Islander culture, art and music, in a local park. But the flyer rubbed me up the wrong way; I felt like it was too aggressive. The hashtag was #fuckthedate, and it invited me, in big red letters, to, 'Sit down, shut up and listen.' Poor, privileged white me, having to feel uncomfortable about being told to leave my opinions behind. 'Don't expect a pat on the back,' warned the flyer. I agree with calls to change the date, but I didn't go to the march.

My reaction was a textbook example of what Eddo-Lodge is talking about when she writes, 'They've never had to think about what it means, in power terms, to be white, so any time they're vaguely reminded of this fact, they interpret it as an affront. Their eyes glaze over in boredom or widen in indignation. Their mouths start twitching as they get defensive. Their throats open up as they try to interrupt, itching to talk over you but not to really listen, because they need to let you know that you've got it wrong.' I don't want to be this person. To listen is to learn. Perhaps it's time to go back to school.

Enrol in resistance school

'The greatest power to change policy ... or really make any kind of structural change, comes from the people who are most directly affected getting together and confronting those in power,' says Saru Jayaraman, waving her arms for emphasis so that her big, silver hoop earrings swing. 'Because they are not fighting for somebody else. They are saying, "Me, myself, I, who you think has no power—I now have power, because I am showing up with other people who are also affected." Does that make sense?'[6]

It does.

This, she says, is organising. 'Organising is the basis for social movements. It involves collective action led by the people who are most affected. So, if you're fighting to raise the minimum wage, as I do, the people who are most affected are the people who earn the minimum wage.' Jayaraman is a union organiser in the restaurant industry. When others show up on their behalf, or on behalf of an issue, that's activism, she explains. Activism is important and useful, 'but organising must be led by the people most affected,' she says again, stabbing the air for emphasis, 'engaged in direct action targeting those with power ... with the goal of winning concrete improvements in people's lives and challenging the power structure.' You've got to have skin in the game.

I'm attending Jayaraman's second-semester lecture at the Resistance School at the University of California, Berkeley, although I'm a bit late. It happened, in real time, four months ago, but thanks to the power of the internet, plus the fact that it's free, I am able to join the 175,000 students who've already benefitted from this program.

The school was set up by a group of Harvard graduates after the Trump election. Their idea was to share some theoretical tools to help people engage more effectively in activism, organising and movement-building, learnings that Orsola de Castro and Carry Somers had to figure out by themselves on their Fashion Revolution journey.

Jayaraman is well known for leading the Restaurant Opportunities Centers (ROC) United, a union for tipped workers in the US food and beverage sector. As the organisation's president, she is a media darling (especially after she attended the 2018 Golden Globes with Amy Poehler); she has given a TED talk and written books. 'You cannot be in the restaurant industry and not have had Saru on your radar,' the guy who started Shake Shack told *The New York Times*.

In college, Jayaraman founded a mentoring program to reduce teenage pregnancy among young women of colour, and after law school, she founded La Alianza para la Justicia (Alliance for Justice) at an immigrant workers' centre on Long Island. There, she was building a litigation framework for workers across several low-income sectors, including manufacturing and cleaning, but it was the restaurant business that really got to her. As the United States' second largest private sector employer, it's home to seven out of the ten lowest-paying occupations.

Jayaraman was never a waitress or kitchen hand herself,[7] but after 9/11 she was asked to help set up a relief centre, ROC, to help those affected from the industry. There'd been a fancy restaurant, bar and conference complex on the 106th and 107th floors of 1 World Trade Center called Windows on the World. Seventy-two workers lost their lives there, and in the weeks that followed, about 13,000 New York restaurant workers found themselves unemployed.

Jayaraman started thinking about how the food movement, while questioning so many aspects of the modern diet, was systematically ignoring one of the industry's biggest components: the people who put the food on our plates. 'If you care about your health, if you care about locally sourced and sustainable, you can't just care about the cows and the pigs and how they're treated,' she says. 'You have to care about the people touching your food.'[8]

Although there are state variations, in 2018 the US federal government requires employers to pay tipped workers at least US\$2.13 an hour presuming tips should take that up to the minimum wage of US\$7.25 an hour. If it doesn't, employers are supposed to cover the difference. But at ROC, Jayaraman hears the same stories over and over again: of wait-staff having to audition for their wages several times a night, hoping customers will tip enough; and of bosses refusing to make up the shortfalls. Of kitchen hands taking home zero dollars after taxes. Of women being harassed on the job.

Food culture began to change in the United States, Australia and the UK in a big way in the early 2000s, as books like *Fast Food Nation* by Eric Schlosser and the movie *Food Inc.* made news, 'and you saw this very organic, no pun intended, movement of consumers going out and asking every time they ate out, "Is this locally sourced? Is this organic?" And then restaurants responding and changing their menu items,' says Jayaraman.[9] Wasn't it about time we started asking questions about food's human supply chains?

'The abuses endured by American farmworkers, meatpacking workers and restaurant employees violate even the most watered-down corporate-flavoured definition of "sustainability",' writes Schlosser in the foreword to Jayaraman's 2014 book, *Behind the Kitchen Door*.[10] 'Our food system now treats millions of workers like disposable commodities, paying them poverty wages, denying them medical benefits and sick pay, and tolerating racism and sexism on the job.'

What Jayaraman is doing for restaurant supply chains echoes what Fashion Revolution does. It's important stuff; just don't call it a movement, she says, even though she sometimes does herself. 'The work that I do is organising.'

Today's class is called 'Transforming Resistance into a Social Movement'. It's about organising around issues to create change. Since this is school, we're using Sidney Tarrow's framework. Tarrow wrote the classic textbook, on every sociology student's reading list, called *Power in Movement: Social movements and contentious politics*. He defines movements as 'collective challenges, based on common purposes and social solidarities, in sustained interaction with elites, opponents and authorities'. We build them, he says, through 'contentious collective action', and the context for contentious action is risk—you're required to put something on the line.

Challenging ruling power structures takes courage, and it can be dangerous. In the most extreme cases, as with the Madres of the Plaza de

Mayo, or the French Resistance members who fought the Nazis in Vichy France, it means putting your life on the line. Protestors can face imprisonment, unemployment, eviction. They might risk trolling, ridicule, social isolation or being disowned by family. They also, of course, risk winning. Through their actions, they might reverse injustices, usher in fairer regimes. They might change the world.

Before we can do that, says Jayaraman, it helps to understand what a social movement is. First, in her opinion, it's long-term. The Civil Rights movement, for example, was sustained over several decades. The women's and green movements began in the 1960s and continue to evolve, and the climate movement has been building since the science went mainstream the '90s.

Second, it must bring together large numbers of people from different backgrounds, locations, generations, income brackets and groups, to fight for system change. 'Thinking that a social movement occurs over a couple of years, or even a couple of months, or with one organisation, limits our ability to think in terms of what is actually possible in terms of transformative structural change,' she says.

Tarana Burke, who started Me Too in 2006, echoes this when describing its current incarnation, which exploded in 2017: 'A moment is not a movement. In the spectrum of a movement, I would say this is a victory. This is a moment that we can build from but we don't stop here.'[11]

6
We stand with you

"'Are you going to stand up?" the driver demanded. Rosa Parks looked straight at him and said: "No." Flustered and not quite sure what to do, [the bus driver] retorted, "Well I'm going to have you arrested." And Parks, still sitting next to the window, replied softly, "You may do that.'"
—from *Rosa Parks: A Life*, by Douglas Brinkley

'I feel like there is a constructive fury that has resulted in a resolute pursuit of equity … This is not just my hurt, this is more than my hurt. This is not just my anger, this is our anger, and instead of it just being a feeling, it's becoming an action.'
—Actor Tracee Ellis Ross on Time's Up Now

'What I know for sure is that speaking your truth is the most powerful tool we all have.'
—Oprah Winfrey, receiving the Cecil B. DeMille Award at the 2018 Golden Globes

Oprah for president

Saru Jayaraman arrives at the Beverly Hilton on Wilshire Boulevard and steps, for one night only, onto the surreal ride of Tinseltown celebrity. She's got this. Frankly, she looks like a movie star. Although most of the photographers haven't a clue who she is, they recognise her date, Amy Poehler, who co-hosted the Hollywood Foreign Press Association's annual ceremony for three years in a row. 'Amy! Over here!' They pause and pose in their black dresses. Poehler points out someone out in the crowd, and Jayaraman squints, recognises them. 'That's fabulous,' she says.

Jayaraman is attending the 2018 Golden Globes to support the Time's Up Now campaign. Like almost every other guest, she is wearing black 'in solidarity'. Think of it like a red carpet funeral procession, albeit a rather jovial one. The metaphorical death being celebrated is that of the culture of workplace sexual harassment, abuse and discrimination.

Awards shows have long been used to draw attention to injustice, with varying degrees of success. The previous year Meryl Streep used her Globes speech to dress down Trump for mocking a disabled person. Leonardo DiCaprio turned his 2016 Oscars speech into a plea for collective action on climate change. Others have used their absence to make statements. Jada Pinkett Smith, Will Smith and Spike Lee boycotted the Oscars, also in 2016, to protest against white bias. In 1973 Marlon Brando stayed home, sending activist Sacheen Littlefeather to refuse his Oscar for *The Godfather*, citing the industry's persistent discriminatory treatment of Native American people. In those pre-internet times, such a large captive audience was a golden opportunity. In 1993, Richard Gere noted that since 'there were one billion people watching this thing,' he might as well take the opportunity to condemn human rights violations in China and Tibet.

Over the years, guests have worn red ribbons for AIDS awareness, blue ones for the American Civil Liberties Union and '*Je suis Charlie*' badges (after terrorists attacked satirical French newspaper Charlie Hebdo). There were also 'Time's Up' pins, and the inevitable sneers—feminism reduced to a trendy accessory—but in its scope, this activation is markedly different.

Time's Up Now began with hundreds of women in the entertainment industry forming a leaderless collective (it is volunteer-run and made up of working committees)[1] shortly after *The New York Times* published the first explosive story detailing sexual harassment allegations against Harvey Weinstein on 5 October 2017. ('Any allegations of non-consensual sex are unequivocally denied by Mr Weinstein. Mr Weinstein has further confirmed that there were never any acts of retaliation against any women for refusing his advances,' a spokesperson responded to *The New Yorker*. In May 2018, Weinstein was arrested in New York and indicted on first- and third-degree rape charges.) That opened the floodgates: scores of women who'd worked on projects produced and distributed by his studios, Miramax and the Weinstein Company, emerged with 'me too' stories, ranging from bullying and intimidation to rape. Stories poured out about other powerful men too.

On 12 October, the fashion model Cameron Russell, well known from *Vogue* covers and luxury advertising campaigns, took to Instagram to expose the problem in the fashion industry, posting about photographers abusing models, and their agents and others enabling them. 'Hearing about Harvey Weinstein this week has sparked conversations about how widespread and how familiar his behavior is,' she wrote. The first screen shot she shared was of a text message, sent by a model who was just fifteen years old, with a chaperone in the next room, when she was sexually assaulted by a photographer. This model wished to remain anonymous—the photographer was still working.

Russell, thirty and pregnant with her first child, had 'me too' stories of her own: 'On many occasions, I've been called a feminist for reporting unwanted groping, spanking, pinching, pressure for dates, phone calls and texts of a sexual nature, lack of appropriate changing areas, etc.' she posted. Russell is a feminist, proudly so. 'And because the response has always been "are you surprised?" or "that's part of the job" I tolerated them.' Russell invited models who'd had similar experiences to message her, anonymity assured. 'I will post your words,' she promised, 'so the industry can see the size and scope of this problem.' In forty-eight hours, she'd shared seventy-seven separate stories. The suggestion that models will never work again unless they accept unwanted advances or agree to explicit poses that make them feel uncomfortable is a depressingly recurrent theme.

Another *New York Times* exposé, 'Weinstein's complicity machine', describes a network of 'enablers, silencers and spies' who allowed the producer's behaviour to continue unchecked for decades. Those speaking out, as the actor Ashley Judd did, risked blackballing.[2] (Judd told friends, family and others in the industry that Weinstein had sexually harassed her in 1997, and in 2015 she went public with the story in *Variety* magazine, although she didn't name him. She believes Weinstein sabotaged her career after she rejected his advances. In April 2018, she filed a lawsuit suing him for defamation as well as sexual harassment.)

On 10 November, an open letter from the National Farmworker Women's Alliance broadened the conversation. This wasn't just a Hollywood or a Planet Fashion problem.

Dear Sisters,
We write on behalf of the approximately 700,000 women who work in the agricultural fields and packing sheds across the United States. For the past several weeks we have watched and listened with sadness

as we have learned of the actors, models and other individuals who have come forward to speak out about the gender based violence they've experienced at the hands of bosses, co-workers and other powerful people in the entertainment industry. We wish that we could say we're shocked to learn that this is such a pervasive problem in your industry. Sadly, we're not surprised because it's a reality we know far too well. Countless farmworker women across our country suffer in silence because of the widespread sexual harassment and assault that they face at work.

We do not work under bright stage lights or on the big screen. We work in the shadows of society in isolated fields and packinghouses that are out of sight and out of mind for most people in this country. Your job feeds souls, fills hearts and spreads joy. Our job nourishes the nation with the fruits, vegetables and other crops that we plant, pick and pack.

Even though we work in very different environments, we share a common experience of being preyed upon by individuals who have the power to hire, fire, blacklist and otherwise threaten our economic, physical and emotional security. Like you, there are few positions available to us and reporting any kind of harm or injustice committed against us doesn't seem like a viable option. Complaining about anything—even sexual harassment—seems unthinkable because too much is at risk, including the ability to feed our families and preserve our reputations.

We understand the hurt, confusion, isolation and betrayal that you might feel. We also carry shame and fear resulting from this violence. It sits on our backs like oppressive weights. But, deep in our hearts we know that it is not our fault. The only people at fault are the individuals who choose to abuse their power to harass, threaten and harm us, like they have harmed you.

In these moments of despair, and as you cope with scrutiny and criticism because you have bravely chosen to speak out against the harrowing acts that were committed against you, please know that you're not alone. We believe and stand with you.

In solidarity,
Alianza Nacional de Campesinas

Actor Rashida Jones summed up the mood: 'There is no change unless you bring every single person along who has spent time being marginalised, harassed, assaulted ... There are so many people who have been ignored as we deal with the long tail of the patriarchy. So for [Time's Up], intersection-ality is the hub, is the absolute centrepiece of everything that we do.'[3]

Still, Hollywood, being so visible, was a smart place to start.

Rose McGowan—the actor-turned-activist who on 12 October, via Twitter, accused Weinstein of rape—describes Hollywood's 'systemic misogyny' in her autobiography *Brave*. The Directors Guild of America, which represents working Hollywood directors, 'is 96 per cent male,' she writes. Hence, we 'are fed a steady diet of largely male "thought" and bias about what women are and can be.'[4] McGowan likens Hollywood to a cult, and argues that its commodification of women as sex objects normalises rape culture and casual sexism, not just on sets and at castings but wherever its influence reaches. It peddles stereotypical tropes that paint men as macho, vocal and active and women as passive, silent objects; just 'girls', valued only for their nubile beauty and desirability—while it lasts. Perpetuating these ideas broadly and negatively affects how all genders regard themselves and their roles, responsibilities and rights. 'Hollywood creates a fucked-up mirror for you to look in,' writes McGowan.

Unimpressed when reports first surfaced of the Globes fashion 'black-out', she tweeted: 'Actresses, like Meryl Streep, who happily worked for The Pig Monster, are wearing black @GoldenGlobes in a silent protest. YOUR SILENCE is THE problem. You'll accept a fake award breathlessly & affect no real change. I despise your hypocrisy. Maybe you should all wear Marchesa.' The Pig Monster is McGowan's name for Weinstein, who by February had been accused of misconduct, varying from requests for massages to intimidating advances to rape, by more than seventy-five women. His ex-wife Georgina Chapman (they've since divorced) is the co-designer of fashion brand Marchesa, and Streep the star of several films produced by Weinstein. Streep said she'd been unaware of claims that he was a sexual predator.

But McGowan was wrong about the silent protest; the action was carefully planned to be noisy and strategic, not an end in itself but, rather, an unbeatable piece of marketing for Time's Up and the launch of its Legal Defense Fund. Within two months, they'd raised US$21 million through Go Fund Me to subsidise legal support for those who've experienced work-place sexual harassment, everywhere. They'd persuaded lawyers to do pro bono work and received 1600 requests for assistance from people working in sixty different industries. By 1 March, a thousand potential plaintiffs had been connected to lawyers.[5]

The Globes action began with Best Actress nominee Michelle Williams calling up Tarana Burke to suggest she be her date. Burke's initial response was, 'Why? I'm trying very hard not to be the black woman who is trotted out when you all need to validate your work.' Williams won her over, and the pair decided to flood the red carpet with activists. As Burke said to Williams, '"I know some badass women activists from around the country, across the spectrum, all races and classes, different issues"—and we wondered what it would look like if we used the time usually allotted to [red-carpet trivia] for our issues.'[6]

In the end, eight actors joined forces with activists/organisers and issued a collective statement outlining their reasons. There'd been too much Weinstein talk. It was time 'to shift the focus back to survivors and on systemic, lasting solutions'. They hoped 'to broaden conversations about the connection to power, privilege and other systemic inequalities'.[7] This was a tipping point, made possible by the Women's Marches and Me Too. The work now was about building a broad, inclusive movement to address workplace inequalities and abuse, especially in industries where women are most disadvantaged, like farm work, tipped work in the restaurant and service industry, and domestic work. So, who came to the party?

Mónica Ramírez was a no brainer. The civil rights lawyer, who co-founded the National Farmworker Women's Alliance, partnered with Laura Dern (who won a gong for her work on the female-led show *Big Little Lies*).

Burke reached out to Rosa Clemente, the journalist, former Green Party candidate and social-justice campaigner behind the Puerto Rico on the Map project. 'I know Susan,' said Clemente of her date Susan Sarandon. 'We're Green Party folks. She supported me when I ran a long time ago.'[8] The pair used the Globes to talk about the situation in Puerto Rico post–Hurricane Maria, where, Clemente said, half the people on the island were still without power, and 90 per cent lacked reliable access to clean water.

Jayaraman and Poehler were a good fit since Poehler worked in restaurants before she found fame. 'I was a white woman who had certain privileges allowed to me, and I worked with very reasonable restaurant owners,' she explained at a rally she attended in New York with Jayaraman a month later. 'But I did, like every woman in this room, deal with incredible amounts of harassment from customers and co-workers.'[9]

Ai-jen Poo, executive director of the National Domestic Workers Alliance, checked her voicemail one day to find a message from

Meryl Streep: '[I] heard her soft voice, familiar from so many of my favourite films, introducing herself. There she was, asking to discuss the possibility of attending the Golden Globes together. Yes, Ms Streep, we can definitely discuss that.'[10] They met over cups of tea to brainstorm how to use the occasion, together, to get the message out about the conditions faced by America's two and a half million domestic workers: the nannies, care workers and cleaners 'who do the work that makes all other work possible'. Ninety per cent are women, and most are women of colour. Just one in ten has access to healthcare, and 30 per cent are undocumented. According to Poo, this is a workforce defined by its invisibility, toiling 'behind closed doors [in] isolated environments. You could go into any neighbourhood and not know which homes are also workplaces; it's not like there's a list or a registry anywhere.'[11] People smuggling and slave-like conditions are a risk. Harassment and worse must be frighteningly common.

Emma Watson brought Marai Larasi, who runs the London-based Black women's rights organisation Imkaan. Emma Stone brought the tennis legend Billie Jean King, who in the 1970s fought for equal pay for women athletes, and continues to be an outspoken advocate for equality and LGBTQ rights.

Shailene Woodley, another *Big Little Lies* cast member, partnered with Calina Lawrence, a singer and member of the Suquamish tribe who campaigns for Native treaty rights. Woodley is an activist herself. She was arrested protesting against the Dakota Access Pipeline in 2016.

While Oprah Winfrey didn't bring a change-maker in physical form, she brought several in spirit. Winfrey was honoured with the Cecil B. DeMille Award for being awesome over a long period of time. In her acceptance speech, she acknowledged all the women who'd shared 'me too' stories, and those who've endured abuse and assault but 'whose names we'll never know'. There was one in particular she wanted to mention: Recy Taylor, who had just died at the age of ninety-seven.

In 1944, Taylor, a young mum, was walking home from church when she was gang-raped by six armed white men. 'They threatened to kill her if she ever told anyone, but her story was reported to the NAACP [National Association for the Advancement of Colored People], where a young worker by the name of Rosa Parks became the lead investigator on her case, and together they sought justice,' said Winfrey. 'But justice wasn't an option in the era of [the] "Jim Crow" [segregation laws]. The men who tried to destroy [Taylor] were never prosecuted ... For too long, women have not been heard or believed if they dare speak the truth.' To men who abuse their powers, Winfrey had this to say: 'Their time is up.'

You can work all hours on something vital and important, like trying to help the Recy Taylors of this world, and no one outside of your own circle will notice, then a seemingly little thing, unplanned, goes and changes everything for everyone. Not that Rosa Parks did what she did a decade later in a vacuum.

As a Black woman living in Montgomery, Alabama, Parks was sick and tired of the injustice that was her constant companion. Her husband was a union organiser and civil rights activist, and Parks knew that key figures NAACP were planning to challenge the city's racism. Discrimination wasn't just rife; in the Southern states it was written into law. In Alabama, segregation was enforced in many public places, including restaurants, theatres, bathrooms, parks and cemeteries, and on public transport, and Black voting rights were severely restricted by racially motivated criteria.

Montgomery's buses had designated rows for Black passengers at the back, leaving the front seats reserved for white passengers. Some seats in the middle were undesignated, so first come, first served. On the evening of 1 December 1955, Parks was travelling home from work (she was employed as a department store seamstress). She boarded the busy 2857 to Cleveland Avenue and took a seat in the undesignated section. The bus was soon full. When a white man boarded, the white driver asked Parks and three others to move to the back and stand.[12] She refused. The driver, a known racist bully who'd picked on Parks before, called the police, and Parks was arrested and briefly imprisoned. Her mother's first question when Parks called home was, 'Did they beat you?'

'People always say that I didn't give up my seat because I was tired but that isn't true,' said Parks later. 'I was not tired physically. No, the only tired I was, was tired of giving in.'[13]

The Women's Political Council gave out flyers calling on Montgomery's Black citizens to protest: 'Don't ride the buses to work, to town, to school, or anywhere on Monday.' A system of carpools was organised, and taxidrivers reduced their fares. That night a local pastor spoke at a political meeting at the Holt Street Baptist Church. 'The great glory of the American democracy is the right to protest for right,' he said. It was Martin Luther King. The boycotts lasted a year, until the Supreme Court ruled segregation on public buses unconstitutional. With her act of peaceful resistance, Rosa Parks helped change the world.

'I just hope,' said Winfrey at the Globes, 'that Recy Taylor died knowing that her truth—like the truth of so many other women who were tormented in those years, and even now tormented—goes marching on. It was somewhere in Rosa Parks' heart almost eleven years later, when she made the decision to stay seated on that bus in Montgomery, and it's here with every woman who chooses to say, "Me too." And every man, every man who chooses to listen.'

It was all over social media. Here, surely, was the sort of person America wanted to see in power. In a *New Yorker* piece titled 'The Fever Dream of Oprah for President', Doreen St Félix commented:

> Lately, we've been especially deprived of the sort of galvanizing that Oprah can induce. We have been lacking, too, the delights of a well-wrought oration … One could immediately sense the shift in the room. In our fidgety political climate, any sort of cogent articulation from a person of power has the ring of a stump speech … The notion of a Winfrey Presidency took hold instantly. 'She launched a rocket tonight,' Meryl Streep said, after the ceremony ended.[14]

'I can't believe I have to explain why Oprah shouldn't be president,' countered *Vice* writer Eve Peyser.[15] 'Can we let celebrities just be celebrities? … Have we learned nothing from Donald Trump?' Not to worry. Winfrey dismissed the idea. She has no interest in the job, she said.[16] And yet. I feel like America could do worse than elect Oprah for president. Sorry, not sorry.

How Me Too went viral

Alyssa Milano was getting ready for bed on 16 October 2017 when she got a text. It was from Charlotte Clymer, a transgender woman, who when identifying as Charles Clymer in 2014 ran a Facebook page called 'Equality for Women' and managed to offend some members so much they started a hashtag #StopClymer. But if Clymer was off message back then, she was on it now. Her text to Milano was a screen grab of something she'd seen on Facebook. It read, 'Suggested by a friend: if all the women who have been sexually harassed or assaulted wrote "me too" as a status, we might give people a sense of the magnitude of the problem.'

Milano thought it was a fine idea. Just the other day, she'd joined a 24-hour Twitter boycott after the platform had temporarily silenced McGowan. Officially McGowan's account was suspended because she violated the rules, but she was convinced it was a result of her speaking out about Weinstein.

For a while, Milano had avoided commenting publicly about the movie mogul—she is mates with Georgina Chapman (they'd worked together on *Project Runway*) and wanted to give her and her kids some space—but she was ready now. On 9 October, Milano had published her thoughts on her website: 'Men like Harvey Weinstein are around every corner,' she wrote. 'Statistics say that 1 in 3 women are sexually harassed in the workplace. Really think about that. Really allow that statistic to become a part of you. Also, while you process it, think about the gender inequality women— particularly women of color—face in salary and opportunity. Actually, fuck the statistics, just do better, world.'[17] And so Milano forwarded Clymer's message, with the additional line, 'If you've been sexually harassed or assaulted write "me too" as a reply to this tweet.' Then she went to sleep.

She woke the next morning to 30,000 replies. Within twenty-four hours, there'd been more than twelve million #MeToo posts across social media. What Milano didn't know as these events unfolded was that Tarana Burke was behind Me Too.

Burke is a New Yorker who went to college in Alabama, where she founded the African American Student Alliance then built her career working with marginalised communities, first in housing, then with youth. In the mid-2000s, she was working with kids in Selma when she and a friend got to thinking about how the girls had different needs from the boys. Their solution was a program that focused on girls' self-worth. They called it Just Be. 'The world tells Black girls that you're more worthy if you're smart, [or] you're more worthy if you're pretty, or if you're light-skinned,' she explains on the podcast *The Call*.[18] 'It's qualified by something. What we wanted them to understand is, you are worthy just as you are, in your own skin, how you exist, right here, right now … Let's give this context.' Also, many of the girls Burke met through the program were survivors of sexual violence. She knew what that was like.

As a child, Burke had been molested by a gang of neighbourhood boys. What she needed back then was an adult to confide in, someone trustworthy to make her see that it was not her fault. Later, she was lucky enough to meet a group of women who helped her recast her narrative, not as a victim but as a survivor. It was this, above all, that Burke wanted to bring to the marginalised girls and women she was working with in Alabama.

She visited a local rape crisis centre to get some information and met a frosty, older white woman who all but closed the door in her face. Burke got back in her car, seething, and decided then and there, 'I'm going to do this myself. Like, I can't depend on these white people to support my girls.'

One of the first steps Burke took was to write down her own experiences. There was another episode that haunted her: an encounter at a youth camp with a thirteen-year-old. Heaven was a handful: clingy but prone to mood swings. When the girl asked to speak to Burke in private, Burke knew something terrible was coming. 'For the next several minutes this child, Heaven, struggled to tell me about her "stepdaddy" or rather her mother's boyfriend who was doing all sorts of monstrous things to her developing body … I was horrified by her words, the emotions welling inside of me ran the gamut, and I listened until I literally could not take it anymore … which turned out to be less than five minutes.'[19] Burke cut the girl off, and referred her to a colleague she deemed better equipped to help, but she never forgot Heaven's disappointed little face and visible shock at being rejected. 'I could not muster the energy to tell her that I understood, that I connected, that I could feel her pain,' writes Burke on the Just Be Inc. website. 'I could not find the strength to say out loud the words that were ringing in my head over and over again as she tried to tell me what she had endured … I watched her put her mask back on and go back into the world like she was all alone and I couldn't even bring myself to whisper … me too.'

Burke introduced Me Too at a workshop in 2006, as 'an outreach mechanism' to create a safe space for girls to admit they needed help with the trauma of sexual violence. Then, for more than a decade, she got on with the work of guiding them towards healing and self-empowerment.

The night after Milano sent her cataclysmic tweet, Burke was scrolling through Twitter when she noticed the hashtag. Initially, she panicked. 'I felt a sense of dread, because something that was part of my life's work was going to be co-opted and taken from me and used for a purpose that I hadn't originally intended.'[20] Milano, Burke stressed in a Twitter post on 22 February 2018, 'has been an ally and a friend from the moment she found out'. And yet she worries that the broader media storm risks erasing the years of work done on the ground 'invested in the lives of Black and brown girls'. It has to be more than a slogan. 'The work of Me Too is about supporting survivors.'

In 2017 *TIME* bequeathed its Person of the Year status on a group: the Silence Breakers, 'the voices that launched a movement', which the editor-in-chief calls 'one of the highest-velocity shifts in our culture since the 1960s.'[21] The cover features five women's faces (and one woman's arm, that of an anonymous Texan hospital worker): Ashley Judd; Taylor Swift, who took a man to court for grabbing her in the street, and won; Susan Fowler, who blew the whistle on the culture of sexual harassment at Uber; lobbyist Adama Iwu; and a farmworker using a pseudonym. The inside story profiles others including Burke, McGowan and Milano, but the change has been driven by thousands of voices. *TIME* describes it as 'a reckoning' that 'appears to have sprung up overnight. But it has actually been simmering for years, decades, centuries.'[22] Or millennia?

I reckon we can trace this stuff back to when someone wrote a book about the world's first woman being created from the rib of the world's first man 'as his help'. Adam and Eve lived in a beautiful garden until an incident with some fruit after which their god banished them—Eve was to blame, apparently. (It's always the woman's fault.) The Almighty told Eve that Adam 'shall rule over thee'. It became a global bestseller, this book, and so the story grew in power and influence, and was twisted and built-upon by those on top. Meanwhile women, being subjugated by male privilege and kept busy raising the children needed to perpetuate the human race, missed out on most of the power play that kept men ahead in courts and councils. And we ended up with the patriarchy.

At least most of us did. The Mosuo people who live near China's border with Tibet in what's known as 'the Kingdom of Women' are one of just a handful of matriarchal societies. Mosuo women, as the traditional heads of their households, control the finances. They may choose and change partners as they wish, and there are no words for 'father' or 'husband' in their language.

Most everywhere else, the men are in still charge, despite the progress made by the feminist movement. The patriarchy is a power structure that's dominated by men. Gender-based discrimination and violence are two of its side effects. #NotAllMen, but so what? As Chris Hemmings, author of *Be a Man: How macho culture damages us and how to escape it*, writes:

While it's perfectly obvious that not *all* men are sexist, it would be absurd to argue that sexism isn't a mostly male pursuit. Equally it's true that not *all* men are violent, but in the same breath almost 90 per cent of violent crimes are carried out by men … and almost 97 per cent of sexual assaults have a male perpetrator.[23]

As Rose McGowan puts it, 'Do I make you uncomfortable? Good.'[24] Yes, this reckoning has been a long time coming, but it shifted gear in 2017. As I write, there's a constant flow of new developments involving studio execs, politicians, comedians, news anchors, radio hosts, film directors, photographers, NFL players, celebrity chefs, Australia's once-favourite TV gardener. Then there are those '100% fabricated and made-up charges'[25] against President Trump that keep making 'fake news' headlines.

The Women's Marches undoubtedly catalysed the mass take-up of Me Too. As the Hollywood pus was being drained, I remember thinking, Surely rock'n'roll is next. In November, close to 2000 Swedish women in the music industry—'artists, musicians, composers, students, record company employees, trainees and others'—endorsed an open letter condemning widespread sexual misconduct and signing it off, 'We know who you are.' Australian women in music had their own push, with the hashtag #MeNoMore. At the 2018 Grammys, artists wore white roses in solidarity. This had its critics (too tame, too quiet—where was the risk?), but as the Australian feminist and author Tara Moss says, 'Every conversation makes a difference. Stand up for women, and believe them. Stand up for women, men and children who speak out against abuse. Show them respect. Be part of the change.'[26]

I contacted Moss to get her take because she began speaking out against sexual harassment and violence before this new atmosphere of solidarity kicked in. As a model, her experience was similar to Cameron Russell's in that it involved a string of early gropings, leerings and harassments. Once, in Milan, four men in a car chased her down the street as she was walking home. Today Tara Moss is a women's rights advocate, a bestselling crime novelist, a rape survivor, and someone who knows firsthand how speaking out about sexual violence can lead those who feel threatened to try to silence you.

Echoing Jayaraman, Moss says that 'change is cumulative and collective', and not easily won. 'Those who haven't experienced sexual harassment or abuse often underestimate how common it is, or how much pressure it puts on the survivor/victim. When I wrote about my experiences as part of my memoir *The Fictional Woman*, I had genuine concerns about losing public work contracts. I worried that people would look at me differently, and I was right about that, but I was also lucky in that the public response was overwhelmingly positive—albeit with some rape threat trolls and so on—and I did not lose the jobs I needed to support my family.'

Both Moss and Tarana Burke emphasise that public disclosure is not a suitable path for all survivors. But this new atmosphere is persuading women in large numbers and from all walks of life and locations to break their silence. In February 2018, as Sarah Reyes, a former combat medic in the US army, detailed her story of being raped at work,[27] a 22-year-old Indonesian woman was posting CCTV footage online that shows the moment a man groped her in broad daylight in Depok, West Java. She'd reported it to the police, she said, but they were stalling. In China, censorship can make speaking out difficult: feminist websites have been shut down and activists arrested,[28] but in January, after the #MeToo hashtag was blocked by Weibo and WeChat, #RiceBunny started trending instead—in Chinese it's pronounced 'mi tu'.

There's no stopping it now. The frames are changing, and even with a backlash, which I suppose we must expect, we've seen it now, haven't we? In clear light. We've all of us—including the abusers and their enablers—have had to take a tough course in looking.

7
Green Piece

'You cannot protect the environment unless you empower people.'
    —Wangari Maathai, founder of the Green Belt Movement

'Power is not just the guy at the top.'
    —Cameron Russell

'The idea was out there and everybody grabbed it. I wanted a demonstration by so many people that politicians would say, "Holy cow, people care about this." That's just what Earth Day did.'
    —Gaylord Nelson

Everything is connected

When asked what needs to happen to keep the Me Too momentum going, Tarana Burke said, 'We have to expand our conversation.' [1] I wonder if Cameron Russell agrees. I call her up in New York and she tells me everything is connected. We will not make progress by isolating Me Too, since the movement is a symptom of a broader power issue. 'I never understood that idea of the "one cause",' she says.[2] 'That doesn't make sense of how we live and how the world works.' So to think of this as purely a feminist moment is to miss something. 'The reality is, if you're not having gender parity, then what are you talking about?' says Russell. 'That should be part of everything, same with Black Lives Matter. The conversation about race is central, and it's not like you can separate race from climate.'

What we are seeing now is a power-shift moment, and if we can manage to keep a hold of it and steer it responsibly, it might take its place as part of a much larger whole—an inclusive reimagining of how the different issues fit together.

Take fashion, says Russell. Why not? She and I, we both work in it. 'It employs so many women who aren't in charge. Eighty per cent of the work is done by women but … those women mostly don't make a living wage, those women are mostly Black and brown women, and when we get down to geography, we are talking about women who are living on the front line of climate change. Let's talk about Bangladesh!' Okay. Sea-level rise is expected to wipe out more cultivated land in Bangladesh than anywhere else in the world.[3] 'So, when we think about, why is our industry not sustainable? And what does "sustainable" actually mean? We have to be holding all of that reality: here's an industry that is using sexism and racism to have a disposable workforce.'

The first model who sent her 'me too' story to Russell made a good choice. Russell is an organiser. She set up the Model Mafia group in New York to engage her peers in activism; she tells them, 'You're not just a model; you're a woman in media.' They run social and climate justice teach-ins, and in 2017 they all piled on a bus and went to the People's Climate March in Washington. Russell has long used her influence to draw attention to the different issues that are important to her, from workplace harassment to body image, diversity and the environment. She reported from the Paris climate talks in 2015 for *Vogue*. Ahead of the Copenhagen talks, in 2009, she and her friends made a video for 350.org, *Supermodels Take it Off for Climate Change*. While it was an effective media hack—'It got climate on Fox News'—she wouldn't make the same film today. 'It was a bunch of pretty white women using their bodies in this very two-dimensional way. I've had a lot of evolution since then in terms of thinking about what models can do and some of the strengths we can bring to the table.'

In her TED talk, 'Looks aren't everything. Believe me, I'm a model', she discusses the genetic lottery and the power of image in perceived success and failure. It was so popular (twenty-two million views at the time of writing), that she took to Tumblr to ask, 'Can we reroute this press deluge … to create opportunities for more of our voices to get heard in the average news cycle?' She answered by starting a magazine with Ethiopian-American creative Hannah Assebe. They called it *Interrupt* and put it in the hands of guest editors and community leaders. 'I'm totally fascinated by undervalued leaders and experts,' explained Russell. 'Why does our media ignore them, why does our electoral system ignore them?'[4]

As a kid, she wanted to be president. 'I genuinely did; I talked everybody's ear off about it and worked on political campaigns in high school.' As she got older, and gained her degree in politics and economics, she changed her mind. 'Power is so much greater than who is elected, and the structures that put them there. We have to look beyond wealth and gender, and all those things that create a hierarchy—that's not how you organise if you want to make progressive change.'

To her mind, it makes sense to start with the environment, since the global-warming fight is so urgent. 'Maybe first we put everything else aside and focus all our energy on stopping the climate catastrophe because it's moving so fast ... And yet, I think that there's a real problem if we aren't simultaneously thinking about saving the Earth and our ability to survive, and also thinking about, if we survive, what kind of life do we want for the people who make it? Do we want to make it past this period of disaster into another world of haves and have-nots?'

Russell was raised in an aware household. 'My mom was very focused on climate, feminism and social justice, but those words were rarely used in my house; maybe they weren't used in the '90s in general,' she says. 'I found out recently that my dad, after the first Earth Day in 1970, decided he was never going to get in a car again, so only biked until his late twenties. His family lived in Baltimore. They would go on vacation to Florida and they would drive and he would bike over many days to meet them. As a kid, I remember him biking to work. We lived in Cambridge, Massachusetts, but his job was way out in the suburbs so he would bike along the highway in the middle of winter.' Earth Day had that sort of effect on people.

Earth Day

Key to the birth of the modern environmental movement, the first Earth Day happened in the United States on 22 April 1970, instigated by a 53-year-old Democrat senator. Gaylord Nelson was a progressive type. As governor of Wisconsin in the early 1960s, he'd overseen the purchase of 1 million acres of wetlands and wildlife habitat for the creation of a state park, funded with a tax on cigarettes. He'd tried to galvanise President Kennedy on the subject of the environment back then, but missed his moment.

Not that JFK was immune. The President had read Rachel Carson's influential eco-book *Silent Spring* and, in the summer of 1962, appointed a committee to look into pesticides. But by the following November he was dead, and within a few months so was Carson. Changes in the law made it a little harder for chemical companies to market harmful products, but broader environmental protections were slow coming.

By 1970 some parts of Los Angeles were so polluted that simply breathing was like smoking two packs a day. The American eagle was on the verge of extinction. The Cuyahoga River in Cleveland oozed rather than flowed, stank and 'bubbled like a cauldron',[5] but wasn't the only river in the country liable to burst into flames.

The idea for Earth Day sparked when Nelson read an article about the anti–Vietnam War teach-ins that were happening at the end of the '60s. 'I put the magazine down, and said, "This is it! Let's have a nationwide, grassroots demonstration on behalf of Mother Earth."'[6] Nelson rejected a proposal from a Washington insider to build the campaign from the top down,[7] and instead enlisted a group of young activists, led by Harvard graduate student Denis Hayes. It had to be grassroots. Nelson didn't want to be the leader.

According to Hayes, the big idea was to 'raise a set of issues, to tie them all together into one fabric, so the people who were fighting to stop pesticides and the people who were fighting to stop freeways cutting through their neighbourhoods, or fighting against air pollution or fighting to preserve a wetland, would realise they had common values.'[8]

Gaylord Nelson's 1970 Earth Day speech was ahead of its time. He urged the building of bridges 'between men and Nature's systems instead of building more highways and dams, and new weapons systems that escalate the arms race'. He said, 'Environment is all of America and its problems … It is a hungry child in a land of affluence. It is housing that's not worthy of the name and neighbourhoods not fit to inhabit. Environment is a problem perpetuated by expenditure of tens of billions of dollars a year on the Vietnam War instead of on our decaying, crowded, congested, polluted urban areas that are inhuman traps for millions of people.'[9]

Students, in the midst of the counterculture revolution and already well versed in the teach-in concept, got excited. They held tree-plantings, petition-signings and mock trials. In Florida, students tried a Chevrolet for polluting the air. There was trouble at a Boston airport when thirty students held a 'die-in' in front of the Trans World Airlines desk, but the vibe was chilled in New York, where the mayor condoned the be-ins in Central Park and closed 5th Avenue to motor traffic. There were picnics in the streets. Right-on celebrities like Paul Newman and Ali MacGraw turned up. Reported *The New York Times*, 'Thousands crowded into a block-long polyethylene "bubble" on 17th Street to breathe pure, filtered air; before the enclosure had been open for a half hour the pure air carried unmistakable whiffs of marijuana.'[10]

That night on the news Walter Cronkite described the national proceedings as 'predominantly young, predominantly white'.[11] Was he right? *Grist*'s justice editor Brentin Mock surmises today that African Americans may have been put off by concerns that the new environmental causes would divert funding from civil rights work. 'People of color didn't necessarily oppose environmental activism; they just didn't want it to come at the expense of civil and human rights.'[12]

The green movement has a diversity problem. I've been carrying this quote around with me in my notebook, from a story I read in *Quartz*: 'Close your eyes and picture an environmentalist, and you're likely to summon up a white guy in a Patagonia jacket, standing proudly next to his Prius with camping equipment loaded in the back.'[13] A 2014 report, *The State of Diversity in Environmental Organizations*, speaks of a 'green ceiling' preventing people of colour from rising in green organisations today. The researchers, led by environmental sociologist Dorceta Taylor, identify discrimination, unconscious bias and insular recruitment as barriers.

Naomi Klein thinks it goes back to 'the elite roots of the movement, and the fact that when a lot of these conservation groups began there was kind of a noblesse oblige approach to conservation. It was about elites getting together and hiking and deciding to save nature.'[14] In the 1930s, the National Wildlife Federation and the Wilderness Society (United States) were started by wealthy male conservationists. John Muir, the first president of the Sierra Club in the 1890s, was not rich as a young man (he survived on odd jobs in factories and on farms), but the legacy of his boy's own adventures in Yosemite contributes to 'the unbearable whiteness of hiking' today.[15]

Yet, I don't think that holds in Australia. We're just less 'gentlemen-hiker' over here. In the 1970s, it was union men—Jack Mundey and the New South Wales Builders Labourers' Federation—who led the 'green bans' opposing greedy developers in Sydney and saving precious fig trees and urban parklands, and we will hear how the Australian Greens were founded in a future chapter, but it is fair to say that your average tradie, truckie, logger or miner doesn't usually side with the tree hugger.

The original 'tree huggers', incidentally, were Indian villagers who linked arms around trees to save them from the axe, first in 1730 in Rajasthan, led by a woman called Amrita Devi whose Bishnoi faith forbade the harming of trees or animals, and later in the 1970s in the Chamoli district of the Central Himalayas. Devi was beheaded for her troubles, but the Chamoli tree huggers won, inspiring the Chipko (which means embrace in Hindi) movement that eventually led to commercial felling bans in the region.

Dorceta Taylor, as an African American, talks about different frames. 'Our lived experiences with environment are different,' she told Brentin Mock. 'White people bring their experience to the discussion—that's why they focus on the birds, trees, plants, and animals, because they don't have the experience of being barred from parks and beaches.'

Nature writer David George Haskell touches on the 'geographies of fear' in his book *The Songs of Trees*. American history, he writes, combined with continuing inequality, too often 'reserves the feeling of wholesome ease in the outdoors for only a small segment of humanity'. He invokes dark histories. 'The lonely creek is where white men dump the bodies of those they have killed. The trees are hung with Billie Holiday's "strange fruit." The outdoors—fields forests, and green spaces—carry with them memories, and present day threats, of violence.'[16] Women raised on Little Red Riding Hood and *CSI* are taught to fear the wilds as places where no one will hear us scream, while mothers warn their children that sinister molesters lurk in every dusky corner and patch of scrub.

First Nations people tell a different story, one of deep and ancient connections to Nature but also of ancestral lands and the rights to them stolen and threatened. As Amelia Telford, a young Bundjalung woman and the co-director of Australia's Indigenous youth climate-action organisation SEED, reminds us, 'Our land is part of who we are ... For generations, thousands and thousands of years, we've looked after this land sustainably.'[17] Aboriginal people never ceded the sovereignty of their land, and actively resisted its invasion. The story of modern environmentalism is inextricable from the story of colonialism and Indigenous justice. Gaylord Nelson wasn't so forward-thinking on this. Members of the Ojibwe tribe accused him of a land grab in the creation of the National Lakeshore park, and demonstrated when he spoke in Milwaukee on the eve of Earth Day.

And yet people from diverse backgrounds did come together and participate in those early Earth Day actions. An estimated one in ten Americans took part in 1970, including Girl Scouts, housewives, church groups and labour unions. In St Louis, the Metropolitan Black Survival Committee performed skits highlighting local pollution. In Philadelphia, a working-class mum organised a bus tour to her neighbourhood smoke-belching refinery.

Environmentalism led to political action, and the introduction of laws and organisations that made things safer for everyone in the United States, including the creation of the Environmental Protection Agency (EPA), and the signing of the *Clean Air* and *Clean Water* acts. Important green groups were also founded during this period, including Friends of the Earth in San Francisco in 1969 and Greenpeace in Vancouver in 1971.

In the 1980s, 1990s and 2000s, some of the big green groups started to act like big corporations, paying their bosses big green salaries and doing most of their advocacy work in the board rooms. But I would argue that we've entered a new era characterised by the rise of grassroots green. I see its shoots everywhere I look, from niche groups like Model Mafia to broad coalitions like the one fighting the Keystone XL Pipeline in the United States. It is there in the rise of the permaculture and Transition Towns movements, and the classrooms of Australia's first climate-change focused school, Cowandilla Primary in Adelaide. The eco-fight has come home, back to our neighbourhoods and communities, and today it includes everyone.

The second Earth Day in 1990 was global, and now we have it every year, everywhere. The Earth Day Network links 50,000 grassroots groups all over the world. They work on community health issues, green education and creating green jobs and investment as well as the obvious stuff around pollution, deforestation and wildlife conservation. It was never just about 'scenic beauty,' said Gaylord Nelson, the man who didn't want to be the boss. 'The objective is an environment of decency, quality and mutual respect for all other human beings and all other living creatures.'

8

The rise of the climate movement

'Climate change isn't an "issue" to add to the list of things to worry about, next to health care and taxes. It is a civilizational wake-up call.'
—Naomi Klein, *This Changes Everything*

'If you look at the science about what is happening on earth and aren't pessimistic, you don't understand the data. But if you meet the people who are working to restore this earth and the lives of the poor, and you aren't optimistic, you haven't got a pulse.'
—Paul Hawken

'We're in the early stages of a global "Sustainability Revolution" that has the magnitude of the Industrial Revolution, and the speed of the Digital Revolution.'
—Al Gore

Moving mountains

Last night I woke in fear at 3 a.m. My hair was pasted with sweat to the back of my neck, and I physically jolted because in my dream I'd been falling. Don't you hate that? It takes you a moment to right yourself, to realise that you didn't fall anywhere; the mattress is still beneath you. I'd dreamt I was climbing a mountain, and I had this very clear sense of elation, of reaching or conquering something. It was quite easy, this dream-climb, I was sprinting through it, but as I approached the summit, I realised there was none—the top of the mountain had been removed, sliced clean off.

Reading before bed has been my habit for thirty years, so I'm pretty good at keeping the stories out of my dreams. Occasionally, however, a book refuses to respect those boundaries and crosses realms. The culprit, this time, was Naomi Klein's *This Changes Everything*, and it's where I learned about 'mountaintop removal' coalmining (MTR).[1] It is exactly what it sounds like. Think can-opener rather than drill. Or a bomb. After the mining company razes the forest and all that lives in it from a mountain's slopes, they dig a big hole in the top and pack it with explosives. The draglines that clear the rubble can be as large as a city block.

The practice began in the Appalachian Mountains of West Virginia, Virginia, Kentucky and Tennessee in the 1970s and scaled up in the '90s, so that by 2012, rock, soil, bits of broken trees—or the industry's weasel word for it: 'overburden'—had obliterated more than 1600 kilometres of streams.[2] Communities living nearby face soil and water contamination, and increased instances of lung disease, cancers and birth defects.

A 2016 study likens the devastation in Appalachia to the havoc wreaked when a volcano erupts, concluding, 'the entire landscape is fractured … effectively resetting the clock on landscape and ecosystem coevolution.'[3] The volume of rock removed from West Virginia (where MTR is concentrated; it was banned from most of Tennessee in 2016) 'would bury Manhattan' and has made some regions 40 per cent flatter than before. This is not what my second-favourite '60s folk singer Donovan meant when he sang his great Zen song, 'First there is a mountain, then there is no mountain … '

That we should value our mountains goes without saying. They are not just great places to hike or ski or film *The Sound of Music*, but places of great poetry and spiritual symbolism. In meditation, we are told to 'be like the mountain' and let the weather of our thoughts simply pass. Tibetan Buddhists and Indigenous peoples like the Standing Rock Sioux hold mountains sacred. The Inca shamans believed the mountain gods had the power to heal, while in the Bible mountains often represent celestial things. Every religious text includes mountain stories, from the Qur'an to the Bhagavad Gita.

Climbers often experience moments of great profundity on the slopes where, as the explorer Edmund Hillary (the one who climbed Everest) noted, 'It is not the mountain we conquer but ourselves.' I'm the least sporty, least religious woman I know, but I came the closest I've ever been to feeling god's presence on the Annapurna trail in Nepal. My god, incidentally, if she were to exist, would be Gaia, the ancestral mother of all life, the primal Mother Earth goddess. Or else Bob Dylan. We seek out mountain wildernesses to find meaning, and something greater than our egos. The Renaissance poet François Rabelais was referring to death when he wrote, '*Je m'en vais chercher un grand peut-être*' (I go to seek a great perhaps), but that phrase has been adopted by adventurers ever since.

Spiritual matters aside, mountains perform vital practical roles. Almost all of the world's major rivers begin in mountains. Mountains 'make' weather, in that warm air cools as it rises up and over them, and since this cooler air is able to hold less moisture, it starts to rain. Wooded slopes do the vital work of storing water from heavy rains, reducing floods in the lowlands. Mountains also provide habitats for a wealth of flora and fauna, some of it found nowhere else. Paleontologist Tim Flannery, who in the 1980s discovered sixteen species of mammals in the mountain rainforests of Papua New Guinea, warns that 'throughout the world every continent, as well as many islands[,] has mountain ranges that are the last refuge of species of remarkable beauty and diversity.' Climate change is crowding them out; as temperatures rise, the only way is up: 'We stand to lose it all, from gorillas to pandas to New Zealand's vegetable sheep (a unique tussock plant).'[4]

Naomi Klein dubs our age the extreme energy era and categorises mining that reconfigures mountains as 'high-risk extreme extraction'—along with fracking, tar sands–mining and deep-water drilling. I would add to that list: drilling in places that have until now been protected, places where it surely offends whatever deity you believe in (unless you worship only money).

The Ecuadorian government is drilling for oil in a UNESCO Biosphere Reserve in the Amazon rainforest. The Trump administration seems intent on opening up the Arctic National Wildlife Refuge in Alaska for drilling and has granted new exploration permits for the Arctic Ocean. At the time of writing, Chevron has abandoned plans for exploration in the rough, remote deep of the Great Australian Bight, where wild weather increases the risk of spillage, but says the decision has nothing to do with environmental concerns, just oil prices. Norwegian company Statoil is still keen to drill the Bight. A spill in these waters off the South Australian coast, which are a haven for whales and sea lions and, according to Greenpeace, harbour more unique species than the Great Barrier Reef, would be catastrophic, uncontainable and irreversible.[5] These heinous ideas, these great affronts to Nature designed by big, irresponsible business, are powering a resistance and boosting the numbers in the climate movement—because this is personal. We have everything to lose.

Fracking, or hydraulic fracturing, involves deep and dicey drilling too, in this case into subterranean shale rock. The rock is then injected with a mixture of water, sand and chemicals at very high pressure to fracture it, releasing pockets of hitherto inaccessible natural gas. Fracking has been linked to increased earthquakes and tremors in places that rarely experienced them before, and while the energy companies insist it's perfectly safe (tobacco giants once told us ciggies were good for our health), studies show how the process can poison groundwater.[6]

France banned fracking in 2011 and, in 2017, passed a law to ban oil and gas exploration and extraction too. Critics point out that since almost all of France's fossil fuels are imported, it's purely symbolic, but President Emmanuel Macron is serious about tackling climate change: his government raised carbon taxes and announced the phase-out of petrol and diesel vehicles.

Scotland and Wales have effectively banned fracking, but in England, alas, it's on. Designated conservation areas have been earmarked for it, and Conservative Prime Minister Theresa May thinks it's fabulous,[7] despite safety concerns and the fact that the wells are unsightly blots on the landscape. How many would be needed to cut the UK's gas imports in half? About 6000, reckon Friends of the Earth. Not surprisingly, the idea is enormously unpopular.

In Australia, farmers are organising to prevent extreme extraction from happening on their land (more on this later), but since the Crown owns almost all of Australia's unmined minerals (even if they don't own the ground in which they lie), it's no straightforward fight. With the exception, for now, of Victoria, which in 2017 became the first Australian state or territory to ban fracking, licenses can be granted without consultation with landowners (unless Native Title is involved); a company rep simply drives up to your house to inform you they intend to drill. And another thing: fracking is also a supervillain when it comes to emissions. Klein claims 'methane leaks at every stage of production, processing, storage, and distribution.'[8]

Big energy is chasing ever more elaborate methods to extract fossil fuels while ignoring the science, which is unequivocal: we should be leaving this stuff in the ground if we're to have a hope of keeping climate change to liveable levels.

Of the greenhouse gases that trap heat in the atmosphere—carbon dioxide (CO_2), methane, nitrous oxide and synthetic fluorinated gases—CO_2 is the clear leader. Fossil fuel and industrial processes are the main source, accounting for 65 per cent of global emissions.[9] CO_2 is also emitted from natural sources, through breathing for example, and when dead plant matter decomposes. For a detailed explanation of how the atmosphere, or what was once called 'the Great Aerial Ocean', and the carbon cycle work, I recommend Tim Flannery's *The Weather Makers*. 'Earth's thermostat,' as he writes, 'is a complex and delicate mechanism,' and without its proper functioning there would be no life on this planet.[10]

Over billions of years of history, the Earth has experienced ice ages and warmer periods, and levels of CO_2 and other gasses in the atmosphere have fluctuated for natural reasons—after volcanic eruptions, for example. However, since the Industrial Revolution, when humans began to pump CO_2 into the atmosphere at scale by burning fossil fuels (coal, gas and oil) to power electricity, manufacturing and transport, the Earth has been warming up. Taking the year 1800 as a baseline, by 2005, when Flannery published *The Weather Makers*, temperatures had risen by 0.8 degrees Celsius. Ten years later, the United Kingdom's Met Office reported that the global average surface temperature rise had passed 1 degree.

So, if we're to keep warming below 2 degrees, we've already spent half our budget, right? Wrong. In fact, we've spent more. CO_2 is a long-lived gas—it hangs around. About a quarter of fossil fuel CO_2 emissions remain airborne for several centuries,[11] which means a sizeable fraction of the gas that's up there right now, causing the Earth to warm, was emitted years ago. And today's emissions have yet to make their warming effects felt. This does not mean we should admit defeat; it means we have even more reason to curb emissions as swiftly and decisively as possible. We won't turn the thermostat down, but we can stop it turning up and up, and up.

The Intergovernmental Panel on Climate Change (IPCC) was established by the United Nations and the World Meteorological Organization. It's made up of 195 country members, and hundreds of scientists from all over the world, who volunteer their time to provide a global assessment of climate change, its impacts on society and future projections. Their first Assessment Report in 1990 asked how much the average global temperature would rise by the end of the twenty-first century if we continued to emit at current levels (the report called this scenario 'Business-as-Usual'). The answer was about 3 degrees (or 4 degrees over pre-industrial levels). The revised estimate from the fifth report in 2014 was between 2.6 and 4.8 degrees relative to a 1986–2005 baseline (the next report is due in 2021). However, some projections are as high as 6 degrees.[12] There are complicated reasons for these variations (again, Flannery is your man for a detailed breakdown on how computer modelling works, where it's done and what limits it). Suffice to say, it's getting hot in here.

The impacts of such a hike are barely imaginable, but author and international relations expert Parag Khanna has given it a go with a colour-coded map published by *New Scientist*.[13] This imagines what our world might look like warmed by 4 degrees: Most of Europe has become a desert. Sydney, Melbourne, Brisbane and everywhere in between are uninhabitable and large areas have been given over to solar energy production— Antipodeans now live in high-density cities in Tasmania and New Zealand, while western Antarctica has become a metropolis. [14] Polynesia has vanished beneath the sea. Southern China is a dust bowl and almost no one lives there anymore. Ditto all of South America; except for Chile and the southern part of Argentina, it is uninhabitable. Bangladesh has been largely abandoned, along with southern India, Pakistan and Afghanistan, where 'isolated communities remain in pockets'. Europeans have moved north, as the rivers have dried up, to farm in Russia and Siberia. Snow is just a memory for the Alps. New York is a ghost town, Miami underwater.

Okay so now you know, but can I suggest that you don't look up the map? We don't have time to waste freaking out about it. We need to get on with saving our future.

How are greenhouse gases pulled out of the atmosphere, and what else, apart from burning fossil fuels, puts them there in the first place?

The oceans do much of the grunt work of sequestering carbon dioxide, and in coming chapters we will explore how ocean change is hindering their ability to do so, and what activists are trying to do about it.

Fossil fuels are the ancient carbonised residues of once-living things, formed hundreds of millions of years ago and buried at great depths. In a former life, coal was prehistoric vegetation. Today's land-based plants absorb and store CO_2, which is pretty darn useful. Over the past forty years, the world's forests have absorbed about a quarter of our carbon emissions. When plants die and decompose, they release that gas, but in the natural scheme of things, there is balance—old trees die, new ones grow. Deforestation, whether by land-clearing, industrial logging or forest fires, upsets the balance, accelerating the release of previously sequestered carbon back into the atmosphere. Some of it, for example that stored in Tasmania's monumental old-growth trees, has been locked in there for hundreds of years. Cutting them down is a bad idea, but that's not the only way trees die en masse. The IPCC expects more forest dieback in many regions over the twenty-first century, due to increased temperatures and drought.[15] Is planting more trees the answer? Flannery reckons we'd need to reforest an area the size of Australia, over a fifty-year period, to draw down one-tenth of the volume of carbon pollution humans emit each year.[16]

Soils are also carbon stores. So, for example, as Canada's boreal forests shrink, we lose not just the trees that help clean our air by 'breathing in' carbon right now, but the ancient storage facility beneath. What does this do? It turns up the heat. For someone who didn't pay attention in science lessons, the facts and figures behind all this can be confusing, but I like David George Haskell's description from *The Songs of Trees*: the conversion of a forest 'from a carbon sink to a carbon source adds yet more eiderdown to the atmospheric quilt.'[17]

Farming is another contributor to the build-up of greenhouse gases, thanks in no small part to livestock, and in particular the world's 1.5 billion cows. This is the basis of the argument that if you really care about climate change you should be vegan. Cows' burps, farts and manure emit methane. While there's way more CO_2 in the atmosphere, methane is much more effective at trapping heat, which is why Naomi Klein is worried about methane leaks from fracking. Farming is also the major source of nitrous oxide pollution, which primarily comes from fertilisers.

The last part of the greenhouse gas picture belongs to human-made fluorinated gases, which do not occur naturally in the environment. Remember when we worked out that CFCs from fridges and spray deodorants had damaged the ozone layer? Their replacements, HFCs (hydrofluorocarbons), are no angels either. While in terms of volume they are minimal, they have a strong greenhouse effect and are long-lived. Other synthetic fluorinated gases escape when producing things like aluminium and are used in the electronics sector.

Carbon dioxide levels are now at their highest in around 2.5 million years. Using ice cores drilled from Antarctica, where the ice trapped air bubbles as it froze, scientists can work out how much CO_2 was in the air 800,000 years ago. Rocks and deep sea sediment cores take us back further still. In March 1958, the first readings were taken directly from the air by a scientist called Charles David Keeling at the Mauna Loa Observatory in Hawaii. Keeling recorded the concentration of CO_2 in the air in parts per million (ppm) by volume. Monthly recordings have been taken from Hawaii ever since, with labs set up in additional locations from 1967 onwards. This ppm thing has become a rallying point for climate activists.

Before the Industrial Revolution, atmospheric CO_2 concentrations were about 280 ppm. Keeling's first reading was 315. By 2008 they'd reached 385. That was the year American climate scientist James Hansen and his team at Columbia University published their paper 'Target atmospheric CO_2: Where should humanity aim?' They concluded that 350 ppm was the tipping point. Any more and we risk dangerous levels of warming. 'If humanity wishes to preserve a planet similar to that on which civilization developed and to which life on Earth is adapted,' they advised, 'CO_2 will need to be reduced from its current 385 ppm to at most 350 ppm.'[18]

Hansen describes how climate sensitivity increases as temperatures rise, risking reinforcing feedback loops that could lead to much more rapid warming. So, for example, as polar sea ice shrinks, the white surfaces that reflect heat back out from the Earth (what we call Earth's 'albedo') are reduced. When dark seawater takes the ice's place it absorbs more heat, which leads to increased warming, which kills more trees, which releases more CO_2, which leads to even more warming ... Basically, we don't want to go there.

On your marks

London's November temperatures were about average in 2015. On Saturday 28th, the city reached 10 degrees: quite cool, take your coat, and if you're headed to the Tate Britain, a camera too. For here, in the 1840 Room, in the company of Lord Frederic Leighton's bronze of an athlete wrestling a python and surrounded by paintings dating from the Victorian Great Exhibition era, thirty-five activists in dark clothing form an arresting tableau. A woman washes her hands in a small bowl brought along for the purpose, pulls on latex gloves, then proceeds to ink her first volunteer, who has unzipped his hoodie and slipped half of it off to reveal a bare shoulder. She asks him, sotto voce, 'How are you feeling?'

'Pretty excited,' he says. 'I love this stuff.'

'Do you?' she whispers.

'How many tats have you got already?

'Three.'

'Any of them to do with climate change?'

'The one that Mel practised on my leg,' he laughs.

'Okay,' she says, adjusting the light on her headband. 'I'm ready, if you are.'

When she's done, his tattoo reads, '351'. It represents the CO_2 ppm number the year he was born.

Organisers from the group Liberate Tate staged the happening to draw attention to the fact that the gallery's major corporate sponsor was BP. Protests began after the *Deepwater Horizon* spill in 2010, when activists tipped molasses down the Tate's stairs. The next year, the Reverend Billy and his Earthalujah Choir turned up at Tate Modern to perform an exorcism. After the Birthmark protest, a Liberate Tater explained, 'The black mark on our skin reflects the taint of BP on Tate.'

A university art teacher was among the tattooed that Saturday. He recognises the performance as an 'audacious and poignant' way to challenge the idea of an oil company sponsoring public art. As for the tattoos, 'As birthmarks, memorialising the constant increase of greenhouse gases since the Industrial Revolution, they connote our individual complicity in the accumulation of atmospheric CO_2, as well as serving as constant reminders of our capacity to become better stewards of our planet and its future.'[19] The idea caught on. Youth delegates came home from the Paris climate summit with birthmark tattoos. Students lined up to get them outside a Canadian university.

In 2017 BP ended its 27-year sponsorship of Tate.

Under pressure—governments act

The United Nations climate change conference was held in Paris in December 2015. This was the twenty-first time the Conference of the Parties (COP) had met to discuss the climate issue—hence, it is known as COP21. It was this lot who'd negotiated the Kyoto Protocol, which in 1997 sought to limit emissions and put the obligation on developed countries on the basis that they're historically responsible for current levels.

Kyoto was ratified by the European Union, Australia, Norway and various other countries. Russia and Japan did not follow through. Canada committed but withdrew in 2011, and the United States never signed it in the first place. When COP15 happened in Copenhagen in 2009, environmentalists pinned their hopes on a new agreement with universal buy-in, but went home disappointed.

For many in the climate movement, Paris, COP21, felt like the last chance. There was reason for cautious optimism. Within a year of the summit, 176 countries had signed the Paris Agreement, committing to aim to keep global warming below 2 degrees above pre-industrial levels, and 'to pursue efforts to limit the temperature increase even further to 1.5 degrees'. It is, however, non-binding: signatories agree only 'to put forward their best efforts through "nationally determined contributions" and to strengthen these efforts in the years ahead'. It's easy to see how they might do the bare minimum. Switching to renewables means redrawing the economy; jobs and profits will move, and the big fossil fuel companies will fight like hungry tigers to prevent it. The United States, as the world's second largest carbon polluter, pledged to aim to reduce emissions by 26 to 28 per cent by 2025. Barack Obama signed that one. Trump wasted no time in announcing he'd withdraw as soon as possible (although the deal prevents exit before 2019).

In 2018, CO_2 levels in the atmosphere passed 410 ppm. NASA's 'moderate emissions scenario' projects 650 ppm by the end of the century.[20] Two years on from Paris, 1.5 degrees sounds like an impossible dream. Business as usual is leading us inexorably towards greater warming than that. But the extreme extraction strategy of the giants (ExxonMobil, BP, Shell and Chevron are among the ten biggest companies) aren't business as usual—they're business on steroids, they're incredibly risky business, worse than Tom Cruise dancing in his underpants.

I'm finding it stressful to research this. It's properly scary. Weather systems are complicated, but a pattern is clearly forming: climate change is exacerbating extreme weather events. We saw it with hurricanes Harvey, Katia and Irma. We're seeing it with fires. Seven of the ten biggest California wildfires have occurred in the last ten years. Longer, hotter heatwaves are driving up the bushfire risk in Australia. Globally, the ten warmest winters ever recorded have all occurred since 1998. The Arctic sea ice is declining. I watch over and over the heart-wrenching *National Geographic* footage of a starving polar bear dragging its emaciated hind legs across a grassy plane in search of food that isn't there, and I cry. Summer for the bears has always meant going without food while they wait for the ice that is their hunting grounds to form, but now that's taking longer, and they are wasting away. No wonder there are still climate-change deniers out there.

Denial is a coping mechanism for things we find too difficult to face, which explains why social scientists at Yale estimate that 30 per cent of Americans believe global warming isn't happening, while more than half think it's not caused by human activity. According to CSIRO, just 45 per cent of Australians agree that climate change is happening and is caused by humans.[21] About 8 per cent believe it isn't happening, and 38 per cent that it is, but as a result of 'natural fluctuations'. The remainder haven't a clue.

Australian IPCC scientist Lesley Hughes draws this analogy: Imagine you're standing in front of a Qantas plane with 100 engineers. Ninety-eight of them tell you they are very worried that the plane is going to crash. Two of them disagree, saying it's going to be fine.[22] Would you board that flight with your family?

I try to talk to my husband about the Qantas plane and about Parag Khanna's map, and suggest we start looking for property in Hobart. 'The whole of New South Wales might turn into a desert,' I say. 'Good for nothing but solar energy production.' For some reason this puts my husband in a bad temper. He reminds me that last week I regaled him about the Dr Evil possibilities of geoengineering that might see renegade governments or sinister billionaires take it upon themselves to inject sulphur into the stratosphere to mimic the effects of a giant volcanic eruption, thus dimming the sun. He tells me his own convoluted story about how his late grandmother won an encyclopaedia as a prize in 1932, and there were no entries for jet engines or DNA. 'What's your point?' I say.

'My point is that we have no idea what will be known in a hundred years' time.'

'It's eighty-two years.'

'You are unbelievably frustrating. That, I know,' he says, and goes back to browsing air conditioners online.

Is this how you feel?

'If you feel sorrow, anger or fear about global warming, you're not alone,' Dr Anthony Leiserowitz reassures me in dulcet tones. I'm not reclining on a leather sofa in a psychiatrist's office but sweating through a 47-degree Sydney summer's day, the second hottest on record, listening to audio from the Yale Climate Connections website. As Leiserowitz says, 'Immersing yourself in the subject can take its toll.'

The overwhelm is real. Support groups are beginning to crop up. In Salt Lake City, one uses the classic twelve-step program to structure bimonthly

'Good Grief' sessions, where sufferers meet, share and presumably blub. This kind of personal work takes effort and courage. No wonder some prefer to switch off, or pretend it's all in hand; that science or governments or Richard Branson will somehow save us. Just in time.

Since the publication of her 2016 book, *Hope and Grief in the Anthropocene: Reconceptualising human–nature relations*, Australian geographer Lesley Head has given talks about how hard we find it to acknowledge climate grief. 'There is a deep cultural pressure in the West to not be a "doom and gloom merchant",' she writes, but 'at least some of us should be thinking systematically about worst-case scenarios' and figuring out what our responses should be.[23]

I would argue that a lot more of us ought to be organising to pressure our governments to take action. Although we are mourning considerable losses, it is not game over. There is work to do. Urgent work. Denial isn't just pointless; it's dangerous.

Australian ethicist Clive Hamilton hammers this home in his book *Earthmasters: Playing God with the climate*:

> The psychological strategies we deploy to deny or, more commonly, to evade the facts of climate science, and thereby to blind ourselves to our moral responsibilities or reduce the pressure to act on them ... include wishful thinking, blame-shifting and selective disengagement. For selfish reasons, we do not want to change our behaviour or be required to do so by electing a government committed to deep cuts in emissions.[24]

Meanwhile those who profit from the existing fossil fuel–based system attempt to discredit the science. The Heartland Institute is famed for its defence of the tobacco industry. One of their best guys on this in the '90s was the American physicist Fred Singer, who called the link between passive smoking and cancer 'junk science'. Singer appears in a controversial 'documentary' called *The Great Global Warming Swindle*. While the Heartland Institute no longer discloses where its funding comes from, past donors include ExxonMobil, tobacco giant Philip Morris and oil barons the Koch brothers. Since 2009 they've released reports from something called the Nongovernmental International Panel on Climate Change, which claim to debunk the IPCC findings. The IPCC reports are produced by more than 500 unpaid scientists; the NIPCC reports are written by three (and one is our old mate Fred Singer), paid by Heartland, which is paid by oil companies. I know. Even so, this stuff gets reported on, and people get duped by it. I mean, it's a scientific report, right? Who are we meant to believe? Most of us haven't a clue what scientists are on about, but we know we're meant to trust them.

Joe Duggan thinks scientists have a communication problem. 'Your average person doesn't understand that, in the academic field, when we say we're 95 per cent certain something is happening, that means we are, essentially, certain. The tendency, outside of science, is to say, "Ah, but what about the other 5 per cent?"'[25]

Duggan, an Australian, worked in marine research after getting his degree (he majored in zoology), then took time out as a builder's labourer. 'My science work didn't centre around climate change, but in the research world you understand that it affects everything, and in my sphere, the dark little brother of climate change—ocean acidification—had massive repercussions.' On building sites he was 'reminded how ordinary people talk. The contrast could not have been starker in terms of communication. When you work on a building site, you need to speak and interact in a clear, straightforward way to get the job done. No more flourishes; what you say is exactly what you mean.'

He decided to return to academia, this time to study science communication. 'There's a whole bunch of reasons for the disconnect between what scientists know and what the general public believes,' he tells me. 'I thought one of them might be that scientists aren't communicating the way everyone else does. Scientists deal in evidence and data, not emotions, and that's as it should be. Their work should be precise and meticulous, not riddled with feelings, but if you give them a moment to reflect on what their climate science findings mean to them, it's a different story.'

Is This How You Feel? began as a website and became an exhibition that opened in Melbourne during National Science Week. It consists of handwritten letters from scientists in response to the question 'How does climate change make you feel?' Duggan's aim was to battle public apathy and disengagement by humanising the scientists: 'They're not robots. These scientists are mothers, fathers, grandparents, daughters. They are real people. And they're concerned.'

In her letter, Lesley Hughes describes how she dreamed of being a biologist as an animal-loving kid: '[My] bedroom was full of jars and boxes of things that crawled and slithered and hopped. The notion that I could actually be paid for doing this, as an adult, was truly wonderful.' And how she feels today at the thought of climate change–induced species extinction: 'We have so much to lose.'

British geographer James Byrne writes that worrying about climate change keeps him up at night. He admits to anger and sadness, but also excitement. 'We can fix this!' he writes.

Michael Mann, professor of atmospheric science at Penn State, lists his emotions as: concern ('that we will leave behind a fundamentally degraded planet for our children'), bemusement ('because the scientific case is clear'), frustration, disgust, anger and hope. 'Yes, most of all, I feel hope.'

Duggan expected fear to dominate the letters, but was pleased to see that hope is very much in evidence. That CSIRO report that speaks of denial also confirms anger, fear and powerlessness are the most commonly felt emotions in response to climate change, but—and here's the clincher—active engagement on the issue results in 'a higher sense of hope'.[26] We feel better when we get off our arses and try to fix it.

We can all take steps to tackle climate change. We can give our votes to politicians who prioritise it, lobby government, local councils and business, and join environmental groups. We can switch to a green energy supplier, divest our funds from fossil fuel companies and pressure institutions to do the same. We can switch off the lights (not just for Earth Hour), fly less, buy less, shop local, eat less meat or go vegan, and talk about those things so that, gradually, we change the culture. We can cycle, walk, take public transport. We can be the change. Sure, I am just one person, but *we* are a community of people, connected to many more.

Action stations

The universe has sent me May Boeve on a rare visit to Sydney from the United States. 'David won. Remember that,' she tells me. 'You have to keep telling yourself: "David won, David won." It's a useful mantra when a task seems daunting.'[27] Not that Boeve does daunted. The woman who was made executive director of 350.org when she was twenty-seven is confident that the Davids of the climate-change movement will ultimately beat the lumbering old fossil-fuel Goliaths.

Renewables now make economic as well as moral sense. Solar power costs have fallen dramatically. Tesla has built the world's largest lithium-ion battery in South Australia, linked to a wind farm, while *Bloomberg* reports that electric cars might soon be cheaper than gas-guzzling ones.[28] Petrol and diesel cars aren't just on the way out in France; the United Kingdom, Norway, the Netherlands and India are all up for banning them, while loads of other countries have set targets for increasing the percentage of electric vehicles on the roads. Global coal demand has either reached its peak or is about to, depending which report you read. While the International Energy Agency expects that oil and gas use will continue to rise as populations grow, renewables are getting cheaper and more accessible all the time,[29] despite many fossil-fuel operations being propped up by government subsidies and sweet deals.[30]

Resistance is spreading. Cities are suing over extreme weather events. In September 2017, San Francisco filed a lawsuit against BP, Chevron, ConocoPhillips, ExxonMobil and Royal Dutch Shell, claiming that 'Global warming is here and it is harming San Francisco now' and 'this egregious state of affairs is no accident'.[31] Burning fossil fuels is the primary cause, they assert, and these companies have known for years and have done nothing about it.

The People vs Big Oil. It's a Hollywood script writing itself. In January 2018, New York's mayor Bill de Blasio joined in: 'This city is standing up and saying, "We're going to take our own actions to protect our own people!"' In February it was Paris's turn, when the city council announced it was looking into the viability of a case—floods in recent years have seen curators rushing precious artworks out of the Louvre. Bill McKibben must be punching the air.

In 2012, McKibben wrote an article for *Rolling Stone* calling for mass divestment to hit the fossil-fuel companies where it hurts: in the wallet.[32] Since serious change requires a movement, and movements (usually) require an enemy, he nominated the industry as 'Public Enemy Number One'. Why should these companies be allowed to dump their waste—CO_2 emissions—for free, for years? We could use some moral outrage. It worked against South Africa during the apartheid era. That article got *Rolling Stone* ten times more Facebook likes than Justin Bieber's cover story.

McKibben made a movie called *Do the Math* and went on the road with it. 'Shall we work through the numbers?' he says.[33] 'There are three, and they're easy.' Two degrees is how much the world has said it's safe to let the planet warm. The second number is how much carbon we can pour into the atmosphere and have a reasonable chance of staying below 2 degrees: 565 more gigatonnes (a gigatonne is a billion tonnes). Under business as usual, we'll be there by the late 2020s. Scary? The third number is the really frightening one. This refers to how much carbon the big fossil-fuel companies already have in their reserves, and it's 2795 gigatonnes: 'Five times as much as the most conservative governments on Earth think it would be safe to pour into the atmosphere.'

In 1989 McKibben wrote the first book about global warming for a mainstream audience. He was inspired by a fierce drought that had hit the American grain belt the year before.[34] That summer, James Hansen had given a testimony on 'the greenhouse effect' to the Senate Committee on Energy and Natural Resources. Global warming, Hansen said, had begun. McKibben set about investigating, and the result, *The End of Nature*, is as sobering a read as the title suggests.

The author assumed that once everyone heard what was going on with the climate there would be rapid action taken by governments and business.[35] Yeah, about that. For the next decade he published more books, went on speaking tours and penned stirring opinion pieces for important magazines, but McKibben knew one man could not build a movement alone. He needed an army. An army with energy, enthusiasm and brains to spare, and with skin in the game. If climate change breaks Earth's thermostat, this group 'won't have much of a planet on which to make use of their degrees,' he said. He needed university students.

In 2003 May Boeve was an eager, blue-eyed, blonde undergraduate newly arrived at Middlebury College, Vermont, and keen to make a difference. She was that sort of kid. 'From an early age, I was aware that something was not right with the way the world worked,' she says.[36] As a four-year-old growing up in Sonoma, California, she'd gotten her mother to help her write a letter to George H.W. Bush asking him to make cruelty to animals—'including bugs'—illegal. 'When I was ten, I started an animal rights club, and we raised money with a lemonade stall at my dad's church. Even then I knew fundraising was important.' They made $18. 'I had a financial-planning thing going,' she says. 'It involved three peanut butter jars—one for savings, one for spending, one for giving. The giving jar always went to PETA.'

Her father was a pastor in the Dutch Reformed Church, and her mother a writer. 'She writes mostly about food now, but she also wrote a book about her brother, who was the first American civilian killed in the Vietnam War.

He was a volunteer in the program that the Peace Corps was modelled on. The experience turned my mother into an anti-war activist very early on.'

Boeve says her parents helped shape her view of the world and her role in it. 'I was raised in engagement with bigger issues; that's what we talked about at the dinner table. I guess because of my mother, the '60s was very shaping for me as a young person. You always grow up thinking that your generation is the worst and all the fun was had before you came along, right?' As a kid, Boeve was the one listening to her mother's Joni Mitchell records imagining herself at a hippie sit-in. 'For me the idea of being part of a social movement was a really big deal—that was the world I wanted to live in—so when there was this emerging climate-change movement, I do remember very clearly thinking: here's my chance.'

At Middlebury, Boeve's animal thing morphed into a gardening thing, and she helped set up a worm farm in the college greenhouse. One summer she and her friends took a road trip in a bus fuelled by vegetable oil. They stopped to talk in 150 venues along the way, collecting names for a Clean Car Pledge to encourage American companies to make fuel-efficient vehicles. When the tour wound up in Detroit, they presented 11,000 signatures to the United Automobile Workers union. So this is how you change the world; take on awesome challenges while everyone else is at the beach. And do it with grace.

While Boeve is now one of the most respected climate-change activists of her generation, and is entirely at home with putting politicians in their place—'I want you to know, if you fail to rise to the challenge,' she told Todd Stern, then the United States Special Envoy for Climate Change, before he left for COP15, 'that you are personally responsible to all the millions of people who have tried to let you know how important this issue is'—what strikes me most about her in person is how warm and empathetic she is. The future is female. We both wish it would hurry up. 'Trump has waged war on climate,' she says.[37]

Bill McKibben, as Middlebury's scholar-in-residence, was an influential presence while Boeve was at college, but he wasn't the one to start her on the climate path. That was an economics professor who ran a class called 'Building the New Climate Movement'. Boeve didn't actually take it—she'd enrolled in something called 'Voices of Rock in Latin America'—but she attended anyway, and joined in the class project. 'It was to create a campus-based activism group. It soon became the most fun part of my week.' Some Sunday evenings they'd have 100 students show up. They did things like camp outside in terrible weather to push the slogan 'Keep winter cold!' and campaign to persuade the university to go carbon neutral. Did that happen?

'How could it not?'

Middlebury is now famous for incubating 350.org. As graduation grew closer, Boeve and her inner circle were reluctant to give up their climate-action group. 'We wanted to stay together. We had this idea to move somewhere in the United States where there was a lot of coal and stop it being mined. We got the maps out, looked for the place with the highest concentrations of coal reserves, green energy potential, students and micro-breweries.' If all else failed, there was beer. They never made it to Billings, Montana.

'That same summer Bill had just come back from a trip to Bangladesh,' explains Boeve. 'Seeing the floods, the dengue fever and considering the implications of that—mosquitos now live in places they didn't used to—he came back thinking, "I can't just write books anymore."' He asked Boeve and her friends Jeremy Osbourn, Will Bates, Jamie Henn, Kelly Blen, Jon Warno and Phil Aroneanu to help organise a march across Vermont. In September 2006, their five-day trek culminated in a rally of 1000 people in Burlington's Battery Park. McKibben was shocked to discover this was the biggest climate-change march in American history. Clearly, something had to be done.

Their next move was to create a viral protest, under the banner Step It Up. It being 2007, they used MySpace. Humble beginnings—just seven people sitting in a room with their laptops emailing everyone they knew—but the April timing was great. Cities were already pledging to reduce emissions. In February, *An Inconvenient Truth* had won an Oscar, after taking US$45 million at the box office worldwide. A study found that watching the film caused a 50 per cent relative increase in the purchase of voluntary carbon offsets within a 10-mile radius of the screening.[38] Unlike the Women's March, Step It Up had a single clear policy ask. They were demanding a more serious commitment from Congress to reduce emissions, way beyond what Kyoto called for: they wanted an 80 per cent reduction by 2050. It didn't happen, obviously, but it did make it harder for politicians to ignore requests for action on climate.

By 2 March, the team was expecting 757 different actions, including an underwater rally by scuba divers off Key West and a parade of 'clean' cars in San Francisco. By 13 April, there were 1300 events planned in fifty states. Step It Up had 'no business being particularly successful because we have no money and not really any organisation,' said McKibben, but rather like Earth Day, 'people were ready to act.'[39] Many participants had never done anything like it before.[40]

Boeve attributes its reach partly to the students' 'beautiful naivety. What we didn't know we made up for in enthusiasm. We were really bubbly; we had a sense of humour, but no sense of what was too big to ask for. It was like, let's get everyone together and demonstrate our beautiful movement, which was awesome—that's exactly what we should have done. It was not pointed, or if it was pointed at anyone, it was pointed at politicians, with the idea that we could encourage them to do the right thing.'

A second action day that autumn led to the foundation of 350.org the following year, with McKibben and Naomi Klein on the board. Boeve says it thrives because it rejects the top-down 'Big Green' model; it's about interconnected networks rather than central control. She spends most of her time on the phone talking different groups into coming together, although she did manage to get herself arrested in front of the White House protesting the Keystone XL Pipeline. 'To make this work today, it has to be about allies and collaboration,' she says. '350.org is not a movement. It's part of one.'

As McKibben once said, 'For the foreseeable future, weekends are for fighting tyranny,'[41] but today Boeve has a day off. She's going to the beach with the 350 Australia team. She didn't bring a sunhat. 'There's still a hole in our ozone layer,' I tell her.

'I'll be fine,' she says, showing that a bit of that naivety clings on. She heads off down the street then doubles back. Boeve can't resist an organising opportunity. 'You know there are 1200 proposed new coal plants throughout the world? You have them here. You can stop them. You should get in touch with Lock the Gate. There's a big Australian action day coming on the 24th of March. It's called Time 2 Choose. It's going to be amazing. Make sure you're there, Clare.'

I'll be there. It's impossible to resist May Boeve.

9

Fight Club

'I wish I had more middle fingers.'

—Rose McGowan

'At the very least, we have to put up a good fight.'

—Bill McKibben

When the system lets you down

Students Liz Morley, twenty-one, and Breana Macpherson-Rice, twenty-three, are trying to explain the origins of their climate-change activism. Digging around for her earliest eco experience, Macpherson-Rice comes up with, 'I was part of the compost team at school,' then adds, 'I didn't start it,' lest I give her credit where it's not due.[1] They are scrupulously honest; it's a matter of principle, because those they oppose deal in half-truths and outright lies, like Trump's tweets about cold snaps ('It's freezing and snowing in New York—we need global warming!').[2]

Macpherson-Rice answered McKibben's call to join the divestment movement as soon as she heard it. She's read all his books and volunteers for 350.org. The composting 'was just something we did during lunch breaks. I'm not sure I can honestly tell you I cared deeply about it.' The caring bit came later. She'd just arrived at university and was taking international studies. 'I always thought I would grow up, get a great job and travel the world. That's how I imagined my life playing out,' she says. A lecture threw that dream into sharp relief by describing how our warmed world might look by the end of the century, with refugees rather than gap-year backpackers on the move, forced from their scorched homelands by desertification and sea level rise. 'It was something in the way that the lecturer explained it,' says Macpherson-Rice, 'or maybe I was just ready to hear it, but it clicked: We've been lied to. Our future is not secure. It will most likely be characterised by climate disaster, worsening social problems and more extreme weather.'

She switched courses to study environmental humanities at the University of New South Wales, only to find the institution had investments tied up in the fossil-fuel industry. 'It was during Orientation Week; I got chatting to these kids from Fossil Free UNSW. I was horrified.' She signed up and was soon made campaign co-ordinator.

Elizabeth Morley was acutely aware of the environment as a child growing up during Australia's Millennium Drought. The nightly news told of farmer suicides and reservoirs drying up. 'I was obsessed with saving water,' she says. 'I worried that the country would run out and we'd all die.'[3] She was still in primary school when she watched *An Inconvenient Truth*. 'I was very upset by it. I thought the world was going to end, but in high school I kind of forgot. Everything around me seemed fine.'

As it does right now in Sydney's leafy Glebe. Pop songs play on the radio; the weather has broken after a four-day hot spell, and there's a pleasant breeze. Across the street, a handsome man walks a lolloping orange-haired dog. Next door, the bookstore brims with browsers. You'd never know to look at it that this is our dangerously warming world.

The teenaged Morley figured there was nothing to see here 'around the time that the carbon tax was being introduced in Australia. I felt like the government was acting and scientists were being listened to; that they had this thing under control.' But just as Jayna Zweiman did with feminism, Morley had a wake-up call. One minute you're just a kid, happily trusting that the old people are acting responsibly; the next, you grow up. Fast.

Carbon pricing was introduced in 2011 with the Gillard Labor government's *Clean Energy Act*, but repealed in 2014 by Tony Abbott (the Liberal–National Coalition accepted at least $1.8 million in direct donations from mining and energy companies that year). Australia did sign the Paris Agreement, committing 'to taking strong domestic and international action on climate change' and reducing emissions, but guess what happened the following year? Emissions rose.

I ask Morley if she was paying attention to politics again when the carbon tax was killed, and she says, 'Of course,' and I ask her how she felt, and she says, 'Angry. The injustice really got to me. They knew it would lead to where we are today, the path was clearly set, but they decided to keep going because it made them richer.' I ask her who she means by 'they' and she says, 'Our politicians, on both sides, who do not act in our best interest, but profit at our expense; and the fossil-fuel industry, and everyone who gets paid by them.'

The year of the Paris Agreement was also the year Morley read *This Changes Everything*. She was in her second year at UNSW, majoring in Japanese. 'Naomi Klein's book was the big turning point for me in my adult life; like, god, our future is not secure. Our lives are not going to be like our parents' lives were. I can't have these assumptions that we'll grow old in a world that's safe and familiar to us, like previous generations did.' She, too, switched courses (to environmental humanities and economics) and now talks about the urgent need 'to dismantle the power dynamics that exist in perpetuating the use of fossil fuels'. All she needs is a beret. Don't get the wrong impression; these women aren't dangerous revolutionaries. They are mild-mannered, open, friendly and considered. Diligent students. When contemplating arrest as they planned their 36-hour occupation of UNSW's council chamber in 2016, they were confident that their exemplary academic records would work in their favour should the police be called in. 'We are the kids who get good grades,' says Morley.

Macpherson-Rice: 'On most people's inbuilt crim-scoping radar, I score a "more-likely-to-get-mugged-than-break-the-law". Let's be frank—I'm a bit of a nerd.'[4]

The sit-in was a last resort. They'd tried asking nicely. Their requests for meetings with the Vice Chancellor were repeatedly knocked back, even after they'd surveyed 1300 students and found that 78 per cent supported divestment. 'We got nowhere,' says Macpherson-Rice. 'So we collected signatures for an open letter. We got staff and academics on board. We presented it to the Vice Chancellor, but within a couple of weeks he'd made his response.' It was no. 'We finally decided to take the route of the "hard" tactic,' says Morley. 'Direct action.'

The sit-in was part of a national day of student climate action. In Victoria, arts major Aoife Nicklason was one of nine students who clambered, naked, onto the roof of the University of Melbourne's storied Old Quad building, with a message painted on their bums: 'Drop your assets.' They guessed right that 'the internet's obsession with butts (thanks for that one, Kimmy K)' should guarantee news coverage.[5] Most memorable headline? 'Melbourne University students get high, naked.' Nicklason wrote for a student news site, 'For our voices to reach as many people as possible, our activism must be as diverse as possible. So write a letter to the editor, tweet about it, make a YouTube video, talk to your mum, do some performance art.'

Beware, though: mums don't always understand. One Mother's Day, Macpherson-Rice did not get home for lunch. Instead, she put her war paint on—a red cross on each cheek—climbed into a white hazmat suit and joined a blockade of the Sandgate Bridge on the Newcastle coal rail line. The protestors sang and ate hummus as the police removed them one by one, charging them with trespassing. That same day, a flotilla of several hundred activists in kayaks blockaded Newcastle harbour. The chant? 'We are unstoppable! Another world is possible!'

I ask Macpherson-Rice if her parents were mad at her for getting arrested. 'Mum was just really worried about my future,' she says. 'I get it, but … '

'This is more important?'

She shifts in her seat and moves her elbow onto the table, revealing the birthmark '355' on her outer wrist. She sees me see it, and smiles. 'We used data from Tasmania so it's a bit different from other people's.'

Parts per million recordings began in the southern hemisphere at Cape Grim on the north-western tip of Tasmania in 1976, the year I was born. If I were the tattoo type, my ink would read '329'. Measurements are always slightly lower here than in the northern hemisphere, because there is less land mass (hence less population and industrial activity), and the ocean—a carbon sink—covers a larger area. 'The tattoo means a lot to me,' says Macpherson-Rice. 'It's a reminder, a constant one, and also a conversation starter.'

'I remember you saying you got it on that side of your arm so you're not always having to look at it; otherwise you can't escape it,' says Morley.

'Yeah but mostly it's so other people see it. My cousin was like, "What that's about?" and when I explained, he said, "What's the ppm thing now?" So I told him, "Now it's 403. Time is running out."'

A few months on, as I put the finishing touches to this book, the levels have crept above 404. Take a look after you've read this. You can download the data from the Cape Grim CSIRO website. The trend, you will see, is clear: the only way is up.

Stop Adani

'Welcome to the O,' says a bright kid in cut-off denims, a red T-shirt and Perspex 'Stop Adani' earrings. These slogan accessories are a hot trend—the designer was commissioned to make them by the Australian Youth Climate Coalition (AYCC). I've seen eight pairs already today.

There are more than a thousand of us here this morning. As the organisers round up stragglers, we get into formation, laughing and talking as we spell out the letters: S-T-O-P-A-D-A-N-I to make a human sign. The mood is good-natured and fun. Two guys have dressed up as Malcolm Turnbull and Gautam Adani carrying bags of money, but there are also folks in sea-creature costumes. One woman has come as a giant prawn. White foam laps yellow sand on the iconic Bondi Beach, as the ocean stretches beyond—it's the perfect front-page picture. A drone buzzes overhead as we break into a chant, 'Stop Adani! Stop, stop Adani.'

Over sixty community events are happening across Australia, including human signs on beaches at the Gold Coast, Noosa and Cottesloe. It's all over social media. As May Boeve told me, the emphasis on visuals really works. 'The other side is always going to have more money than us, but we have creativity and the human spirit,' she said. 'The way that you depict that visually is very significant.'

In Bondi, speeches begin, but there's a problem with the sound system and half the crowd slips away, although not before I ask a couple of old-timers why they came. Turns out they've been involved with Greenpeace since forever. The Stop Adani Alliance unites thirty-seven organisations, including Greenpeace, Friends of the Earth, 350.org, GetUp!, 1 Million Women and the AYCC. My new Greenpeace friends echo Bob Brown's assertion that 'in forty years' time, people will be talking about the campaign to stop Adani like they now talk about the Franklin. "Where were you and what did you do?" they will ask.'[6]

The campaign to protect the Franklin River in south-west Tasmania made Bob Brown's name. He was working as a GP in Launceston in the early '70s when he fell in love with the state's majestic landscapes, buying a bush property in the Liffey Valley. In 1976, he rafted the Franklin, dubbed the 'last wild river', and was smitten by its pristine beauty. That same year, he and some friends got together in his kitchen and formed the Tasmanian Wilderness Society. The membership fee was $2.[7] Their first campaign was to try to stop a concrete bridge being built over another river, the Picton (they lost). When plans were announced to dam the Gordon River right below the Franklin, they were ropeable.

Australia was one of the first countries to sign the World Heritage Convention, and in 1981 World Heritage status was granted to the Great Barrier Reef, Kakadu National Park and the Willandra Lakes Region. The Tasmanian Wilderness was now proposed, but powerful forces opposed adding this vast area of old-growth forests, ancient caves, rivers and gorges to the list—there was money to be made.

The state-owned Hydro-Electric Commission planned to dam the Gordon River for a power plant, which would have drowned 30 kilometres of the Franklin and surrounding temperate rainforests. The environmentalists had seen it all before when damming flooded Lake Pedder. Plenty of locals were up for this new scheme, persuaded by the promise of job creation, but the Wilderness Society argued that as one of the last remaining waterways 'not marked by the hand of modern man',[8] the Franklin must be preserved. Recalls Brown: 'It seemed hopeless. We had the three newspapers in Tasmania, the unions, except for the ETU [Electrical Trade Union], the business sector, both houses of Parliament, both political parties, all in the favour of the dam. We came to Canberra and the then Prime Minister, Mr Malcolm Fraser, said it was a state matter. We had one effort in the High Court, we tried to argue that the Commonwealth should not be lending money to Tasmania to damage a potential World Heritage area, [but] that … got short shrift.'[9]

Colour television helped push the issue into public consciousness across Australia (the campaign to save Lake Pedder had been waged in black and white). Footage of the area's extraordinary beauty captured hearts and minds; what civilised society would willingly trash this? 'Flooding the Franklin would be like putting a scratch across the Mona Lisa,' said Brown. In June 1980, an estimated 10,000 protestors marched through Hobart. As if to prove this was no hippie rabble, Brown marched in a suit and tie.

Another founding Wilderness Society member, the caver Kevin Kiernan, had been busy rediscovering Aboriginal caves in the lower Franklin. In March 1981, wallaby bone fragments and Aboriginal butchering tools dating from the Pleistocene were found at the Kutikina Cave site. It made headline news. Members of the Tasmanian Aboriginal community told a Senate inquiry that they and the river and the caves were one: 'Their destruction represents a part destruction of us.'[10] The dam issue became so divisive that the Tasmanian government called a referendum. On 12 December 1981, voters were given a choice of two different dam-scheme options, but no option to object outright. More than 30 per cent wrote 'No Dams' across their ballot papers, resulting in the toppling of the premier.

As far as I know, no one made earrings featuring the distinctive yellow triangle of the 'No Dams' logo, but there's a sticker in the collection of the National Museum of Australia. Craftivists sewed banners with it. But while the debate raged, the bulldozers moved in. By the time UNESCO granted the Tasmanian Wilderness its World Heritage status, construction on the dam had already begun.

In response, the blockade kicked off in December 1982. According to the Wilderness Society, 6000 people registered to take part. About 1400 were arrested, and nearly 500 jailed. Brown was one of them. On his release from Risdon Prison in January, he was elected to the Tasmanian Parliament as the MP for Denison.

The federal election happened in March. In the run-up, the 'National South-West Coalition including Tasmanian Wilderness Society and Australian Conservation Foundation' took out a full-page ad in Fairfax newspapers. 'Authorised by Dr Robert Brown, Parliament House, Hobart', it featured Peter Dombrovskis's photograph *Morning Mist, Rock Island Bend, Franklin River* with the caption, 'Would you vote for a party that would destroy this?' The answer was no. Bob Hawke's incoming Labor government passed the *World Heritage Properties Conservation Act 1983*, which along with amendments to the *National Parks and Wildlife Conservation Act 1975*, outlawed clearing and excavation in the area. The dam was finished.

'Those who say the [Adani] mine can't be stopped have forgotten the unbeatable power of the majority of people standing up for what they believe in,' says Brown.[11] Most Australians don't support the Adani mine or public money being spent on it.[12] The AYCC helped persuade Australia's biggest four banks not to fund the project, with volunteers postering Westpac ATMs under cover of darkness with altered options. 'Select an amount or enter another amount then press okay,' became, 'Fund Adani's dangerous mine near the Great Barrier Reef? or Protect our climate and rule out the Adani coal mine?'

Inevitably some went further and, as Brown did in the '80s, risked their liberty for the cause. In January 2018, five Frontline Action on Coal activists blockaded the Adani-owned Abbot Point Terminal, shutting it down for eight hours. A Queensland police chief spoke darkly of the possibility of a vigilante response.[13] These protestors—city blow-ins, spoiled students— were threating the jobs of Aussie battlers. Was it 1464 or 10,000 jobs?

No one knew. But as the tabloids beat up fears of unemployment among locals already suffering from the effects of a recent cyclone, the true story of Adani's supposed job-creation plans emerged. They would use driverless trucks, and 'everything will be autonomous [automated] from mine to port.'[14] As Adani's hand-picked economist Jerome Fahrer told the Queensland Land Court, 'It's not many jobs. We can agree on that.'[15]

The Wangan and Jagalingou Family Council represents the traditional owners of the Galilee Basin. They say the mine would 'tear the heart out of the land' and its scale would have

> devastating impacts on our native title, ancestral lands and waters, our totemic plants and animals, and our environmental and cultural heritage. It would pollute and drain billions of litres of groundwater, and obliterate important springs systems. It would potentially wipe out threatened and endangered species. It would literally leave a huge black hole, monumental in proportions, where there were once our homelands. These effects are irreversible. Our land will be 'disappeared'.[16]

Lock the gate

Bleary-eyed at 6 a.m., I climb onto a bus to go camping with strangers. Among us are a couple of young activists, a beautiful French girl, a stand-offish filmmaker, two mums with grown-up kids and a corporate lawyer. An older couple is planning a posh cruise to Malta after this. Why did they come? They are worried about their grandchildren's future, they tell me. 'We want to see for ourselves what sort of state we're leaving the place in.' At the front of the bus sits a Knitting Nanna, proudly sporting her 'Viva La Nannalution!' T-shirt. She and her friend sing in an eco-choir, performing original songs with names like 'Green Like Me' and 'Machines Are Closing In'.

We are taking Lock the Gate's two-day 'Hunter Valley vs Coal' tour. Our destination is a picturesque winegrowing region of New South Wales, home of the romantic mini-break. Slick Sydney couples nip off here for dirty weekends, seduced by the promise of a deluxe spa-bath suite with views over 'wonderfully verdant rolling countryside'. Providing they face the right direction.

What the tourism blurbs do not disclose is that Nature is under attack in these parts. Multinational mining corporations have transformed large tracts of it into a toxic dust bowl where nothing green grows. Once they're done, in say twenty or thirty years, these companies can get away with leaving what they call the 'final voids', which can stretch several kilometres across and hundreds of metres down. There are forty-five of them approved or planned for New South Wales; added together, they have a bigger surface area than Sydney Harbour. In all the talk of the jobs mining may or may not create, there is little discussion of the long-term future— where will people work when all that's left is these gaping wounds? Here? Not likely.

It has been suggested that the voids might one day be turned into jolly tourist lakes,[17] but that's wishful thinking. In the case of the enormous Warkworth mine next to the embattled village of Bulga, the pit lake would take 800 years to reach equilibrium (when the water levels are stable).[18] Other lakes should stabilise more quickly: in fifty years over at Liddell, and 300 years at Maules Creek on the Liverpool Plains, where more than 250 people have been arrested for trying to protect the surrounding Leard State Forest since the mine was approved. However long they take to form, pit lakes will be salty and laden with heavy metals. Around their shores, the mountains of dumped overburden make landslips likely. It's hard to imagine how these places can fail to become dangerous no-go zones. How all this will affect the groundwater is unknown, but here's something we can be sure of: the reason the mining giants are in no hurry to restore this land to the state in which they found it is money.

In the United States, mining companies have been required by law since the 1970s to backfill final voids, and this is factored into a mine's initial approval. That is not the case in Australia. Here, mining companies routinely revise their plans after approval, and it is easier to argue that unforeseen costs make backfill untenable, or that they might come back and dig a bit more in the future.[19] Marketing materials try to put a pleasant spin on it. One company even suggests we might look on these unholy holes as 'benefits'—they could become wildlife conservation areas! It's all bullshit except the bit about the impracticality of 'significant cost implications'. When the easily accessible coal runs out, and a mine is no longer commercially viable, it's standard practice not to fill the voids. If no one's making you and this ain't your backyard, why bother? Just pack up and go home.

I've read about open-cut coalmining, but up close, it's chilling to witness so vast a killed field. Those who believe in good and evil might see the devil himself in these desolate expanses of wasteland, which were once green valleys, thriving communities and bushland. On windy days, dust turns the sky grey. The haze is easily mistaken for smoke, and on more than one occasion emergency services have been called out to a fire that doesn't exist. In one month alone, there were seventy-two poor–air quality alerts for the Hunter Valley. Meanwhile, blast plumes from the mines contain toxic oxides of nitrogen, which give them an orange tinge. These plumes sometimes travel several kilometres before dispersing. Low-level exposure can cause eye and airway irritation, but breathing this stuff in at high levels can result in a build-up of fluid in the lungs, and even death.

The racket adds another dimension to the stress of living here. Former teacher AnneMaree McLaughlin lives in Bulga and wears ear plugs to bed to reduce the noise from the Warkworth mine next door, where bulldozers, dump trucks, draglines and excavators move rock and earth 'all day [and] all night'.[20] Recently, she joined a 'protest orchestra' outside the EPA's Newcastle office. Her neighbour George Tlaskal brought his chainsaw (leaving the blade at home) while others rattled cowbells and yelled through megaphones to give the bureaucrats inside a taste of what it's like to deal with an uncontrollable din.

Neighbourhood getting you down? Move. The mine owners would prefer it, and typically help some on their way by throwing money. In the beginning, the owners of strategically placed properties can clean up, providing they sign a gag clause. Life gets trickier for those who hold out, or live in properties the mine doesn't desire.

Mark McAlpin's family settled in Bulga in the 1840s. His ancestor's picture is up on the wall of the Bulga community hall, our first stop on the bus tour. McAlpin loves where he lives, but it's breaking his heart. 'I can't sell my property, not that I want to, because it's worthless now,' he tells me. 'What can I do? We're in a state of limbo, with everything decaying around us, including my mental health.'

AnneMaree McLaughlin smiles as she hands me a plate of plump scones, but the set of her shoulders speaks of a deep weariness. The mining company has bought the local pub and is trying to close a public road. Rumour has it they're in talks to buy the service station. What's up for sale next? The sky? I ask her about the stress, and she admits it gets to people, then visibly straightens and says, 'Look, we're not going to lie down and take it. You don't just go gentle into the night; you've got to stand up, because it's unjust.'

One by one, members of the community head to the front of the hall and tell their stories. 'We had a ministerial deed of agreement which says this area [Saddle Ridge, which shields the village of Bulga from Warkworth] shall never be mined,' explains John Krey, who heads up the Bulga Milbrodale Progress Association. 'Well, the government set about, over a period of two years, changing all the rules.'

This has long been mining country. The first coal was exported from the Hunter in 1799. What's different in the era of extreme extraction is the scale. Warkworth and neighbouring Mount Thorley have been mined since the 1980s. They were merged into a single operation in 2004, when approvals were granted to Rio Tinto for a major expansion. Around the same time, the federal government announced a massive expansion of the Hunter Valley Coal Chain infrastructure.

George Tlaskal spent two decades working for mining companies as a research scientist, and he and his family moved to Bulga in 1987, but by the time he came to write a submission to the NSW Planning Assessment Commission (PAC) about yet another proposed expansion of Warkworth in 2014, things had gotten out of hand: 'Until recently, we had coexisted with the mines reasonably well ... In 2003 [the mine] was about 8 km away and we were protected from their noise and dust by the natural formations of the Saddle Ridge and by the Warkworth Sands Woodlands conservation area ... in perpetuity.'[21] So they believed. The rare woodland, which grows on ancient aeolian sands, is a wildlife corridor and refuge for migratory birds. Its stands of rough-barked apple and coastal banksia trees are listed as a critically endangered ecological community. But the law, as it turns out, can be sculpted and changed by those who apply enough pressure.

'Five years ago world coal prices nearly quadrupled and Rio Tinto doubled the rate of production [at Mount Thorley Warkworth] to make the best of it,' writes Tlaskal.[22] '[An] area that was planned in 2003 to last to 2021 was mined almost entirely in half the time.' So Rio Tinto applied to extend the mine to within 2.6 kilometres of Bulga. The PAC granted permission, but residents challenged the decision in the NSW Land and Environment Court, and won. The judge ruled that 'The Project's impacts would exacerbate the loss of sense of place, and materially and adversely change the sense of community, of the residents of Bulga and the surrounding countryside.' Sorry. No mine extension.

Rio Tinto appealed in the Supreme Court, but there too the judge came down in favour of the Bulga community. There was no room to move until the government changed the law to make it a legal requirement for all approval authorities to prioritise development of 'significant resources' of coal over other considerations. Rio Tinto was permitted to extend the mine. Tlaskal had long suspected they were 'trying to get out of coalmining in the Hunter since it is no longer profitable' and that the expansions were 'supposed to make the sale of the mine easier'.[23] Sure enough, in June 2017, Rio Tinto flogged its subsidiary Coal & Allied, which controlled the Mount Thorley Warkworth mine, to the Chinese company Yancoal for US$2.69 billion. They didn't even want it after all that.

The PAC has approved a new plan for the Warkworth Sands Woodlands. The mining companies are to be allowed to destroy bits of it, providing they attempt to restore them elsewhere. Most everyone agrees this very old, established woodland cannot be regenerated in a different place. So it's goodbye to the speckled warblers and vulnerable squirrel gliders who call it home. It's farewell to the critically endangered regent honeyeater. Things aren't looking too good for the endangered swift parrot in these parts either. The large-eared pied bat, the brown treecreeper, the grey-crowned babbler? Might be time to move house. Perhaps time is also running out for the increasingly rare Bulga fighter. Tell me: in their position, would you not leave if you could?

In the community hall, Uncle Kevin Taggart, a Wonnarua elder who lives in nearby Broke, takes the stage. 'In my opinion, it's environmental terrorism,' says the 67-year-old. He has lived in this area all his life. Eighteen months ago, he and his sister Pat Hansson, a gardener, were forcibly arrested for protesting the expansion of Warkworth. Were they threatening violence or damage to property, perhaps? Nope. They were sitting with a few old mates in fold-out chairs boiling billy tea on the side of a public road. A couple of mine managers turned up, told them they were in a 'blast exclusion zone' and asked the group to move along. When the tea-drinkers refused, the miners called the police. The white fellas were given a telling off, but five officers dragged Taggart up and cuffed him. Pat says she went into a fit from the stress of it. The siblings were charged with disobeying police direction and resisting arrest. In court, the magistrate acquitted them, saying it was 'remarkable' that police became involved.[24] But was it? When you consider that Taggart has been outspoken against the mine for the past several years? It does not do to make a fuss, does it? Find yourself on some sort of list, I'll wager. The mining giants know exactly which mosquitoes are irritating them.

We are seeing extraordinary new laws being introduced in Australia that erode our civil rights to object to injustice. In 2014 Tasmania criminalised peaceful protest that might hinder access to business or disrupt commercial operations. When Bob Brown fell foul of the new laws, he challenged them in the High Court and won, but while that decision was pending, New South Wales introduced its own new measures. In 2016 Mike Baird's government jacked up the fines protestors could incur by trespassing on mine sites, while reducing what those mining companies must pay for operational misconduct: their ceiling used to be $1.1 million; now it's five grand—less than the upper limit for fines incurred by individual protestors. The bill expands the definition of 'a mine' to include gas and gas-exploration sites. Its potential impacts on Lock the Gate are clear. If the government sells a licence to explore on your land in New South Wales, and you don't welcome the cur in for a cuppa, you could face up to seven years in jail. Baird's message was clear: your democratic right to disagree with him was subject to conditions. At the time of writing, his successor Gladys Berejiklian has done nothing to suggest she feels differently.

'Me and Pat were brought up the Aboriginal way, to look after the land, to respect it,' says Uncle Kevin Taggart. 'And look what's happened, just look what's happened.' The carp are gone from Cockfighter Creek,[25] the air is polluted, the woodlands and road are threatened. Before he passed away, Taggart's father asked his kids to look after the land the way their ancestors did. 'We've all got to get together and speak out,' says Taggart. 'I wouldn't be up here speaking [if I had a choice]; I'm nervous, but I'm trying my best for this country.'

When Hansson takes the mic, she is composed and delivers a practised speech. 'What we are experiencing in this area is very confronting, heart-breaking ... I believe I have a spirit sickness. Our once beautiful country as I knew it growing up has been destroyed by coalmining.' Doing nothing, she says, 'is not an option.'

The Lock the Gate Alliance is a grass roots Australian organisation linking local groups that are fighting 'inappropriate' mining projects in their communities. It includes the Hunter Valley Protection Alliance, Friends of the Earth and loads of Knitting Nannas chapters, as well as local conservation societies, environment centres and even slow-food and farmers' market groups. Founded in 2010 to fight coal seam gas in Queensland and the 'super mines' in New South Wales, it is also active in Western Australia and the Northern Territory, where fracking is the enemy.

Lock the Gate brings together the sorts of people who don't normally share a beer: farmers, tree-changers, country shopkeepers and Indigenous elders are working with career conservationists, greenies, inner-city activists and even the talkback-radio menace Alan Jones. The latter might think climate change is 'a hoax' and have opposed the carbon tax, but he grew up on a Queensland dairy farm and bristles against this 'mining invasion' of his home turf.[26]

The man behind Lock the Gate was Drew Hutton, a seasoned campaigner who, over a fifty-year career, 'sat on a thousand picket lines, handed out probably a couple of million leaflets and knocked on tens of thousands of doors.'[27] Although he retired in 2017, the organisation still bears his distinctive signature.

Hutton's activism was forged in ultra-conservative Queensland during the Bjelke-Petersen era, starting with the anti–Vietnam War protests—the biggest march in Brisbane happened in 1967 when 4000 students marched from the University of Queensland into the city without a permit, prompting a crackdown. Long-haired layabouts making trouble were just the excuse the Premier needed to introduce draconian measures designed to boost his image as a strongman.

In 1971 there were protests against racism in Sydney and Melbourne when the all-white South African rugby team toured, which led to the first real organising contact between the young, white Left and Aboriginal activists. With the Springboks due in Brisbane, Joh Bjelke-Petersen over-reacted big-time. He introduced a state of emergency, busing in 450 extra police officers from rural areas. Some of these country coppers went on a rampage, chasing, pushing and kicking protesters under cover of darkness in scenes you have to see to believe. (And see them you can: check out the footage on YouTube; it's hard to believe this is Australia not some fascist dictatorship.) Bjelke-Petersen said it was 'great fun' and 'put him on the map'. Hutton, then a 24-year-old teacher, was appalled. He joined a revolutionary organisation called the Self-Management Group (SMG) and set about trying to design a more socially just society. The SMG was obscure. No one much was listening, although Hutton did once chain himself to a tree in the Queen Street Mall to protest Bjelke-Petersen's lack of respect for free speech.

In 1984 Hutton formed the Brisbane Greens from the ashes of the SMG, and eight years later joined Bob Brown and others in co-founding the national Australian Greens. Hutton stood for state government many times but never won a seat. Queensland wasn't ready for him. Until it was.

Tenacious, absurdly thick-skinned and driven by conviction, Hutton was just the guy to drum up support for Lock the Gate by knocking on doors, many of which, initially, were slammed in his face. 'Most farmers are patriotic, law-abiding, polite; they're respectable, everything I'm not,' he told *Australian Story*. 'They blamed me for the tree-clearing laws, [and] in terms of being a greenie, I was number one.'[28] But there's nothing like a common enemy to unite people.

Bev Smiles, sixty-three, enjoys the dubious distinction of being one of the first people to be prosecuted under Baird's anti-protest laws. Worst-case scenario, she'll be seventy when she gets out of jail for attempting to protect her village from total annihilation by big coal. But Smiles, with her story-book name and kindly country nanna's face, is a sophisticated operator. 'I'm the radical ratbag they all suspected me of being. This is a test case on this draconian new law.'[29]

At 5 a.m. on a cool April morning in 2017, Smiles, Bruce Hughes and Stephanie Luce approached the Wilpinjong mine entrance. They'd brought their banners—'Enough is enough', 'Save Wollar'—and it was turnover time; the workers employed by the mine's owner, American giant Peabody Energy, would be swapping shifts.

The Missouri-based company controls nine mines in Australia, and in 2016 sold 187.8 million tons of coal, raking in US$4.7 billion—despite having filed for bankruptcy protection in the United States that year. Its website displays pictures of happy women on serene green backgrounds, and claims that Peabody is a 'leading voice in advocating for sustainable mining'. Happy women are a good sell. Angry Bev, not so much.

A former state Greens candidate, Smiles campaigned against the expansion of the Yancoal-owned Ashton mine at nearby Camberwell. When Peabody applied to extend Wilpinjong to within 1.5 kilometres of her home in Wollar, she was indignant. She'd had enough of watching her neighbours bullied into moving away, or left with stranded assets and no compensation. When the PAC approved the extension, she got arrested on purpose. 'My message is: "You can put me in jail. Do what you want." I'm prepared to go to jail over this because what else is there left for me to do? Facts and evidence mean nothing in the way these things are dealt with. I'm happy to be a martyr to the cause.'

I wake at the crack with a stiff neck from a night spent on the floor of the Wollar Memorial Hall. I creep out leaving the few other tent-less campers to their slumbers. Outside, the air is crisp and the sun slants through the gums, turning their leaves golden. At the end of the road, the police are waiting. Doubtless, I fit their profile of a threat: like Bev Smiles, I am a woman. And I'm carrying dangerously hot opinions and coffee. Their vehicle blocks the road as I approach.

'Lovely morning!' I call. 'Isn't it?'

One of them looks sheepish as he mumbles, 'G'day.' The other stares me down, mute. I turn into Armstrong Street, where there's no one home. An eerie silence hangs over the empty houses and school. It's a ghost town. Of the 115-odd homes here, four remain occupied. The police follow me for a bit, then seem to give up and head off in the other direction. A yellow road sign reads, 'Expect the unexpected.'

Looping back around towards our camp ground, I see the police again. They turn into the road to meet me, and we edge slowly closer together. I give them a wave. I still haven't seen another human soul. I pass more sad, boarded-up houses, then I hear a radio—there's someone here after all. Colin Faulkner sits in his front yard reading a novel. Sometimes, of a morning, he hears rocks being dropped into the dump trucks, but today is Sunday and it's peaceful. The cops inch past us and we smile conspiratorially. A soft breeze nudges the sign on Faulkner's gate post back and forth. It reads, 'This is mine, not the mine's.'

On 5 June 2018, the case against Smiles was dismissed on technicalities. 'Justice prevailed for us today,' she said, but the magistrate told the court he did not need to consider the protest rights issue in making his decision. It remains untested.

10
Youthquake

'Millennials: The Me Me Me Generation'
—*TIME* cover, May 2013

'We don't want these people in charge of us anymore.'
—Emma González, to CNN after the Parkland school shooting,
February 2018

'The winter is over, change is here. The sun shines on a new day, and the day is ours. First-time voters show up 18 per cent of the time at midterm elections. Not anymore. Now, who here is going to vote in the 2018 election? If you listen real close you can hear the people in power shaking.'
—David Hogg, March for Our Lives speech

Generation We
Lock the Gate joined 350.org, the Wilderness Society and others to stage a rally in Sydney on 24 March 2018, and 7000 marchers took to the streets, including a cavalcade of farmers on horseback. It was a beautiful event with a strong message—that it's 'Time 2 Choose' a green-energy future—but one thing struck me: how old everyone was. White hair was everywhere. Where were all the young people?

Walking home, I passed a man in a wheelchair and his daughter, both wearing 'No Coal Seam Gas' T-shirts, and we got chatting. 'He's turning eighty-five next week,' she told me. 'We've come down from the Northern Rivers.' They were looking forward to a family reunion the following day. 'I couldn't get the kids to come here. They're excited to see him,' she nodded at the old man, 'but they weren't interested in the rally. I get the feeling they think we're slightly mad.'

Bev Smiles, Uncle Kevin and Auntie Pat, Bob Brown and Drew Hutton are seniors; who are they passing the baton to? I've seen how older people often dominate by numbers at rallies. Stop Adani in Bondi was also heavy on the greys, punctuated by bright young things from the AYCC, but in nowhere near equal numbers. Millennials were out in force in Bondi, but thronging the cafés rather than lending their support on the beach. Afterwards, I asked a group of women in their late twenties how come they hadn't joined us, and they had no idea what I was talking about; in their case at least, the message wasn't getting through.

Obvious reasons for older people doing the grunt work of organising include ageing populations (certainly the case in the Hunter communities I visited) and the fact that retirees have time on their hands. Some students have hours to spare too. Parents with young families, however, are usually time-poor, as are ambitious professionals in the building stages of their careers. That explains why it's so often grannies and kids who volunteer. In the United States, those aged between thirty-five and fifty-five are most likely to volunteer, but older people tend to put in more hours. Everywhere, women volunteer more than men. In Australia, of the nearly six million people who volunteered in 2014, the highest rates were among young people aged fifteen to seventeen (42 per cent of them volunteered).

Millennials are by no means apathetic, but many are disengaged from the existing systems, which fail to speak their language. A million fewer American youngsters voted in the 2016 presidential election than in 2012 (when Obama was voted back in), seeing neither side as representing their values. If they regard politicians as unrelatable and self-serving, is it any wonder? Traditional politics is too often a closed shop, still so pale and male, and the next generation is seeking alternative ways to engage. It's not just voting they are light on; group and union membership, contacting public officials, attending public meetings, and working with neighbours are all on the decrease, which helps explain why the Stop Adani and Time 2 Choose protests were skewed towards older protesters. Maybe street protests are learned behaviour: the boomers got their practice in the '60s.

'Kids today! They're surgically attached to their phones. Obsessed with social media. And porn, probably. They have no manners! What's with selfies? Selfish, more like. In my day … '

Every generation of old codgers thinks its society's youth are feckless layabouts who will send the world to hell in a handbasket. Socrates complained that ancient Greek children loved luxury, and had terrible manners and contempt for authority. Plato moaned that 'they riot in the streets with wild notions' and 'have decaying morals'. In the 1920s, parents feared their offspring would turn into immodest flappers and risky partygoers. In the 1960s, when large numbers of students and young people drove the new civil rights, feminist, peace and environment movements, they sent the older generation into a panic. Youth had 'gone wild'. British rock stars were 'invading' America. Teenagers were 'sex-obsessed', while protestors were nothing better than rioting criminals. It's inevitable, then, that millennials cop criticism, but it's not justified.

A much-discussed 2013 *TIME* cover bears the memorable line 'Millennials are lazy, entitled narcissists who still live with their parents.'[1] The inside story, penned by a Gen Xer, told of 'a crisis of unmet expectations' for kids born between 1981 and 2000, thanks to their being raised on a diet of constant praise and affirmation: 'Though they're cocky about their place in the world, millennials are also stunted, having prolonged a life stage between teenager and adult.' Please. It is not bruised egos that disappoint this generation; it's the fact that the last lot failed to clean up after themselves and the planet's conking out.

'No one agrees about what makes each generation unique. For instance, are young people today narcissistic and coddled, or are we creative and energetic?' writes sixteen-year-old Logan Casey, with impressive maturity, in *The New York Times*. (He was part of the paper's Student Council program for the 2015/16 school year.) 'Generalizations snowball and millions of people are made to share one identity. These stereotypes can reinforce prejudices and make groups into easy scapegoats.'[2]

I work with students all the time, and I've never met a single one who didn't care about global warming or social justice or trying to build a better future. While millennials are indeed a large and diverse demographic, studies show how they value authenticity and transparency, and are more likely to be recyclers and conscious consumers. Coming of age in the Anthropocene, they exist online in a way that their parents did not. Add these ingredients to the pot and stir, and you get a very different dish from the one served up by *TIME* magazine.

The Millennial Impact Project runs an annual survey that since 2009 has quizzed over 100,000 American millennials on their attitudes to civic engagement, showing how this generation is combining social media with traditional forms of participation, while 'redefining terms long accepted in the cause and philanthropy space: Activist. Cause. Social issue. Ideology.'[3] The 2017 report concludes that their interest in the greater good is driving their cause engagement today, and their activism (or whatever you want to call it) is increasing.

Gens Y and Z are the most globally connected ever—they are building community online. They may well be induced to march (as we are about to see); they might even sue the government for its failure to protect their right to a healthy environment. But it starts, builds and evolves with social media. Older people trying to figure out what makes Gen Z tick (and how to sell to them) have noticed that they regard equality as a non-negotiable, and are getting involved in social activism at a much earlier stage in life. *Forbes* hints that it's the Malala effect.[4] As one young journalism student puts it, 'Millennials have developed our own activist platform. Homophobia, racism, cultural appropriation, transphobia, negative body image, police brutality, gun control, and women's reproductive rights are some of the social and political issues that affect our lives, and we are willing to fight for them to great lengths until national action is taken.'[5]

Jeremy Heimans is a New York–based Australian who co-founded GetUp! in his twenties and has co-authored a book called *New Power* with Henry Timms. 'Old power works like a currency,' they explain:

> It is held by few. Once gained, it is jealously guarded, and the powerful have a substantial store of it to spend. It is closed, inaccessible, and leader-driven. It downloads, and it captures.
>
> New power operates differently, like a current. It is made by many. It is open, participatory, and peer-driven. It uploads, and it distributes. Like water or electricity, it's most forceful when it surges. The goal with new power is not to hoard it but to channel it.[6]

Kid warriors

'Different generations have left different marks on the planet that are unforgettable,' says Xiuhtezcatl (pronounced *shoe-tez-caht*) Martinez,[7] a 'conscious hip-hop artist' who encourages kids to change the world through his music, book, social-media platforms and Earth Guardians organisation. He began his activism aged six, after seeing the Leonardo DiCaprio documentary *The 11th Hour* and telling his mother, 'I need to talk to people.'

Martinez, with his chiselled jaw and glossy curtain of long, dark hair, was an unnervingly confident thirteen-year-old in 2014 when he delivered his TEDxYouth talk about his deep connection with the natural world, grounded in his Aztec heritage. 'I have the power and I have the responsibility to do something about it, not just for myself, not just for my generation, but for every generation to come,' he said. To wit, he performed an eco rap with his little brother Itzcuauhtli (*eat-squat-lee*) called *Return to Nature*, then evoked Gandhi: be the change that you wish to see in the world. 'So what that means for me, is that we cannot wait for other people to do it,' he said. 'A lot of people think that … the power to make a difference … comes from political leaders, from governments, from presidents but they are wrong because the power to change the world is in each one of you.'[8]

Earth Guardians was started by his mother in the 1970s, and she's obviously been a big influence, but Martinez decided 'to keep the momentum going' on his own terms by bringing in fifteen kids from his neighbourhood of Boulder, Colorado. Since then, they've campaigned against fracking, to get pesticides banned in local parks and to introduce a fee on plastic bags, but the big one was suing the government.

On International Youth Day in August 2015, twenty-one young people from across the United States, including Martinez, 18-year-old activist Kelsey Juliana and 'Future Generations through their guardian Dr James Hansen', filed a lawsuit against the US government for causing climate change and therefore violating the youngest generation's constitutional rights to life, liberty and property. Their charge was very similar to the one brought by San Francisco against big oil: that for over fifty years 'the United States of America has known that carbon dioxide pollution from burning fossil fuels was causing global warming and dangerous climate change, and that continuing to burn fossil fuels would destabilize the climate system on which present and future generations of our nation depend for their wellbeing and survival.' And they did nothing about it. The case, known as *Juliana v United States*, is set for trial in October 2018.

Little Itzcuauhtli has also been busy. In 2014, aged eleven, he was listening to adults discuss extreme weather, ocean acidification and mass extinctions at an eco-conference when he decided, 'I have to do something drastic to change the outcome of the future. What can I do as one person to help change the direction we are headed?'[9] He decided on a 'talking strike' promoted through a new website called Climate Silence Now. Itzcuauhtli— an outspoken kid who loves to chat—held his tongue for forty-five days.

Can you imagine how much strength of character it took to stay quiet? He wrote on Facebook that the experience was 'a bumpy road', but 'though I have lost friends at school, I have made many new friends from all over the world who have signed up to join me.'

One of them was the actor Mark Ruffalo, who'd met the Martinez boys at the People's Climate March earlier that year and was moved to encourage others to share Itzcuauhtli's vow of silence for an hour on 10 December. Ruffalo's 'first reaction was concern. No eleven-year-old should be sacrificing his voice in hopes of ensuring a habitable planet for his future. As a father, I worry about the other children around the globe who feel that same weight.'[10] Martinez shared part of a note from Ruffalo: 'I also am made heartsick by your despair, little one. Your silence is a symbol of the silence that will come from doing nothing. You are silent for species that will go extinct and for the countless lives lost in super hurricanes, droughts, floods and ecosystem failure due to the folly and inaction of our leaders.' But, Ruffalo told the world, 'Here's the thing: Itzcuauhtli could have gone into despair when he thought about his future, but he didn't—he took action. And by doing so he believes we will take action too. When he writes of world leaders, he isn't just talking about heads of state, he's talking about you and me.'

March for Our Lives

By the time she reaches the fourth name, she has to wipe her tears with her fists. 'Scott Beigel would never joke around with Cameron at camp.' But they keep coming, the names of her dead friends. 'Helena Ramsay would never hang out after school with Max. Gina Montalto would never wave to her friend Liam at lunch. Joaquin Oliver would never play basketball with Sam or Dylan. Alaina Petty would never. Cara Loughran would never.' Emma González reads out the names until she is done. Seventeen. 'Meadow Pollack would never.' Then she waits, and the wait is excruciating. Many in the 500,000[11]-strong crowd are weeping. The tears roll down González's face, but this time she does not wipe them away, only blinks and looks into the crowd as a chant rises: 'Never again, never again, never again.' Finally, a beeper goes off to signal that her silence is up. 'Since the time I came out here, it has been six minutes and twenty seconds,' she says.

Six minutes and 20 seconds is the time it took a disturbed nineteen-year-old with a legally purchased AR-15 rifle to kill fourteen students, two sports coaches and a geography teacher at Marjory Stoneman Douglas

High School in Parkland, Florida, on Valentine's Day 2018. So here we are at another rally on 24 March 2018, this one dominated by young people.

March for Our Lives saw students and their families descend on Washington, where, as with the Women's March, Trump was conspicuous in his absence. Again, sister events ran in other cities, with New York's mayor saying 150,000 turned out there. Their message? 'Not one more. We cannot allow one more child to be shot at school.' #NeverAgain.

González, eighteen, went from regular high-school senior to massacre survivor to key leader of the youth-driven gun-control movement in under a week. Her image—big eyes, defiant expression, close-cropped hair; she'd recently shaved if off, dismissing it as 'an extra sweater I'm forced to wear'—was seared onto the public consciousness when she delivered her first emotional speech at a rally in Fort Lauderdale three days after the shooting, saying she'd happily ask Trump 'how much money he received from the National Rifle Association.'

America is a dangerous place to be a student. Thirty per cent of American schools have a police officer on staff.[12] Parkland sparked a debate about whether to arm teachers, as shooting incidents continued to happen in schools and universities. According to Everytown for Gun Safety, there were seventeen separate incidents in the nine weeks following the Parkland massacre. From the outside looking in, the situation seems unfathomable. Hundreds of students have been killed and injured by guns in American educational establishments since the University of Texas massacre in 1966. They include the four unarmed college students murdered by the national guard at Kent State University in 1970, during a protest against the Nixon administration's bombing of Cambodia. They include the twelve students (one teacher was also killed) who were murdered at Columbine High School, Colorado, in 1999 by two teenagers. They also died. And now the fourteen Stoneman Douglas kids. That's not even the worst student death toll; it is only the worst since the one at Sandy Hook Elementary School in 2012, when a twenty-year-old gunman slaughtered twenty first-graders and six adults. He then shot his mother before killing himself.

In the last six years, there have been at least 239 separate school shooting incidents in the United States.[13] (Not all of them ended in fatalities, and not everyone agrees on how to count them. It's in the interests of the pro-gun lobby to exclude suicides, shootings where kids were only maimed and incidents that happen on school property but don't involve students.)

The Sandy Hook murderer suffered from untreated mental illness, a fact exploited by those intent on delivering that infuriating response, 'Guns don't kill people; people kill people.' Let us be clear: Guns kill. That is their purpose. Selling guns in supermarkets will result in people being shot with them. This is not a matter of opinion. It's a cold, hard fact.

And yet the March for Our Lives kids aren't even requesting guns be outlawed; they're mostly not questioning the Second Amendment. They ask only that gun control be tightened to prevent more kids being killed with weapons designed for military use.

According to *The New York Times*, 'The AR-15 re-entered the gun market after the end of the federal assault weapons ban [introduced by the Clinton administration in 1994 amid concerns over mass shootings—the ban expired in 2004], at a time of heightened interest in the military. It was popularized by the rise of a video game culture in which shooting became an accessible form of mass entertainment.'[14] The Iraq War was all over the news. These idiots were buying this gun because it made them feel like heroes. One of these guns was used at Sandy Hook. One was used at Australia's Port Arthur massacre in 1996, resulting in a swift change of the law here.

Since 1968, more than 1.5 million people have died in gun-related incidents on American soil. Read that number again. It takes a while for it to sink in. That's more than the total number of American service members killed in all wars in US history. America is at war with itself. Yet large sections of US society are insistent that their right to bear arms is sacred and unassailable. For any reasonable person who is not American, this makes zero sense, but if you're an American who believes you ought to be allowed a handgun in your handbag, can we at least agree that selling gas-operated, semi-automatic weapons to unstable young men does not make the world a safer place?

The March for Our Lives campaign is asking for stronger gun laws, a ban on the deadliest weapons, and universal background checks. Since Sandy Hook, various states have introduced and/or extended background-check requirements for gun-buyers, but Republicans and the NRA continue to fight them. A month after Parkland, for example, it looked as if Minnesota might pass new gun-control legislation, but by April it was defeated.

Not that background checks prevented the Parkland shooter, former Stoneman Douglas student Nikolas Cruz, from tooling up. The suburban gun store in question, situated on a nondescript strip mall next to a spa, was required only to check that he did not have a criminal record and had not been found mentally defective by a court. And so Cruz, despite being troubled and known to police, was able to buy a weapon with barely more difficulty than if it were massage oil.

Cameron Kasky, seventeen, survived the shooting. In the car on the way home with his dad and brother, he began sharing on Facebook. In one post, he wrote that 'doing nothing would lead to nothing.'[15] The next night he invited some friends over, including seventeen-year-old Jaclyn Corin, and they came up with #NeverAgain. According to Corin, 'Our first meeting was small—there were a handful of people lying around Cameron's living room, trying to figure out next steps (if there were any). But with each meeting, we'd invite a few more students to join us, until we had about twenty people at our meetings.'[16] Reaching out to peers who were on social media, they found sharing their responses was easy, as was connecting with millions of kids across the nation who cared. By the day of the March for Our Lives rally, González had 1.4 million Twitter followers.

As the funerals of their friends were being held, Corin put out a call for 100 students to travel to Tallahassee to lobby the state legislature, posting on Instagram, 'Please contact your local and state representatives, as we must have stricter gun laws IMMEDIATELY.' #NeverAgain organised via a huge group-text thread.[17] The group agreed on their aims from the outset—to build an inclusive, student-led movement to campaign for action to stop 'the epidemic of mass shootings'—and naturally began to message and hear from other kids who'd experienced gun violence.[18] Within days, they had their plan for March for Our Lives. Social-media graphics, posters and voter tool kits were made available online. A supporter donated an office space, which became both war room and hangout. They crowd-funded US$2.7 million in a week, but there were no parents or seasoned campaigners running the show.

David Hogg, seventeen, had ambitions to be a filmmaker or journalist before the shooting, and brought out his phone and started interviewing his friends as they were hiding from the gunman in a closet. He told CNN he'd had one thing on his mind: 'Tell the story.'[19]

Two members of the core team are twenty-year-old ex–Stoneman Douglas students, now in college and apparent media whizzes, but really, what would take your mum six months to build on Squarespace any one of these kids could whip up in an afternoon. Corin calls social media 'our weapon'.[20] They've all been raised on the 24-hour news cycle and knew it was now or never, plus content creation comes naturally to them.

Vanity Fair also points out that Columbine survivor Laura Farber took nineteen years to make a documentary based on the experience, while Hogg, 'filmed his ordeal as he lived it, huddled in lockdown, laying down the commentary track in real time and conducting his first on-camera interviews. He fled the school, made it home, then rode his bike back that same afternoon to grab B-roll.'[21]

González is obviously no fan of Trump's, but the group agreed early on that the movement must be non-partisan, and both Hogg and Kasky proved themselves shrewd political communicators, hammering this home repeatedly in their media appearances: 'This isn't about Red and Blue; this is about protecting the kids.' It is also about inclusivity. Whether by intuition—as the brainchild of the most diverse and inclusive generation yet[22]—or design, having taken the learnings from the Women's Marches on board, the rally was anchored by speakers from different communities and backgrounds. Naomi Wadler, at just eleven, opened her speech with 'I am here today to acknowledge and represent the African-American girls whose stories don't make the front page of every national newspaper. These stories don't lead on the evening news.'

One month after the Parkland students ran from their school under siege, thousands of others across America walked voluntarily out of theirs (many risking suspension) as part of a solidarity initiative called Walkout Wednesday. This was organised by the Youth Empower offshoot of the Women's Marches—yet more evidence of the new cross-movements coming together. Asked how he felt about it, Kasky said, 'It was inspiring, the fact that students all over the nation were taking leadership positions that we were thrust into.'[23]

The Parkland students are accidental activists. Corin told *The New Yorker* that she had not been 'even a little bit' politically active before, although she was well versed in the gun-control debate having written a school paper on it. As junior class president, she had perhaps been a little bit famous, but now her face is everywhere. 'Before February 14, 2018, I spent my days at dance class, watching Netflix in bed with my dog, and studying.' Imagine the pressure. She, González and Kasky went on the *Ellen* show, where Kasky admitted he felt guilty that it took experiencing gun violence in his own community to turn him into a campaigner, but as he said in his Fort Lauderdale speech, 'We're just kids.'

These kids—who have been through serious trauma, mind you—present as wiser, and more collected, reasoned and determined than many seasoned campaigners and politicians. This is what Kasky told the crowd at March for Our Lives: 'To the leaders, sceptics and cynics who told us to sit down and stay silent, wait your turn. Welcome to the revolution! It is a powerful and peaceful one because it is of, by and for the young people of this country.'

Everywhere students are speaking out, on Facebook, Twitter, Instagram, YouTube and Snapchat, in classrooms, in the streets and to the media. 'We're not only fighting for ourselves, we're fighting for the future kids,' Parkland student Giuliana Matamoros told *New York* magazine.[24]

'This isn't just about our school,' said her friend Lyliah Skinner. 'It's about every single place that you can go to and not feel safe because: gun violence. Our school gets more attention because of our demographic. We are a predominantly white school, rich, Republican, and that's not fair because places like Chicago, Baltimore, Detroit, this is every day for them.'[25] Skinner had been hiding in a classroom for more than an hour when police burst in, ordered the students to drop to the floor, then led them out with their hands up. Hands up don't shoot. Kids in the crowd at March for Our Lives had the slogan written on their palms. 'Today,' said Kasky, 'is a bad day for tyranny and destruction.'[26]

'Many fellow survivors and I have not kept quiet,' writes González in a piece for *Teen Vogue*, which put her, Corin and other young activists from different communities on its digital cover. Fourteen-year-old Jazmine Wildcat is a Native American gun-control activist from Wyoming. Nza-Ari Khepra, twenty-one, began campaigning after her best friend was killed in Chicago when she was just fifteen. 'We have taken the media by storm through appearances and interviews, met with state and federal lawmakers to beg them to enact much stricter gun control laws, and been joined in protest by students around the nation and the world who've held school walkouts and demonstrations that exhibit the energy and power of young people in full force,' writes González.

After watching David Hogg give his brilliant, courageous speech—'Ninety-six people die every day from guns in our country,' he said, and 'yet most representatives have no public stance on guns and to that we say, no more'—I checked Instagram to see who else was moved to tears. I typed in his name with a hashtag. What came up? Nazi memes showing Hogg dressed as Hitler or Hogg with Hitler, calling him 'CNN's Minister of Propaganda'; posts from gun-toting freaks spouting venom and threatening worse, and I thought, here it is again, the pus from the boil that's being lanced. It gets ugly before it heals. The people holding the power who are set to lose it, and the bullies and the bigots who've benefitted, they can get very nasty indeed.

A politician who was the only declared candidate for Congress in his Maine constituency called Hogg a 'bald-faced liar' and González a 'skin-head lesbian'. She said simply, 'I'm not going to even address the fact that he said it in the first place.' Hogg, however, responded on Twitter: 'Hey friends in Maine! Who wants to run against this hate loving politician He is running UNOPPOSED, RUN AGAINST HIM I don't care what party JUST DO IT.' Within days, the politician was out of the race.

'We are going to make this the voting issue; we are going to take this to every election, to every state and every city,' said Hogg on stage at March for Our Lives. 'And to those politicians supported by the NRA that allow the continued slaughter of our children and our future, I say: get your resumes ready.'

The kids are alright

'I think fourteen is the best age to get involved in activism,' says Anna Rose, who was twenty-two when she co-founded the AYCC with another Australian university student Amanda McKenzie. 'In your teens, you have a lot of empathy. You haven't been beaten down by the world. You're also idealistic enough to believe you can make a difference, and you've got time.'[27] At thirty-five with a child of her own, does she still believe she can make a difference? 'I do,' she says. 'I am.' It's shortly after Christmas and we are whispering in the kitchen of Rose's holiday rental while her baby sleeps. 'Also, you can't get arrested until you're sixteen,' she laughs.

Rose was environmentally aware from an early age. Her grandparents and uncle were farmers, hit hard by drought. 'I lived with my mum and dad in Newcastle, but I spent a lot of time on my grandparents' farm. They ended up selling, and the drought was a factor. My uncle kept his farm, but the cattle had to go away on agistment; there wasn't enough water.'

Like Elizabeth Morley, Rose remembers frightening stories on the news about farmer suicides. Also, she says it was impossible not to think about pollution and the environment growing up near the largest coal-export port in the world. Rose was fourteen when a campaigner from the Wilderness Society visited her school, and told her there was something she could do about it. 'I'd been distressed about the drought and environmental destruction and just sitting with that and feeling powerless, and along comes this guy with this speech that offered a solution. I went up afterwards and asked him, "What can I do?" He said, "Well, you're at school, so start where you are."'

Rose set up a green group with her classmates and convinced the school to back a 'sports' option called Environmental Activities. They planted trees and recycled. Rose also volunteered at the Wilderness Society. 'They had a shopfront—I was selling tea towels—but the campaign office was out the back.' When she heard about BHP Billiton's plans to mine the Stockton Bight sand dunes, less than an hour away from her school, she got Environmental Activities involved. The kids' campaign tactics included dressing up as koalas (which landed them in the local newspaper) 'and a lot of letter-writing'. By 2001, before Rose graduated, a coalition of the Wilderness Society, local residents, passionate kids and the traditional Worimi owners had defeated BHP. The government declared Stockton Bight a conservation area.

At university Rose gravitated towards the eco kids, but not exclusively. 'I'm a joiner,' she says. 'I joined everything.' Links with the Circus Society turned out to be more helpful than they sound. When Rose steered a campaign to persuade the university to switch to clean energy, 'we got all the clubs and societies involved, cheerleaders, footballers, deans of faculties. It was inclusive, and that's why it succeeded. Everyone has a particular talent or network or idea.'

In 2005 Rose was elected environment officer for the National Union of Students. Everywhere she went, she met passionate students, but there was a missing link. Of course, some people simply didn't care, but she figured there must be students who would have liked to join a green group but either didn't dare or were put off for some reason. Did the existing groups seem too serious or too splintered? Like they would take up too much time? Or did they appear to be dominated by the super-dedicated activist types already involved? Were people like Rose inadvertently sending the message that it was all or nothing? And what about all the kids beyond the university, all the working young people, and those still at school? If Rose wanted to change the world, she needed to reach out wider.

She knew the two obvious routes to participation: one, someone invites you; two, you seek it out. (The seeking, she explains, usually happens after reading a book or watching a movie that enlightens you.) 'But mostly it's the invitation. More people asking means more joining.'

No one invited Amanda McKenzie. Reading *The Weather Makers* did it for her. She was on holiday in Tasmania's Styx River State Forest at the time. 'You have to lean back to see the tops of the trees they're so tall, and I remember sitting in that forest thinking, This has been here since before Europeans even knew this place existed, and we could destroy the planet in a generation.'[28] Uh-oh. McKenzie, now CEO of Australia's Climate Council, was then a 21-year-old arts/law student. 'I spent the next six months worrying, sometimes waking up at 4 a.m., then I decided, Enough! I just need to do something.' McKenzie and her sister started writing educational presentations and delivering them in schools. After each talk, McKenzie would say, 'I'm going to start an organisation for young people who care about climate change. I'm not sure what it's going to be exactly, but if you're interested, come and see me afterwards.'

Rose was at COP11 in Montréal as part of the youth delegation when the seed for the AYCC took root in her mind. She reckoned the climate-change issue could use a national coalition of youth groups, and when she got back to Sydney in December 2005, she persuaded a small group of friends to help her organise a founding summit. They secured a $10,000 grant from an insurance company.

'That was a lot of money to give student newbies,' I say.

'By that time, I'd been involved in activism for close to decade,' says Rose.

McKenzie was one of thirty-five people who attended the founding summit in November 2006. She joined the steering committee. Rose became national director. Their first big activation was a youth conference called Power Shift (based on an American model), designed to connect and inspire young climate activists from across the country. It culminated in a flash mob on the steps of the Sydney Opera House, choreographed by the team from *So You Think You Can Dance?*

Today the AYCC is Australia's largest youth-run organisation, with over 150,000 members aged between twelve and twenty-seven. It runs training programs; it works in high schools to help kids get their heads around the climate-change issue; it supports the SEED Indigenous Youth Climate Network (Rose is Amelia Telford's mentor) and, of course, it campaigns. The AYCC was crucial to the five-year-long campaign to persuade the South Australian government to build a solar thermal power plant, the biggest in the world, at Port Augusta. They made submissions, they door-knocked, they crowdfunded TV ads, and organised a 328-kilometre march from Port Augusta to Adelaide. It took them fifteen days. Probably, someone even dressed up as a koala. 'The press needs something to take pictures of other than men in boring suits,' says McKenzie.

Rose left the AYCC when she reached its age limit. She went on to write a book about her efforts to change the mind of a climate-sceptic politician, ran Earth Hour in Australia for a couple of years, and now works with Farmers for Climate Action. I ask Rose what drives her, and she looks genuinely puzzled; like, how is that a question? 'Why wouldn't you do this?' she says. 'If I were to analyse it, I'd say it's what I've always done. I was really lucky to get involved early. But bottom line? Once you realise you can change things, why would you not?'

11
SOS—Save Our Seas

'How can I look my grandchildren in the eye and say I knew what was happening to the world and did nothing?'

—David Attenborough

'Once you become an empowered woman it cannot stay contained. It spills over into every aspect of your life and you find your voice and confidence on levels you could never imagine.'

—Natalie Isaacs, founder of 1 Million Women

The weekend that changed me

Both the common catalysts Anna Rose cites for people joining movements (someone invites you, or you read or watch something that compels you to act) happened to me simultaneously, and she was key. In mid-2017, Rose got together with Clare Ainsworth Herschell (who works with young philanthropists in the art world) to concoct a trip to the Great Barrier Reef designed to engage new voices on climate change. Amanda McKenzie and the Climate Council came on board, and that September a group headed to Heron Island, on the southern part of the reef. Apart from Tim Flannery, coral expert Sophie Dove and marine biologist Laura Wells, we were non-scientists: a musician, a children's book publisher, a poet, a painter, a couple of finance and insurance people, a famous freediver, and Sydney's deputy lord mayor.

It was my very good fortune that Ainsworth Herschell invited me (we have a mutual fashion friend), but at the time, I didn't realise it would change the course of my work. I recognised the trip for a good opportunity—I was curious as a journalist, plus I got to interview Flannery—but I didn't expect this book to be the outcome. Turns out that was the plan—the general gist, at least, if not the specifics. As Flannery told me, 'We wanted you all to see what's happening with the reef close up, and become advocates for the cause.' In preparation, I bought a copy of *The Weather Makers* and reacted just like Amanda McKenzie did: I've got to do something.

The boat jumps, thumps, then finds its rhythm scudding across the white-caps at speed. For a second, one of us forgets to hold on then rights himself. It's exhilarating. Half an hour later, here we are, in our wetsuits, masks and lurid green flippers, and we pitch ourselves into the sea. The freediver zooms off chasing turtles, which abound in these waters. Loggerheads and endangered green turtles nest on Heron Island from October to March, when new babies can be seen clambering out of the sand at dusk. They are more graceful than I am, the landlubber who must be taught how to breathe correctly through a snorkel.

I rarely saw the sea growing up in Yorkshire, except in the old 1960s movies that were often on the telly when I was a child. My ocean was a place of shipwrecks, where Jason and the Argonauts encountered giants. 'From the depths of the ocean comes the most terrifying horror of the deep!' Luckily Godzilla was on hand to fight that one. In the TV series *Voyage to the Bottom of the Sea*, a submarine crew encounters an enormous spider spinning an underwater web, monstrous jellyfish and squid. There's another Kraken-like creature in *It Came from Beneath the Sea*—it rises up to smash the Golden Gate Bridge, and my confidence in the water. Then there was *Jaws*, which I watched from behind the sofa, screaming the whole way through.

My reading list was equally full of high drama at sea. At school the teachers doled out maritime adventures that invariably included near-death experiences in storms, from scurvy or at the hands of pirates, smugglers, slave-traders. Tales of miserable old fishermen, thick with whirlpools and whale blubber. I get it; it was to balance out the Jane Austen, but it did little to endear the big blue to me. As a teenager, I had a holiday romance with the Mediterranean, lolling about on boats and under beach umbrellas, but I didn't truly bond with the sea. I viewed it as a postcard, a fish shop, an excuse for a new bikini.

It was only when I moved to Sydney as an adult that I began to swim properly in the ocean, occasionally still humming the *Jaws* theme in my head. Here, I learned what it is to live in a city on the water, where the beach is our collective backyard, and the ocean constantly reminds us to respect and protect it.

To borrow from the poet Pablo Neruda, we need the sea because it teaches us, but we also, quite literally, need it to live. Phytoplankton (tiny marine algae) generates at least half the oxygen we breathe. The oceans are the largest habitat on Earth, covering 70 per cent of its surface. Many of the world's poorest people depend on the fishing industry—often local and small-scale—for employment, and on seafood for adequate protein. But the ocean's bounty is not infinite. According to the UN's Food and Agriculture Organization, more than half the world's fish stocks are 'fully exploited', while another 25 per cent are either over-exploited or depleted. I'll never forget a line I heard in the Australian documentary *Blue*: Greenpeace campaigner Mark Dia is touring an Asian fish market. He says, 'The precarious state of some tuna makes eating them comparable to dining on snow leopard or polar bear.' *My god*, I thought, *we feed tuna to our cat.*

One of the most confronting things I've ever seen is footage, also in *Blue*, that shows 'super trawlers' at work with nets big enough to haul a dozen 747 aeroplanes. Meanwhile 40 per cent of the global catch may be discarded. This 'bycatch' (another weasel word) includes the dolphins, seals, sharks and turtles that are collateral damage, crushed or drowned in those super-sized nets. Smaller fish that are hunted on purpose, like mackerel, are being overfished to the brink of wipe-out in some areas. Without them, animals further up the food chain go hungry, and it will serve us right when that includes us too. Demersal (or bottom) trawling is more like a scraping of the sea floor, with weighted nets, in order to collect prawns and scallops. This is also done on a massive scale and removes everything else in its wake: corals, plants, webs of life that have taken years to develop.

Like open-cut mining, these industrial-practices-on-steroids are abhorrent and immoral, an extreme example of what can happen when greed is left unchecked and governments fail to defend Nature. Writing this is making me angry, as we all should be, for these things are done without broad consultation. Some official ticked some box while we were looking the other way, but who among us would knowingly support this wholesale raping of Mother Earth?

Climate change is also disrupting the oceans. Marine species are migrating in response to warmer waters much faster than land-based animals. In Cape Cod, fishermen are getting bites from species they've never met before, while in Britain, the cod and chips I grew up with might soon be off the menu, as North Sea cod stocks are on the move. In Australia, tropical parrotfish are turning up in southern waters that used to be way too chilly for them, which sounds fun—fish on vacation!—until you know they're munching their way through vegetation that's not adapted to their appetites. Scientists raise the spectre of 'underwater deforestation'.[1]

Increased sea temperatures affect the weather as well as marine life. Warmer water vaporises more quickly, which leads to stronger, more frequent storms. But acidification is the elephant shark in the aquarium. Apart from providing us with oxygen, the other vital job our oceans do to keep us alive involves our old mate CO_2. The ocean is a giant carbon sink. Between 2002 and 2011, it absorbed about a quarter of our emissions. (Plants took up a little bit more; the remaining 46 per cent went into the atmosphere).[2] But just how much CO_2 can the oceans take before things start to go pear-shaped? If Flannery reckons 'the chemistry of ocean acidification is so complex that even scientists in the field have difficulty explaining the precise mechanisms',[3] then I'm not going to try in these pages. What you need to know is that CO_2 causes the ocean's pH levels to go down and the water becomes more acidic.

Since the Industrial Revolution, human activity has already made the oceans 26 per cent more acidic. The UN projects a possible rise to 170 per cent by the end of the century.[4] Given that the current rate of acidification is ten times faster than anything experienced in the last 55 million years, there is no precedent for adaptation. Most likely we're looking at a mass extinction.

CO_2 in the water means fewer carbonate ions, which are what marine creatures use to build their shells. With less of these available, animals like krill, oysters, crabs, clams, scallops and corals have a hard time forming robust shells and skeletons. Worst-case scenario, they can dissolve.

In 2017 the reef surrounding Heron Island is pristine, and I am snorkelling above it with coral expert Sophie Dove, a professor at the School of Biological Sciences at the University of Queensland, as my guide. Today is a good day. We swim through the dark blue water over large plate corals, fat sea cucumbers and anemones, dispersing jewel-bright schools of butterfly and angelfish. I'm glad to see the parrotfish are still in the 'hood, but my favourite is the yellow trumpet fish with his lovely long nose. The corals look lively dressed in their rich browns, greens and oranges.

Back on the island, half of which is given over to a university research station, Dove is leaning over her precious tanks—her mesocosms. They are part of a long-running experiment she and her team have been conducting to see how different corals react when temperatures and acid levels vary. Each tank contains corals collected from the reef, and seawater that the team manipulates—heating or cooling it and adjusting the pH levels. 'In a more acidic ocean, corals grow more slowly,' explains Dove.[5] But the problem that's been getting all the press is the bleaching.

Coral is made up of small polyps, which are home to tiny algae called zooxanthellae. They need each other. The coral provides a haven for the algae, which provide food for the coral. Together, they 'recycle' nutrients in nutrient-poor tropical waters. It is also the algae that give reef-building corals their colour.

When corals get stressed by protracted underwater heatwaves, they expel the zooxanthellae, revealing the white skeletons beneath. This is what we call bleaching. Bleached coral isn't dead coral—yet. If the water cools relatively quickly, the algae return, but if that takes too long, the coral can starve. Dead coral attracts different kinds of algae and eventually begins to rot and crumble away. After a severe bleaching event in 2016, Dove and Flannery went to check out affected areas and found a stinking graveyard covered in decomposing matter. 'It was devastating,' says Dove. On Heron Island, we are saved from that; we are here to see what a thriving reef looks like in all its splendour. The hope is that it will cast its spell, as Jacques Cousteau said, and hold us 'in its net of wonder forever'.

The island is a second home for Dove. 'We've been coming here for years; the children spent all their holidays on these beaches,' she says. Her husband is Ove Hoegh-Guldberg, who as one of the first scientists to investigate the impacts of global warming on reefs, warned us back in 1999 that bleaching events would become more frequent and that most corals are unlikely to adapt. The couple worries that future generations won't be able to see the magical coral gardens that have been their life's work.

The reef is being attacked on multiple fronts: from climate change and from large-scale development of the Queensland coast; from ports and dredging and agricultural run-off; and now from Adani's idiotic plan, which would bring more than 500 extra coal ships through the Great Barrier Reef World Heritage Area each year. I hope by the time you read this, the

Carmichael mine will be the one dead in the water, but even if it is, there will be other such projects. You can bet on that.

The Great Barrier Reef is 500,000 years old. 'It is one of the most extraordinarily biodiverse regions on the planet,' says Flannery. 'We are seeing its destruction within my lifetime.' We must fight for the reef, and for the ocean in general; we must fight with all our might. The good news is: we are. Every day more of us join the blue movement. Existing marine-protection groups are increasing their memberships as new groups spring up. *National Geographic* says, 'Now, more than ever seaweed (marine grassroots) activists have sworn to commit their lives, their fortunes and their honour' to the cause.[6] Most of these ocean guardians are ordinary people working in their communities, especially in Australia, where our biggest cities are on the coast. They are school kids, parents, swim fans, snorkelers, divers, windsurfers, yachties, sunbakers, surfers, dog walkers, beach cleaners, those who like to fish or just like wildlife. Humans with a conscience, determined to stand up for Nature.

They might be tackling marine debris with groups like Clean Up Australia, or forming their own, like Afroz Shah did in Versova Beach, in Mumbai, India. Shah grew up by the sea but had moved away and built up his career as a lawyer in the city. In 2015, aged thirty-three, he returned to the beach, this time to Versova, which is surrounded by slums and was a horrific example of what can happen without adequate garbage-collection services. Shah was shocked to discover it was possible to 'lose' a beach. This one was completely covered in rotting garbage and plastic. What could he do? 'I have to protect my environment and it requires ground action,' he says.[7] At first, he donned gloves and started to clean up himself with just his 84-year-old neighbour to help, but he soon began door-knocking and recruiting assistants in the streets. 'I was rebuked, "It's pointless you doing it," [some people] said, "It will never get cleared."'[8] Oh ye of little faith. Over sixty-one weeks, the Versova Residents Volunteers (plus the odd politician and Bollywood star) cleared 4.2 million kilograms of rubbish off their beach, leaving it clean and beautiful again. Not that it's been an easy journey. The rubbish keeps on coming and the beach cleans are ongoing. In week 109, Shah posted on Twitter that he was giving up after volunteers were 'abused by goons', but months later he was still at it. In week 127 in March 2018, he tweeted joyous news: turtles had returned to the beach to nest. 'We never had single-use plastic,' says Shah. 'Now everything you buy is in plastic, which is devastating for the ocean.' His message is that all stakeholders must band together: 'the guys who manufacture the plastic, the guys who use the plastic, the guys who litter the plastic, the government that is supposed to regulate it, and citizens [who want a clean environment].'[9]

In Australia, the Boomerang Alliance was established in 2003 by veteran waste warrior Dave West. It began with nine allies committed to beating plastic-waste pollution and encouraging recycling. At the time of writing, there are forty-seven. Tim Silverwood, CEO of one of those allied organisations, Take 3 for the Sea, says, 'We have a shared common goal. As activists we don't want to start our own political campaigns in isolation anymore. We've seen it with things like Save the Reef, Stop Adani, and campaigns against the super trawlers. This is the era of collaboration. NGOs that traditionally thought it was in their best interests to operate alone have found new ways to collaborate.'[10] Together is always stronger.

The last straw
As I drive over the hill towards Sydney's Manly Beach, the sea winks at me and two rosellas flash past in their festive finery. Nature is sending a message: protect her. On the shore, as the day's first tourists bubble and fizz from the ferry, I peer over the wall at the water, which laps prettily onto the sand, turquoise and clear. It is Instagram-worthy, marred by no Friday-night detritus. The local council rakes the sand here regularly during high season.

I'm going snorkelling again, this time hunting plastic straws, the so-called 'disposable' kind. That word is misleading. When we 'dispose' of our trash, when we throw it 'away', it heads off out of sight and usually out of mind, but bar what's burned, most of the plastic that's ever been produced still exists in some form. Less than 10 per cent has been recycled. The rest gets buried or hangs around in the environment, some of it for up to 600 years, breaking up into smaller pieces, being mistaken for food by wildlife and getting into places it shouldn't. On average, 83 per cent of tap water globally is contaminated with plastic particles.[11] The scope of microplastic pollution is only now beginning to come to light, and we're way off fully understanding its long-term impacts, but we know plenty about how our rubbish ends up in the marine environment.

At least one-third of discarded plastic packaging escapes collection. The ocean, being downhill from everywhere, is where much of it ends up. Around 10 per cent of ocean plastic debris comes from marine sources— boats and ships (this includes abandoned fishing nets, known as ghost nets).

The rest? That's us. It is our plastic bags that look like jellyfish to hungry turtles. Our drink-bottle lids that seabirds mistake for dinner. Our plastic knives and forks, our takeaway containers, chip packets, lolly wrappers and juice cups, our cotton-bud sticks, plasters, hairbands, six-pack rings, our plastic straws. Every year, human(un)kind dispatches eight million tonnes of plastic garbage into the sea. There's enough plastic there today to circle the Earth 400 times.

Up ahead I spy our party. Around twenty volunteers are gathered around dive instructor Harriet Spark. We are roughly even numbers of men and women, armed with snorkels and masks, and sacks to stash our bounty in. 'Remember this is a STRAWkle,' grins Spark. 'If you see plastic bags, pull them out by all means, but we won't count those.' This is both a data-collection mission and practical activism, run by Spark and her friends Alicia and Danielle. They are hoping to persuade local bars and cafes to quit doling out free plastic straws. All summer on Saturday mornings, they've been combing Manly Cove for evidence. In six weeks, they've collected more than a thousand littered plastic straws.

Straws might seem like a tiny part of the pollution problem but in fact they make the Australian Marine DeBris Initiative's top-ten list of commonly found marine litter. They are generally not recyclable (too light and small for mechanical sorters) and blow easily out of bins and from glasses and trays. Sometimes, of course, we simply toss them into the environment when we're done sucking. A viral video shows a distressed turtle with a plastic straw stuck up its bloodied nose. Look it up only if you have a strong stomach.

According to Linda Booker's documentary *Straws*, the ancient Mesopotamians were the first to suck fancy drinks through specially made tubes; the beverage was beer, the straws gold. Modern straw use took off in the 1950s with the fast-food revolution and has now gone into overdrive. Americans churn through an estimated 500 million straws daily. People with disabilities or illnesses may require one to drink, but for most of us plastic straws are a supremely minor convenience, a trend that grew into a habit that's as stupid as it is pointless, and ubiquitous. You get a straw when you order a glass of water in a restaurant these days. Choose a cocktail and you might get two.

Californian kayak teacher Jackie Nunez was one early organiser trying to stop this madness in 2011. She'd been doing beach clean-ups for a couple of years and had just returned from a holiday in the Caribbean, where the extent of plastic pollution had surprised her. She decided straws were 'a gateway issue'; once you get people thinking about them, they start to question all the other single-use plastic in their lives.

Four years later, Australia got its first campaign when 25-year-old Eva Mackinley was working in a bar and realised the scale of the problem. Drinkers sucked on their straws for less than twenty minutes, then Mackinley would put them in the landfill bin. On a big night out when they're knocking back the rum-and-cokes, what? Ten minutes? Five? She founded an online campaign called The Last Straw to encourage punters to use their lips.

Today the campaigning is reaching critical mass. The hashtag #GiveASip is trending. Actor-turned-UN-environment-ambassador Adrian Grenier is pushing for a 'strawless ocean' via his Lonely Whale Foundation, complete with a video of an octopus swiping straws from drinkers' hands. Buckingham Palace has joined in, phasing out plastic straws from cafés and staff dining rooms. HRH was reportedly persuaded by a conversation with David Attenborough.

Governments are responding. Taiwan has a plan to ban. The European Union has proposed one, while US city councils have begun regulating—you won't find a free plastic straw on Malibu's beaches. In the United Kingdom, a couple of big restaurant chains have quit them, while the Scottish Parliament's ban kicks in in 2019 (they've also outlawed the sale of plastic cotton buds; go Scotland). As I write, news is breaking that Woolworths Supermarkets will stop selling plastic straws in Australia by the end of 2018. In Cairns and Port Douglas on the Great Barrier Reef, a young marine biologist, Nicole Nash, has persuaded cruise boat operators on to ditch them. It's working! Concerned citizens are changing the world.

'#Strawssuck,' says Spark cheerfully. She gives good hashtag; she used to be the social-media manager for the climate activism organisation 1 Million Women and now works for Taronga Zoo. She got the straw bug when a friend went snorkelling and returned with more than memories. 'She noticed one sticking out of the sand, yanked it out, then started seeing them everywhere. She came back with 450 straws!' Spark swam out herself and found more. 'I wrote a blog about it for 1 Million Women that got a lot of traction. People really connect with numbers, when you say, "We found this many" or "We found hundreds."' They put the STRAWkle call-out on Facebook and strangers turned up to help. The week after I take part,

Spark will find herself on the TV news. 'We're creating a suite of content to persuade businesses: contacts and ideas to fix the problem. You have to have solutions.' Spark's are: switch to paper for things like takeaway milkshakes, and no more straws in bars. Diehard fans might buy a reusable metal one. 'I'm not into the guns-blazing approach,' she says. 'Ours is: this is happening and we can help you transition to different practices.'

'Look for the tips of the straws poking out of the sand,' she says. 'The rest will be buried.'

The water is glorious. While tourists exclaim, 'Like a bath!' Spark's friend Alicia is thinking about the tropical fish turning up in Sydney Harbour, and the fact that corals off Fairlight Beach around the corner were bleached in 2016 while the Great Barrier Reef was baking. Here, a heatwave saw surface temperatures stick at 26 degrees Celsius, when they usually peak at 23 or 24. The local corals are less abundant, colourful and diverse (just two species) than their Queensland cousins, and nobody much noticed when 45 per cent of them died. She is trying not to dwell on it. Beach cleans she can do; beach cleans are practical activism. I ask her what she does for a living and she says, 'I'm a coral scientist, or I was. I found it too depressing.' When I get home, I will google her and discover she wrote her PhD on ocean acidification. Her supervisor was Sophie Dove.

In the water, I float, peering through my mask and trying to remember the breathing technique Dove taught me in Queensland, until I spy a thick blue blade of grass 'growing' on the seabed. I manage to get down there and uproot it, and emerge spitting just as one of our group spots a turtle, and everyone races after it. It seems like a sign.

'I'm not a particularly spiritual person,' says Harriet Spark, as we dry off. She describes herself as 'quite straighty-180 about that stuff'—not the type to use terms like Mother Earth or attend EcoSattva training to fight climate change with Buddhist mediation—but there's a proviso. She believes Nature can save people. 'It makes me feel grounded, like a whole person. When I don't go out in Nature, even just a walk or a swim, I can get stuck in my own head.'

Once upon a time, this athletic creature, with her scruffy blonde ponytail and sandy toes, wanted to be a fashion journalist. 'I looked very severe; I had a dark bob, and was willowy and totally different to how I am now. I was miserable.' She was suffering from depression and anorexia. At nineteen, she moved to the Whitsunday Islands on the Great Barrier Reef in a bid to press reset on her life. She got a job on a boat and learned to dive. She stayed for three years.

'On my very first dive, the instructor took me to 25 metres, which you're not meant to, and I saw a turtle for the first time. The reef was so colourful; I dreamed about it at night,' she says. 'It sounds cheesy but the reef helped me through that time in my life when I needed it. It gave me this strong feeling of a world outside of my own problems. There was something about the act of diving that helped make that clear for me, because you are trained to be responsible for yourself when you dive, but also because you're under-water and can't talk. It is meditative, and you feel really in control. You're on a little adventure with yourself and you grow. I was doing it every day. I'm not saying it's a cure-all [for people dealing with anorexia], I understand it's not, but for me …'

Spark came back to Sydney with a lifelong love for the reef. 'I feel like I owe it,' she says. She volunteered with the AYCC, did some dive-instruction work, then went to work for Natalie Isaacs at 1 Million Women.

Isaacs, an entrepreneur who made her name in the cosmetics business then realised how wasteful it was, started the organisation after watch-ing *An Inconvenient Truth*. Her aim? To build a lifestyle revolution to fight the climate crisis, and to do it through the empowerment of women. She believes that every dollar we spend, and consumer choice we make, shapes the kind of world we live in, and that conscious consumerism can make a real difference. '1 Million Women is about individual women changing their lifestyles to save energy, cut pollution and reduce waste,' says Spark. 'And it works; the community is strong. We'd push out something like the call to urge the government to protect the Great Barrier Reef, and there'd be massive uptake. I think that's because it's a very solutions-based organisa-tion, and that's empowering. 1 Million Women doesn't hit you with a lot of depressing facts about the environment then leave you hanging there, feeling hopeless. They say, "We've got ideas for fixing stuff. Join us!"'

There's a pattern here. Spark believes in the power of the positive. Like Betsy Greer and Sarah Corbett, she doesn't relate to the stereotypically negative aspects of protest culture. Asked if she sees herself as an activist, she hesitates. 'I think the word *activist* still carries some extreme or negative connotations, which is not my style,' she says. She is not alone there. To me, the word *activist* is dynamic and appealing, but however much work Sarah Corbett does to convince the world that it can be gentle, for many, *activism* retains its troublemaking perhaps even militant connotations.

'If they build the Adani mine, perhaps I will go up there and chain myself to something,' says Spark, and I can't tell if she's joking or not, 'but in general I am more interested in thinking up creative ways to communicate where I stand on an issue. Like with my jackets.'

In her spare time, she runs a value-driven graphic design and upcycled fashion business called Grumpy Turtle, named after a turtle called Myrtle she once befriended. 'She looked so sulky, then I thought, Actually they all do. Then, Oh man if I was a turtle in this world of climate change and overfishing and plastic pollution, I'd be grumpy too.' Spark is turning heads with the vintage denim jackets she hand-paints and bedazzles. The one she wore to the Stop Adani event in Bondi read, 'Great Barrier Grief' picked out in neon sequins. 'But that was a protest,' I say, remembering.

'I suppose it was,' she says. 'Never say never.'

12
The anti-plastics movement

'As Plasticville sprawls farther across the landscape, we become more thoroughly entrenched in the way of life it imposes. It is increasingly difficult to believe that this pace of plasticization is sustainable, that the natural world can long endure our ceaseless "improving on nature".'
—Susan Freinkel, *Plastic: Toxic Love Story*

'Does anyone else have plastic bags full of plastic bags, or is it just me?'
—meme

Inconvenience truth

I haven't been shopping in ages. Yet as I head down the escalators towards the store I've been obsessing over, the shopaholic's rush of expectation is absent. You see, I don't want anything in the place. Not a single thing. 'Sorry we're open!' proclaims the sign on the door. A boy in school uniform considers a display of sunglasses: classic aviators, a wrap-around mirrored pair. He reaches for some thick, black 1960s-style frames, very Michael Caine. If only they had two lenses. The kid puts them back. Inside the store are plastic cutlery sets and bumper packs of straws. There's a plastic drum of Chupa Chups sticks and wrappers, lollies missing in action. 'How much are these?' I say.

'Very funny,' says the woman behind the counter. She seems a little fractious.

'Do you not like working here?'

'Let's just say, I wish it wasn't necessary.'

Outside a tourist browses the postcards depicting iconic Australian beach scenes littered with empty cans and takeaway containers. We watch her face as she notices the prices: '$2 each, 4 for $10, 6 for $20.' She spins the display round and round, hoping the views might improve.

I grab a packet of burst balloons marketed as 'turtle food' and take it to the counter, pausing by a shelf of chewed gum. 'Ocean fresh breath!' They are merchandised with the used plasters, empty soy sauce containers and lone flip-flops.

'Want those?' says Marina DeBris.

'Not much.'

'Can I interest you in a Santa hat instead?' she smiles, pointing to a row that she rescued from the shallows on Boxing Day: made in China, bought for a few dollars, worn for a few hours, discarded. The hats are furred with seaweed.

'Yeah, no.'

We regroup outside next to the retro vending machine. It's filled with brightly coloured plastic fragments, white polystyrene beanbag balls and cigarette butts.

'Charming.'

'I don't even smoke,' says DeBris. There's something especially hideous about raking the sand for fag ends when you're not a smoker. Butts are the most commonly found type of marine litter, and they contain thousands of tiny plastic (cellulose acetate) particles. In 2015, the annual International Coastal Cleanup collected 2,127,565 cigarette butts. I don't even like to think about the chemicals they're steeped in.

'Inconvenience Store' has just opened at Taronga Zoo, not far from the elephant enclosure. The installation debuted at Bondi's Sculpture by the Sea exhibition a few months back, where it won two prizes, beating tasteful bronzes and a giant hamburger. DeBris is best known for her grotesquely beautiful 'trashion' gowns, made from beachcombed materials (old coffee cups, chewed dog balls, disintegrating shopping bags), but the Inconvenience Store dispenses with good looks.

'It's an ugly issue,' she says, 'but the store is quite the humorous, don't you think? I've been having some amusing encounters. In Bondi a woman asked, "Do you have any hair ties?" I said, "Yeah, over there," and she went and inspected them carefully. I thought, it's going to click soon, she's going to understand, but then she takes one off, brings it to the counter: "I'll have this." I said, "Are you sure?" She said, "Why not?" I told her they were broken and she left in a huff.'

A man asked if she sold water, and DeBris directed him to a cabinet of wave-bashed PET bottles plastered with fake labels for 'Damn Water' and 'Fizzer'. He asked if she took credit cards.

In case you haven't guessed, Inconvenience Store is not a real shopfront. DeBris, an American in Sydney, is a former graphic designer who began her artivism in 2009 in Los Angeles, when she fashioned an outfit out of cigarette lighters, bottle tops, straws and single-use cutlery for the ocean-protection group Heal the Bay. Since then she's made trashion pieces for mock catwalks and provocative plastic frocks to make points. Recently, in collaboration with KeepCup, DeBris made a sculpture of a tornado from 1600 discarded coffee cup lids. Called *Disposable Truths*, it was displayed in a prominent Sydney retail centre.

'This is fun,' says DeBris of her latest work, 'but it's really not funny. We're past the stage of this being something to tiptoe around. Plastic is a plague. It's truly such a massive problem for wildlife, for the ocean, for our food chain, that we don't have time to mess about doing teeny fixes to the old system. We need a totally new way of living.'

The equation of curiosity

Dreams × Adventure (related to the power of stories) = Inspiration. 'Dreams are the breeding grounds for adventures,' explains David de Rothschild.[1] 'Adventures percolate stories, and stories inspire more dreams. And the entire equation is pushed through by asking questions.'

De Rothschild is a British explorer who in 2006 crossed the Arctic from Russia to Canada to raise awareness about climate change. As he packed up his tent each morning, he noticed that the process involved tidying away a plastic bag of plastic waste. In the great garbage-free white it was matter out of place.

Back home de Rothschild began reading up on the plastic problem and discovered that this seemingly mundane, trifling thing that he'd barely given a thought to before was messing with the environment on an epic scale. He read an article by Charles Moore, the oceanographer and racing boat captain credited with discovering the Great Pacific Garbage Patch in the late 1990s. Moore and his crew had finished a race in Hawaii and were on their way home to California when they discovered it: the famous plastic soup, our consumer conscience, lurking in the middle of goddamn nowhere. Since they 'were feeling mellow and unhurried', they'd decided to take an unusual route through the North Pacific Gyre. 'Fishermen shun it because its waters lack the nutrients to support an abundant catch. Sailors dodge it because it lacks the wind to propel their sailboats,' writes Moore.[2] 'Day after day, [his boat] the *Alguita* was the only vehicle on a highway without landmarks, stretching from horizon to horizon. Yet as I gazed from the deck at the surface of what ought to have been pristine ocean, I was confronted, as far as the eye could see, with the sight of plastic.' Moore returned to conduct several studies into plastic in the gyre, revealing mind-blowing numbers.

De Rothschild asked himself, How is it possible that there could be 46,000 bits of plastic in every square mile of the sea? That the mass of plastic in the gyre is six times that of plankton?[3] And what on Earth could he do about it? 'Rather than lecture people, or tell them off, or make them depressed,' he called on his skills as an epic yarn-teller and decided 'to use the power of a great adventure story to get people thinking about plastics in a new way.'[4] He would build a marvellous boat from trash, and sail it on a fantastic adventure.

The *Plastiki* set sail from San Francisco for the Great Pacific Garbage Patch in March 2010. It was built from 12,500 reclaimed 2-litre plastic soft-drink bottles with sails made from recycled PET fabric, and secured with glue derived from cashew nuts and sugar. Sensible people thought de Rothschild's bizarre 60-foot catamaran wouldn't make it the 8000 nautical miles to Sydney. There were times when de Rothschild felt the same way; when he wasn't skyping journalists about his mission, he spent much of the journey feeling anxious.

After four months at sea, the *Plastiki* made it, and in the process made the ocean plastic problem big news. Said de Rothschild, 'I like to think of *Plastiki* as a metaphor for action. We built a boat out of plastic bottles and sailed it across the Pacific. Let's apply the same ingenuity and hard work to the ocean's problems. I hope, most of all, people buy into the audaciousness of the whole thing.'[5]

Later he told a British newspaper it hadn't been enough. 'I guess I was hoping it would achieve more,' he said. 'We got massive amounts of publicity. We raised the bar on the plastic issue. We caused a conversation, but we didn't solve the problem. The oceans are still drowning in plastic.'[6]

An exquisitely simple idea that might just work

De Rothschild, in his darker moments, might question whether his voyage succeeded, but he underestimates its power. Imagine how many kids unknowingly applied his equation of curiosity to dream of building boats of their own. Big kids too. Take 3's Tim Silverwood was inspired by the *Plastiki*, as well as by Charles Moore's expeditions and Curtis Ebbesmeyer's writings.

You might have heard of Ebbesmeyer: another American oceanographer, he's the rubber duck guy. In 1992, when a Greek-owned, Taiwanese-operated cargo ship lost some containers in rough weather, 28,800 Chinese-made plastic toys were released into open ocean. They included 7200 yellow ducks. Ebbesmeyer, the author of a book called *Flotsametrics* about how gyres work, was not the only beachcomber tracking their progress, but he is the most famous.

I'm at the beach now reading the news as I wait for Tim Silverwood. *The Guardian* is reporting that plastic production is set to increase dramatically on the back of the shale gas boom: by 40 per cent over the next decade.[7] The American Chemistry Council confirms 318 new plastic plants have been built or planned since 2010. As part of a US$20-billion investment, ExxonMobil has expanded its facility near Houston, Mont Belvieu. 'The plant capacity will total more than 2.5 million tons per year, making it one of the largest polyethylene plants in the world,' trumpets the press release,[8] like that's a good thing. One of the primary uses for polyethylene is packaging. Not content with mining the fossil fuels that drive global warming, the big oil companies also own the big plastics companies. It is not in their interests to promote recycling. According to the World Economic forum, 90 per cent of all the plastics produced are derived from virgin fossil feedstocks, and 'if the current strong growth of plastics usage continues as expected, the plastics sector will account for 20 per cent of total oil consumption' by 2050.[9]

Silverwood waves and makes his way slowly towards me, stopping every couple of metres to pick something up from the sand. 'That's more than three,' I say, and he laughs. My own pockets also contain more than three pieces of plastic beach litter. I found a fork, a child's neon orange spade, two bottle caps, a coffee cup lid and a chocolate wrapper. Silverwood knows that however many people get on board with Take 3, we'll never clean all the junk from our beaches, oceans and waterways by hand. 'We have to concentrate on not putting any more in there,' he says.[10] The plan is to get people noticing the problem and thinking of new approaches to consumption and waste. 'Education inspires participation.'

A bit like Harriet Spark, Silverwood believes the ocean taught him 'to be part of something bigger,' only for him it happened when he was a nipper. 'You go out there and you have to let go of your fears and your control, and if you can let yourself go and be immersed in that, that's when it grabs hold of you, isn't it?' The ocean gave little Tim Silverwood as a grommet surfer the most fun he had a kid.

Now all he had to do was work out how to pay it back. Silverwood studied sustainable resource management, but found it disillusioning. 'In terms of the work outcomes, they would steer you towards the mining companies, to help with their rehabilitation programs, or to the environment offices of local councils. Local government, where there's an intention to do some good but your hands are tied. Or a corporation that wants to do the bare minimum to mitigate negative pushback? Those choices didn't stack up for me.'

Silverwood went snowboarding instead. His plastic bug bit in India. 'I was in a mountain village; it was beautiful, but one day I looked over the hill and saw all this dumped rubbish. I investigated, found out the story behind it and realised that it was my rubbish too. I'd put it in the bin, but there was no system to dispose of it properly, so now it was littering the Himalayas. I thought, It's going to end up in the ocean in however many years it takes to get there.'

His first idea was to try to make a documentary about it—'I was in my wanting-to-be-a-filmmaker phase'—and although that didn't work out, he understood the power of visual storytelling. He hadn't been back in Australia long when Chanel Nine aired a *60 Minutes* report called 'Seas of Shame', featuring arresting footage of Kamilo Beach on the southeast coast of Hawaii's Big Island, deep in plastic trash. 'It was a revolutionary story for most Australians eating dinner in front of the telly on a Sunday night. Not many had heard of marine debris and not many knew of the Great Pacific Garbage Patch.'[11] Two years after it aired, Silverwood managed to get there to see it for himself. He found Kamilo 'absolutely covered with all manner of plastic debris from toilet seats, toothbrushes, and tennis balls to mountains of rope, piles of crates, umbrella handles and bottles, bottle caps and bottle necks.'[12] The gyre was disturbing in a different way. It's not choked thick with trash as many of us imagine it must be—the 'floating island' isn't solid. As Charles Moore describes it, 'Half of it was just little chips that we couldn't identify.' Silverwood had joined a research team sailing from Honolulu to Vancouver. Sifting through the debris in the gyre, they wore gloves to protect their skin. The plastic draws in persistent organic pollutants (POPs), acting like a sponge in the water. 'The plot doesn't play out very nicely for the species that are nibbling and swallowing this toxic detritus,' wrote Silverwood of the experience. 'Wait a minute, don't we eat fish?'

His journey to that point involved some serendipity and a lot of graft. He was ranting about plastic at a film festival in Avoca on the NSW Central Coast when someone in the audience suggested he meet two women who lived nearby. 'Amanda Marechal is married to a mad-keen surfer, and she'd been going to Hawaii with him, seeing all the trash that washes up when the trade winds blow,' says Silverwood. She and a friend, marine ecologist Roberta Dixon Valk, had started a beach clean-up initiative. They chose Take 3 as their name because Marechal, who is a mum, thought three bits of garbage was the max that little fingers could manage—they knew inspiring children was vital.

'Schools are a core focus,' says Silverwood, who has delivered hundreds of talks to students since he closed the triangle of Take 3. The organisation offers an early-childhood program to inspire mini marine protectors with storytelling and art projects. They work with primary and secondary schools encouraging the kids to develop their own systems to stop plastic pollution and put them into practice. 'That's the way,' says Silverwood. 'We need to give people agency.'

Being a bit fabulous and also based in Sydney, Silverwood was the project partner the women had been looking for. Not that he knew it all. They all learned how to be professional change-makers on the job. 'For the first ten months it was, "What do we do now?"' admits Silverwood.

Their big, beautiful, ridiculously simple message—'Take three pieces of rubbish [away] when you leave the beach, waterway or anywhere, and you've made a difference'—became their touchstone; they knew it was powerful and that its simplicity was a big selling point. They stepped up the beach cleans, worked on their school program and joined the Boomerang Alliance. Silverwood made a fifteen-minute film about plastic pollution that screened at a surf movie festival. He gave a TED talk. They won a $50,000 grant from Taronga Zoo and built a better website, recruited ambassadors and began working with surf lifesaving clubs. Somehow Silverwood found the time to start a company, ReChusable, which sells metal drinking straws and bamboo cutlery.

'When I first started, the enthusiasm I felt around this issue, you couldn't put a cap on it,' he says. 'I was the archetype activist. I was the guy dressing up in plastic bags. I was waving placards in front of parliament, I was sneaking into Coca-Cola's AGM and getting up to ask [then

Coca-Cola-Amatil chairman] David Gonski hard questions, nervous as hell at the time but just compelled to do it.' A decade on, his approach has changed. 'I have a more calculated, pulled-back perspective. My approach now is about the slow road. Change is so inherently hard—not to say that you can't achieve a lot from rapid activist actions—but if we want to change society, to build this into a real movement to ingrain sustainability into our culture, we need the fabric of society to change, and we need behavioural norms to change. That takes patience.'

How Plastic Free July caught on

It started with one woman looking at an empty yoghurt container she was about to toss. 'I thought, How did I come to have this thing in the first place? What other choices could I have made? I went to work the next day and said, "Right, I'm going to refuse single-use plastics for the whole of next month."'[13]

The fact that this woman was Rebecca Prince-Ruiz and she worked in waste education for her local council was good luck for the planet. She'd recently taken a group to visit a materials-recovery facility in Perth, Western Australia, and the scale of it stunned her. 'The sheer volume, particularly of plastic rubbish. I saw it being sorted and baled up to be shipped to South-East Asia for further processing. It's so complex and energy-intensive. I thought, We focus on recycling when we should be refusing.'

The first Plastic Free July challenge in 2011 involved about forty colleagues and friends-of-friends committing to 'choose to refuse single-use plastic' for a month. It was just a few emails really, sharing tips and encouragement, but the idea was sticky. 'I think lots of people feel overwhelmed by the amount of plastic packaging in our lives,' says Prince-Ruiz.

Maybe they also like the feeling of taking their power back. The year 2011 was a rotten one for global stability and natural disasters, with earthquakes in Japan and New Zealand and riots in the UK. Occupy Wall Street stole headlines. The Queensland floods were the worst in memory, while bushfires near Perth destroyed at least fifty houses. Maybe, faced with all that, the idea of being the boss of your own habits was especially appealing that first year.

Prinze-Ruiz thinks the reason people came back to do it again the next year, and the challenge grew wings after that, is that it feels achievable. 'I mean, you can do most things for four weeks, right? It's long enough to change habits but short enough to handle.' Plus it's not like you're trying to kick an enjoyable habit—the plastic-free life feels better on many levels, as we shall see. Today, the campaign has global reach.

When I tried the fast in 2017, it definitely recalibrated my thinking, and while I didn't turn into a full-blown zero-waste warrior, I did give up the big five single-use plastic items (bags, bottles, straws, coffee cups, utensils) for good, and found it deeply satisfying. In terms of difficulty, it was the sneaky little things that got me: the discs of plastic inside metal beer-bottle tops, the plastic labels on glass jars, the bags inside cereal boxes. The fact that I'm lost without yoghurt—Prince-Ruiz makes her own.

'Some of it is about rediscovering the old ways,' she says, 'which people enjoy. With plastic packaging, you can buy food that's highly processed, imported, not in season, whereas by taking on the challenge, you're almost forced to buy local produce and support local businesses. You rediscover the farmers' market, greengrocer, butcher, fishmonger.

'A couple of generations ago, especially in rural and suburban areas, people used to be responsible for their own waste. You composted what you could or kept chickens to eat scraps, and a little incinerator in your backyard for anything you couldn't deal with. Your rubbish was processed by you on site, so you cared more. Now we're disconnected from our waste, just like we're disconnected from our food production, our environment and where our clothes come from. You need to connect to care.'

Prince-Ruiz says giving up plastic is bigger than a lifestyle trend. 'I see it as part of a counterculture, anti-consumerist movement, bigger than that even, in that it allows you to take a step out of the rat race and become more mindful.' And encourages you to question the system. 'You know the recycling symbol around the number you find on plastic packaging?'

I tell her I do.

'The number is just a resin identification code that tells you what type of plastic you're dealing with. Introducing the recycling symbol around it was a genius idea from the American Chemistry Council, but it's misleading. The question isn't: is it recyclable? It's: will it be recycled? Only 9 per cent of the plastic ever made has been recycled,' she says, and most of that is really 'down-cycled' to a lesser grade application. 'So, PET bottles become synthetic fabric or playground matting; they're not just these happy drinks bottles that keep being fed into an endless closed loop. I see Plastic Free July as part of a much broader movement that's seeing large numbers of people question the role of plastics in our lives and its impacts on the environment.'

13
Zero waste

'If you do anything different or outside of the box, or if you're an agent for change, people often feel unsettled.'

—Stella McCartney

'At first, my message was negative—use less—but gradually I realised there was another way of looking at things.'

—Ellen MacArthur

Talking rubbish

Plastic Free July could change your life. Erin Rhoads was a graphic designer when she took up the challenge in Melbourne after stumbling across it online. 'Who knows, maybe I will adopt this forever,' she wrote on her then six-month-old blog, *The Rogue Ginger* (she'd begun it as a travel diary and had managed a few posts about riding her bike and making onion soup). Today Rhoads is Australia's best-known zero-waste blogger, the author of a book called *Waste Not* and an eco-lifestyle guru. 'I'd typed in, "How do I reduce my plastic?" No one had really discovered Plastic Free July yet; it was still very new,' she says.[1] 'I didn't know it was going to be a movement. I just wanted some tips to change my habits and it worked, so I kept going.'

'Hello more vegetables and fruit,' she blogged thirteen days in. Easier to skip premade food since so much of it came in plastic. She cut her take-away habit and discovered her apartment block had a compost bin. Small changes like freezing vegetable scraps to make stock led to more profound ones. 'The more I learned about my power, the more I realised I could take responsibility on these issues,' she tells me. 'Simple things, like I don't have to buy body wash in a plastic bottle, so I don't have to give my tacit consent to the companies that make it. Or I can sit here and have a cup of tea with you instead of rushing off with it in a plastic-lined cup destined for the bin. Rushing, creating this busyness in our lives, why do we do it? We can choose not to. Take a breath, relax. It's all connected.

'Look at how single-use coffee cups have become the poster child for reducing waste. That's good, they suck, but we're talking so much about the cups and not enough about what's going into them,' says Rhoads. 'People grow the coffee beans, spend their lives cultivating the plants; the beans need to be picked, washed, roasted, and whatever else happens to coffee. I'm not the expert, but I can see that the beans take time and trouble to produce. Then in the café a barista spends time and effort making the perfect cup of coffee. Since when did we forget to appreciate all that? We just chug it down and chuck it away. What I'm saying is, we need to reconnect with the processes behind the things we consume. So yes, you could say Plastic Free July changed everything for me.'

After she took Prince-Ruiz's challenge, Rhoads saved a year's worth of unrecyclable rubbish in a mason jar (toothbrush bristles, fruit stickers, those annoying plastic thingos they punch through the price tags in op shops) and took to toting it around schools to inspire kids to be the change. She made her own mascara and used tapioca flour as face powder. In 2015 she helped start Plastic Bag Free Victoria. They collected 11,600 signatories, in person, for a petition to ban the free distribution of single-use plastic bags. 'We took it to the Victorian Parliament; it was the biggest petition in the last decade,' says Rhoads (online ones don't count). It worked. The environment minister announced a ban in October 2017. 'We brought together all the plastic-bag-free groups in the state and we just pushed and pushed. The quickest way to achieve change is through legislation,' says Rhoads.

Okay, but why did she overhaul her entire life, and make zero waste her work and building the movement her mission, when others take the plastic fast for a month and emerge with a KeepCup but otherwise unchanged? We are the sum of our experiences. Plastic Free July was Rhoads's second zero-waste lightbulb moment. Her first came from watching Canadian documentary *The Clean Bin Project*. The film tracks a young couple from Vancouver as they attempt to 'buy no more stuff and produce zero landfill' for an entire year. They set some rules; they could buy work essentials, for example. If they generated waste while they were eating out, they would have to bring it home. Any packaging generated that wasn't compostable, biodegradable or recyclable must be saved up and stored in their personal bins—one each—to be counted and weighed at the end of the challenge. Rhoads found the film, which features an interview with Charles Moore, fascinating. But she also has the right mindset: she's the sort who questions things and wants to live a meaningful life, beyond just having nice stuff, a good job, a fancy car. There were missionaries in her family, and observing the way her relatives lived and viewed service to their fellow humans—'My grandmother went to work in Uganda as a nurse when she was sixty; my cousin did work in South Africa in an orphanage; my uncle went to Haiti to help rebuild after the 2010 earthquake; they all donated their time'—left Rhoads with an understanding that 'we have a responsibility to each other; we don't exist in isolation.'

Rhoads just had to find her thing, which wasn't religious, unless you count the Church of Oprah. 'I watched it with my mum. Until you asked me, it's not like I thought, Oh yes, this thing has its roots in *Oprah*! But you know what? I do think Oprah taught a lot of us how to respond to different situations, and to listen. I think she taught a generation: let's talk. And she didn't discriminate. Her approach was, "You might be rich; you might be poor. I don't care. Anyone can come here and talk through an issue with me."'

There was a particular episode of *The Oprah Winfrey Show* that struck a chord with Rhoads. It featured the Australian doctor Catherine Hamlin, then eighty, who over five decades had operated, free of charge, on more than 25,000 African girls and women at the Addis Ababa Fistula Hospital. 'I remember feeling very moved and determined to help.' Rhoads had a bake sale. 'Obviously that's really small, but it got me thinking about how I can help people with my money, and who and what I want to support with it.' Later, like many a kid just out of college, she wanted to spend it on travel.

India was where Rhoads first started to worry about trash. It's a very visible problem there. Indian street cows have been found with 30 kilograms of plastic in their stomachs.[2] The trip was also formative because it reframed Rhoads's thinking about privilege, consequence, responsibility and changing the conversation, although she admits the penny didn't drop immediately: 'I was twenty-two when I visited India, and it was confronting seeing what real poverty can look like, but it was also about coming to realise, through a few different experiences, how to join the dots.' She pauses. 'How much ideas from my culture have disrupted other cultures, and how it's our fault; that colonial mindset coming along and messing things up. I saw the cows eat the plastic, and everything smells smoky from burning the trash, which is now plastic and toxic, and I thought, Which companies introduced plastic into India? And how come they didn't also bring systems to dispose of the waste? I didn't know the answers, but I knew something was wrong with the overall picture.'

If you want to change the world, start with yourself by all means, but to be truly effective you have to figure out how the system operates and might be improved, then bring others along with you to push to change it.

I tell Rhoads about the months I spent in India in the late '90s when I was around the same age that she was when she went. How I visited ashrams and tried to write a novel and travelled everywhere by train. I've seven years on her, and plastic rubbish wasn't such an issue then. The chai wallahs sold their brews in clay cups, and we merrily chucked them out of the train windows when we were done drinking. Earth to Earth. Dinner was delivered from the canteen on metal platters, which were then collected for reuse. Street vendors still sold snacks in paper bags upcycled from old newspapers, the sewing of which provided work. Now I'm not saying that was necessarily dignified work—what do I know?—but it was part of a functioning system that didn't leave piles of trash a metre high along the railway tracks. By 2016, New Delhi railway station alone was generating more than 4000 kilograms of plastic waste a day. In 2004 the Indian railways minister Lalu Prasad Yadav tried to bring back the clay teacups, but he was accused of keeping the potters in poverty work, polluting the air with smoke from the kilns and subjecting commuters to 'problems like shape, structure, wobbly base, loss of taste of drink, and so on'.[3] The minister also launched a program to replace synthetic train seat covers with homespun cotton, but that wasn't to be either. By the time he was imprisoned for corruption in 2017, almost all the teacups on Indian trains were plastic. But there is hope: on World Environment Day 2018, India's prime minister announced plans to eliminate single-use plastics from the whole country by 2022. Wouldn't that be fantastic? I'm crossing my fingers.

Rhoads and I are meeting for a cuppa—in reusable porcelain, thank you—at Australia's National Sustainable Living Festival, where we're both speaking about waste at separate events. The festival began around the time I was trying to find myself in India and has grown from a small gathering outside Daylesford, Victoria, to a month-long annual jamboree in Melbourne. This year 100,000 people are expected. It is clear just from looking around us that this movement is building, and that the old silos are less relevant as environmentalists across interests are talking, and sharing ideas. Crowds are browsing stalls run by wildlife societies and eco-activists, permaculture and composting experts, urban bee-keepers, foragers and Earthship builders. In one area, the team from Suitcase Rummage has set up, attracting second-hand fashion fans; in another, a 'wild woman' teaches bush survival skills that include tanning your own wallaby hide with a view to sewing it (using the animal's sinew as thread) into a sort of primitive Viking lady jerkin.

'This,' I say to Rhoads, 'is pretty full on.' I've dressed down so as not to scare the hardcore eco people. Rhoads, however, is having none of that— she's straight outta the Hamptons in a blue-and-white frock and toting a raffia clutch embroidered with eyelashes and red lips. She is making a visual point: that if self-tanning a hide is not your thing, there are no style limits to zero-waste and buy-nothing-new living. Her entire outfit is thrifted.

'Your first time?' she says. 'It gets bigger every year.'

'And how big is zero waste? Not just at the festival but in general?'

'Zero waste is huge,' she says. 'Even if it's just taking the elements that work for you, the concept has caught on.'

'And people don't think you're crazy anymore.'

'Look, some of them do,' she laughs, as she takes her eleven-month-old son into her arms. 'But seriously, this is for him. I use this analogy: say you're about to go into a bedroom and it's really messy and someone tells you that first you have to clean it up. You think, I shouldn't have to clean this mess! I didn't make it. You get really frustrated. Well, that's what the next generation is going to be stuck with. My son will be cleaning up our plastic waste, and our environmental mismanagement.'

He was a zero-waste baby, swaddled in second-hand muslins, bathed in a second-hand tub, and dried with towels from an op shop. His pram and other essentials were passed down by extended family. Rhoads used washable cloth nappies. 'Why not? Our grandmothers did it.'

Total garbage

While we're in the mood for taking inspiration from our grandmas, I offer up the story of Kamikatsu, a 'zero-waste town' in south-western Japan. In this beautiful mountainside settlement surrounded by rice terraces, half of the 1600 residents are over the age of sixty-five, a quarter over eighty-five, and they sort their waste into forty-five separate categories. It used to be thirty-four, but they keep finding ways to improve the system.

The villagers introduced their zero-waste goal for economic reasons. Until the '90s, they'd burned most of their trash, but that became a problem as Japan stepped up its penchant for plastic. The government banned open incineration in 1994, so Kamikatsu installed a compliant incinerator, but three years later, the rules changed and they couldn't afford to upgrade. The solution, they decided, was to go cold turkey on unrecyclable trash.

Kamikatsu residents now compost 100 per cent of food waste and make money from onselling carefully sorted glass of various colours, aluminium, steel, various plastics. 'We've impacted people's consumption,' explains Akira Sakano, chair of Kamikatsu's Zero Waste Academy.[4] 'There was a change in the citizens' mind-set not to pollute our Nature too—all the grannies stood up fighting against the incineration.'[5]

Sakano reminds us that zero waste is a symbolic goal: 'It is a slogan, like "zero drunk-driving". Of course, there will always be that one incident, but by saying "zero" you can be creative enough to achieve 99 per cent. You can engage more people, which is the main goal of zero waste.'[6] What the phrase really means is 'zero waste to landfill' anyway, or we might say, zero wasted waste—the logical extension of reduce, reuse, recycle, repair.

Ariana Schwarz, an American zero-waster who blogs at *Paris to Go*, pins it down: 'Zero waste is an industrial term for a consumer movement encouraging manufacturers to eliminate single-use items and non-biodegradable materials. The aim is to push towards a circular economy and increase demand for package-free products or reclaimable packaging.'[7]

If an entire zero-waste village is unusual, zero-waste influencers, families and community groups are no longer rare. Rhoads tells me about early adopter Béa Johnson, the California-based French mother of two dubbed by *The New York Times* the 'Priestess of waste-free living'. It was Johnson who inspired Rhoads to try the mason jar experiment.

In 2008, Johnson started sewing cloth bags from old sheets and taking them along to do her bakery shop. Soon she was buying staples in bulk, and taking her own jars to the deli to eliminate cheese, meat and fish wrappers. When asked why, she found it easier to say she didn't have a trash can rather than go into a long speech about her motivations. These include reconnecting with the people who make, sell and serve our food. She finds zero waste 'a more human way of shopping because it forces you, in a way, to have contact with the person behind the counter ... it gives a better sense of community because you care more about them and they care about you.'[8]

While Rhoads and Schwarz have clearly spent much time considering the environmental and sociopolitical context of what they are trying to achieve (in one blog post, Schwarz writes, 'It bothers me that eco-friendly behaviour is associated with environmental racism, when garbage is so widely used as a tool of oppression'), Johnson seems happy to keep zero waste filed under lifestyle movement and personal growth: it's good for her and her family; it makes life simpler and clearer; it saves them money.

That said, Johnson is happy to share with those who are curious. Her book, *Zero Waste Home*, has been translated into twenty languages, and being the picture of French elegance, she is well-placed to reach aspirational consumers. To watch her in a video climbing the stone steps to her minimal-chic house in high-heeled ankle boots, carrying her cloth-bagged groceries, is to think, Zero waste can be stylish! Nothing wrong with that. In fact, it's the approach I take with my sustainable fashion work.

New York cool girl Lauren Singer has a similar effect. Through her website, *Trash is for Tossers*, sustainable laundry detergent brand The Simply Co., and the Package Free Shop in Brooklyn, Singer is turning a whole new crowd onto the benefits of zero-waste living. Her journey, tips and tricks have been written up in major fashion glossies, helping to bring the mainstream into the movement. When CNN visited Singer's store to check out its wares, which include menstrual cups and bamboo toothbrushes, they concluded: 'Sound like hippy-dippy, tree-hugging nonsense? You're wrong. The zero-waste movement has teeth, and it's coming to a city near you.'[9]

True that. New York and San Francisco (again) have zero-waste goals. For those who can't wait for the municipal plans to come to fruition, there are thousands of Facebook and community groups. The Zero Waste Europe network is active in seven countries, and its members include Retorna, the Spanish NGO that's reintroducing the container take-back schemes that were popular in Spain in the '80s. Zero-waste bloggers are mushrooming. In Australia, there are no fewer than three zero-waste books coming out in a year. Zero waste is the next big thing.

So why doesn't everyone love it? As usual, women's voices are part of the problem. A Reddit feed reveals that some lament the lack of male role models in the scene. One man commented, 'If a bloke takes a casual look into it and literally only sees lifestyle blogs from stay-at-home mums, he's not coming back.'[10]

It is no coincidence that most of the zero-waste advocates I've come across are women. The fact that it's still overwhelmingly women who decide what's for dinner plays its part, and while there must be straight men out there buying gadgets, clothes and whatever it is that keeps them coming back to Bunnings (it's the sausage sizzle, isn't it?), many clearly loathe shopping. The reasons for this are rooted in social conditioning and the patriarchy—in the nineteenth century, for example, the new department stores and arcades provided public spaces for middle-class women, previously cloistered in the home, to congregate—but the fact remains: women shop.

According to *Forbes*, 'if the consumer economy had a sex, it would be female'—women drive 70–80 per cent of purchasing decisions.[11] According to me, we're fed up with excessive packaging being foisted upon us by supermarkets; rant on social media about cling-wrapped bananas and the conversation goes off. We're fed up with over-packaged, processed food laden with sugar and additives, and we're looking for better ways to live in harmony with the environment and each other. Sustainability is not a buzz word for nothing. And thanks to television shows like *War on Waste*, garbage has become a hot-button issue, no longer the preserve of government departments, landfill operators or materials-recovery plants. It's a community problem with community solutions. In a thought-provoking piece for the environmental arts magazine she founded, *Loam*, Kate Weiner writes that:

> Delegitimizing the diversity of philosophies and practices within the zero waste movement is a way to write off the significant social impact of a thriving community that has been largely shaped and sustained by non-patriarchal bodies. Many popular low-waste living practices—such as creating healing herbal remedies and cultivating a trash-light home—are considered 'feminine' pursuits. And so, like everything 'feminine' in our mainstream culture, it's discarded.[12]

More so when it's young women.

Schwarz, then twenty-seven, was featured in a 2016 UK newspaper article[13] about zero-waste bloggers, along with Singer, then twenty-four, Kathryn Kellogg, twenty-five, of Going Zero Waste and Celia Ristow of Litterless, also twenty-four (and a man actually—Rob Greenfield—who wrote a book called *Dude Making a Difference* and begins his biography,

'Not that long ago, my main priorities included binge drinking every weekend, looking good, and macking on pretty much every good looking girl I saw.' Then he grew up, and now does all of the things: zero waste, permaculture gardening, wholefood diet, lived off-grid in a tiny house before he downsized to a backpack.) Anyway, that story was widely read and caused wide annoyance. There's just something about zero waste that riles people. Is it a perceived smugness, perhaps, that makes mere mortals with overflowing wheelie bins feel somehow less? Less exemplary, less disciplined, less spotless-all-white marble kitchen, more pasta sauce on the lapel? Schwarz accepts that 'people like to poke holes in the concept of zero waste' and that some find it 'preachy, self-righteous, or extreme'. Whatever. 'Living in post-industrial society is wasteful,' she says. 'Instead of nitpicking or worrying about things we can't change, we just try to live as responsibly as we can, and help others who want to do the same.'

The bit she does worry about is the charge that zero waste is exclusive, that it's the 'You can't sit with us' of the environmental movement. 'I'm definitely guilty of saying anybody can be zero waste, and I'm sorry for that, because it isn't practical for everyone and not always appropriate.'

You stink

Erin Rhoads's husband is Lebanese Australian, so it felt close to home as they watched Beirut's trash crisis unfold over the summer of 2015. As protestors hit the streets, they chanted, 'The people want to topple the regime!' and the riot squad was called. But the issue that prompted 4000 citizens to risk tear gas and arrest by protesting that August was total garbage, more specifically the uncollected sort. Since June great piles of it had been rotting in the streets and surrounding mountainside. In desperation people were setting fire to it, releasing acrid clouds of smoke. Then in extraordinary scenes, entire streets turned into rivers of trash. The crisis was political, fuelled by corruption, government inefficiency and mismanagement, but the impacts are social.

Piles of garbage, whether illegally dumped, uncollected or whisked away to landfill, emit methane, which adds to global warming. They attract pests and leak bin juice, called leachate, which can poison ground water and agricultural land. When e-waste (old computers, phones, appliances and the like) is buried in landfill, it adds heavy metals to the mix. Nobody wants a landfill in their backyard, but not everyone gets to choose.

In Beirut, activists, organised by the online group You Stink, parked themselves in tents outside the Ministry of Environment, waving placards bearing the familiar slogan, 'Recycle, reuse, refuse.'

When the system falls over as it did in Beirut—or in Naples, Italy, and its surrounding farmland, where the mafia has facilitated the illegal dumping of toxic industrial waste since the 1990s, leading to cancer clusters and export bans on the local buffalo mozzarella cheese—everybody suffers. But when it 'works' (that is, when our garbage is collected on time and dealt with legally and efficiently), most people don't have to worry about it. However, as we have seen with the story of ocean plastic, that doesn't mean it's not causing problems, and as usual it is the environment and the most marginalised communities that are most effected. Recycling is awesome—we should be doing more of it—but it's no magic bullet.

Rich people, as Adam Minter points out in *Junkyard Planet*, recycle more stuff. 'If you take a drive through a high-income, highly educated neighborhood on recycling day, you'll see [designated] bins overflowing with neatly sorted newspapers, iPad boxes, wine bottles, and Diet Coke cans. Meanwhile, take a drive through a poor neighborhood, and you'll invariably see fewer bins, and fewer recyclables.'[14] Wealthy people might be 'good stewards' of their trash, but they also do 'an equally fine job of generating it'.[15] Says Minter, diligent recyclers patting themselves on the back would do well to remember, 'Recycling is just a means to stave off the trash man for a little longer.'[16] If you really want to be environmentally responsible, you'll take Rebecca Prinze-Ruiz's challenge and reduce.

Towards the end of 2017, a *Four Corners* report revealed massive stockpiles of used glass building up in Australian warehouses. Prices had collapsed, and it was just sitting there. But New South Wales laws limit the amount of time waste can be stored, so criminal gangs were running rackets to smuggle it over state borders and illegally dump it. Suddenly, popping our wine bottles into our yellow bin didn't feel so virtuous. At the very same time China was introducing its 'foreign garbage' bans, and in 2018 Australia stopped dispatching its used plastic and cardboard there, amid talk of some councils abandoning kerbside recycling services completely. What are we going to do: deal with our own waste, reshore manufacturing and close the loop? It would be nice. Regulate to boost demand for recycled content in packaging? Dig more landfills? Cutting down our rubbish would obviously help, and you and I can start doing that right now. China, incidentally, is the world's biggest ocean plastic polluter, so they have their work cut out for them trying to fix that. The second biggest is Indonesia. But don't be quick to judge: per capita, Americans consume by far the most plastic, and Australians are among the highest generators of household waste.

Think about all this. Does the zero-waste movement still sound like a privileged white girl's lifestyle choice or a bit of unimportant female fussing? Or does it sound like a smart strategy to remake our world so that all of us might live with less bin juice and greater empathy for Nature and each other? A peaceful revolution fought with cloth bags and common sense? I'm in.

14
Let's build a tiny house!

'If you do only one thing to make your new home more environmentally sound, make it small. Unless supporting the housing industry is the kind of sustainability you hope to achieve, a reasonably scaled home is the best way there is to make a positive difference with real estate.'

—Jay Shafer, *The Small House Book*

'It suddenly struck me that that tiny pea, pretty and blue, was the Earth. I put my thumb up and shut one eye, and my thumb blotted out the planet Earth. I didn't feel like a giant. I felt very, very small.'

—Neil Armstrong

Small is beautiful

Amanda Chapman strikes me as quite tiny herself, and she's building a tiny house! Actually, a tiny house on wheels (THOW). Since old-school bloke-ish dismissiveness of the 'You're just a girl, do you really think you can build a house, love?' variety is still a thing, I like the idea that this woman is no hulking giant physically, because, as we all know deep down, the only size that matters is the size of your dreams, and your determination to act on them.

Surely it also helps not to be an NBA player if you plan to live in a tin shed that's 2.5 metres wide. Chapman disagrees. 'It was designed for a couple,' she says (there was a partner; they split), 'but three people could live comfortably in there, with another bed on the second mezzanine.'[1]

The house will be 7.2 metres long and extend 4.25 off the ground, including the height of the trailer. I, with my only-child issues and third bedroom/home office, suspect it might be easier with just Chapman and her cat, but the easy life is not the aim here. What Chapman is seeking is a more sustainable future.

Another zero-waster, she too was inspired by Plastic Free July and blogged about it. Chapman is building a life that aligns with her values, and one that proves a point: that it can be done. We can downsize and be happier for it; we can live more lightly on the planet and break the cycle of greed that is pushing Nature to her limits. The THOW is Chapman's practical solution. 'I really want to live off-grid and be self-sufficient, and you can't do that when you're renting,' she says. And at twenty-six she can't afford, and doesn't want, a mortgage.

For the past three-and-a-bit years, Chapman has lived in a share house in Onehunga, a suburb of New Zealand's sprawling capital Auckland, where the average house costs nearly a million bucks. The wrecker's ball has not yet won here, and as we drove in we passed rows of century-old weatherboard villas set in large gardens. Chapman's THOW is parked in hers—her landlord is supportive.

Some of the old places have been done up, their timber decks and stained-glass windows restored. Others are shambolic, paint peeling, their many draughty bedrooms for rent at relatively reasonable sums. It's been twenty years since the likes of Chapman and her friends could afford a place like this in Sydney. From the outside glancing in, New Zealand, with its population of just under five million, seems like somewhere the eco- and artistically minded should thrive, but Chapman is not impressed with her rental's faded grandeur and generous proportions, despite space for a vegetable patch. She finds it cold in winter, and can't see the point of a kitchen big enough to rollerskate in. 'No one uses that,' she says, leading us past an enormous drawing room, empty but for a geriatric TV set. Overhead, a fluorescent strip light buzzes. Large houses serve one of two obvious functions: they accommodate many, or they represent money.

Americans build the biggest houses in the world. The average new build there is 240 square metres. Australians and New Zealanders aren't far behind, but a recent story in the *New Zealand Herald* suggests the trends are polarising: houses are either super-sized or getting smaller.

Humans have been living in small dwellings since they worked out how to build walls. No, longer: since they lived in caves. But the tiny-house movement is about people choosing to live in very small spaces, when bigger ones are available to them and/or the norm in their communities.

Modern tiny-house fans began to self-identify as such after the American architect Lester Walker published his 1987 book *Tiny Tiny Houses: or How to Get Away from It All*. He was inspired by seeing how astronauts managed in cramped conditions. 'I've always felt, Why can't we build smaller? … It's so much more efficient, the taxes, the construction, the heat.' What he calls 'the McMansion movement' spurred him to go searching for historic examples of compact cabins and cottages, and to encourage people to build new ones, but Walker is not keen on the THOW concept and has said, 'I think it should be more of a little permanent number in your backyard or in the woods somewhere.'[2] Walker's tiny houses are just neat holiday homes.

Binge-watching US TV show *Tiny House, Big Living*, I'm struck further by the lack of focus on the eco element. The builders are mostly looking to reduce debt or declutter, or think tiny houses are adorable. Janet wants to downsize 'for the challenge'. Ethan thinks THOWs look cool. Mark co-owns a cabinet company that makes posh wine cellars, so building a tiny house with one inside it seems like good marketing, plus he's skint and sick of living with his parents.

In an essay for *Curbed*, a former editor at *The New York Times* Home section ponders possible motivations. 'Is the building type popular because it is economical and sustainable, fostering noble values and family cooperation, or is it immature?' Perhaps the tiny house is like an adult cubbyhouse? 'Does the small scale allow efficient management of resources, or despotic control of one's surroundings?' And, 'To what extent is simplicity really a virtue?'[3]

Thoreau fans certainly think it is. The simplifiers' poster boy, Henry David Thoreau was an American writer who in 1845 built himself a cabin in the woods in order 'to live deliberately'. Single-roomed, 'ten feet wide by fifteen feet long', it had space for a bed, chair, desk and stove, two windows, a wood shed out back and a cellar reached by a hatch in the floor. Thoreau chopped the pines to build it himself, plastered inside and shingled out. There, he wrote *Walden: Or, Life in the Woods*, his paean to the beauty and majesty of Nature and rejection of the distracting fuss of society. Thoreau believed that city life was 'frittered away by detail' and concluded, 'A man is rich in proportion to the number of things he can afford to let alone.' He took this to the nth degree. 'A lady once offered me a mat,' he wrote, 'but as I had no room to spare within the house, nor time to spare within or without to shake it, I declined it, preferring to wipe my feet on the sod before my door. It is best to avoid the beginnings of evil.' For Thoreau, a house was a place to sleep and write. Real life was lived beyond four walls. He anticipated modern conservationists' concerns, writing to a friend in 1860, 'What is the use of a house if you haven't got a tolerable planet to put it on?'[4]

While Jay Shafer doesn't advocate the full Walden hermit path, America's most famous modern tiny-house influencer moves beyond aesthetics and convenience to explore the social and environmental benefits of this mode of living. His advice to would-be downsizers? 'A good way to assess what you're gonna miss is to just go camping for a week.'[5] Shafer's initial motivations were political. He built his first tiny house in 1997, partly as a response to legal restrictions on dwelling size that aim to keep vagrants from living in sheds. Why shouldn't they? Shafer had happily lived in a caravan before. 'A small house is not merely as good as its larger correlate, it is better,' he writes in *The Small House Book* (even the name is simplified). 'A home that is designed to meet its occupants' domestic needs for contented living without exceeding those needs will invariably surpass the quality of a bigger one in terms of sustainability, economics and aesthetics.'

As Chapman knows, building a tiny house isn't always as simple as the life you crave: zoning laws usually restrict new builds to those that meet square-metre requirements, hence the solution of putting these little dwellings on wheels, so that they can be technically classed as recreational vehicles. This approach comes with its own regulations. In Australia and New Zealand, nothing on the road can be wider than 2.5 metres—the reason for Chapman's skinny abode. There are local laws that make it illegal to live full-time in an RV outside of designated zones, and that prohibit camping for an open-ended time on properties, even when they are your own. An ingenious lot, tiny-house fans are finding ways to work with all this.

An Auckland company has been building THOWs since 2016, designed for off-grid living, with solar panels and composting toilets—there's even one to rent on Airbnb so you can try before you buy—but Chapman wanted to build her own.

The first step was internet research, and visiting other people's little pads. She went WWOOFing (volunteering as a Willing Worker on Organic Farms) for a guy building a THOW, and took copious notes. 'Then I literally drew myself a picture of how I wanted my house laid out,' says Chapman. Her ex converted it into a CAD drawing. Chapman's 83-year-old grandfather was a builder, and he's been helping out, 'although he's never built with a steel frame before,' she says.

Taking it slow means she can afford to learn on the job—she taught herself about plumbing via YouTube. She forked out for a new trailer, batteries and composting toilet, but otherwise most of her materials are factory seconds, used or free. She's excited about a lightweight fibreglass bath tub she's just found. 'It fits!' Ah, a bath of one's own; she's living the dream, which for Chapman, who has moved twenty-three times in as many years, is clearly rooted in her rootlessness as much as in her sustainability goals. Amanda Chapman wants to settle down.

'Do you guys want some cake?' she says. I put my hand out. 'Full disclosure: it is dumpster-dive cake.' Momentarily I take my hand back but can't handle the bad manners, so I have my cake and eat it, and it's delicious.

15
Rejecting money

'One-hundred per cent discount on all merchandise is policy at The Free
Store, 901 Cole street.'
          —San Francisco Chronicle, 13 August 1967

'Why? Because we are fucking stupid and ran out of ideas. Now we need
the money back.'
          —Text from posters put up by the KLF in Liverpool in 2017,
          twenty-three years after they burned a million pounds on the
                                              Scottish island of Jura

'We know that wasting food is a total waste of everything, money, labour,
love, energy, resources—the indebted cost of food waste is far, far greater
than chucking out a bag of tomatoes. When you know the story and the life
cycle of that food, I think you've got greater value for it.'
          —Annika Stott, sustainability strategist, OzHarvest[1]

No price tags

I was eighteen when British rave band the KLF incinerated a million
pounds on camera just because they could, and I was livid. If they didn't
want it, why not give it to Greenpeace? Or me? I felt the same when
Malcolm McLaren's son Joe Corré set fire to five million quid's worth of
Sex Pistols memorabilia in 2016. 'Punk has become another marketing tool
to sell you something you don't need,' he said. 'The illusion of an alternative

choice. Conformity in another uniform.' Corré's mother, the passionate environmentalist fashion designer Vivienne Westwood, joined in; she drove to the site in a double-decker bus and delivered a speech about renewables. But as *Vogue* commented, 'How can it make sense to agitate for clean energy from the back of a dirty old bus, and by burning a bunch of acetates and some PVC pants and letting the fumes belch into the air?'[2] I can't help imagining Viv and her boy had strong words behind closed doors: 'Just sell the effing lot at Christie's and give the cash to Cool Earth.' Burning money is a rich man's game.

A 'frugal movement' is brewing in response to soaring living costs and feelings of stuffocation. Headlines like 'Woman saves $37,000 after refusing to buy things for a whole year!' get clicks. They make us wonder what we could do with all that extra dosh: book a holiday? put the kids through school? The woman in question, Michelle McGagh, a journalist and self-styled 'professional tight-arse', paid off a chunk of her mortgage with it, then wrote a book called *The No Spend Year*. Frugalistas seem to be mostly concerned with their bank statements. More interesting to me are those who are rethinking the whole concept of money. I'm talking about the freegans, foragers, barterers and swappers, and the 1960s Diggers.

The original Diggers, also called True Levellers, were a group of egalitarian seventeenth-century English radicals who objected to the enclosures that robbed country folk of common land. Their leader Gerrard Winstanley believed that landlords accrued their wealth 'either by Oppression, or Murther [murder] or Theft'[3] and that all land should belong to everyone equally. What's more, buying and selling, as concepts, were no good because someone always ended up rich, someone impoverished. Radical bloke, Gerrard Winstanley.

Fast forward. In the mid-1960s, a group of young actors formed a guerilla theatre group in San Francisco, taking their name from the English Diggers. These new Diggers wrote their own material and made the streets their stage. One of them, Peter Coyote, went on to become a film star (he played the government agent in *E.T.*), but in the '60s the Diggers were anarchist revolutionaries. 'The Diggers didn't stand for anything but they were about personal authenticity,' said Coyote. Another Digger (non)leader conceded that they had goals, one being to 'put "free" in front of anything you could think of.' Their artist friend Jeff Berner summed it up nicely: 'Clouds are free. Sunsets are free. Birds. Mountains. Rivers are free. Why not objects and people?'

The Diggers viewed money as 'an unnecessary evil', and argued that since 'food, machines, clothing, materials, shelter and props are simply there … [a] perfect dispenser would be an open Automat on the street.'[4] Failing that, there was the Free Store. The first two opened in San Francisco's Fillmore and Haight-Ashbury districts in 1967, and the social experiment spread. Wherever there was a commune, there was a free box. As the hippies and runaways began to descend on the Haight after the first Human Be-in in San Fran's Golden Gate Park, a young doctor who'd turned on to LSD opened the Haight Ashbury Free Clinic with the slogan, 'Health care is a right not a privilege'. Hippies on bad trips were treated gratis with 'a talk-down guide' and a lava lamp. If they returned from their travels hungry, they could rely on a bowl of Digger stew.

In October 1967, *The New Yorker*'s popular 'Talk of the Town' column wrote up a free store downtown, explaining, 'Diggers are hippies who help other hippies, so everything in the Free Store is given away.' The shop stocked used clothing, and 'piles of miscellaneous junk spread out on rough wooden tables, which line the walls. In one window, a bright-coloured hand-lettered sign reads, "DON'T WASTE. GIVE TO THE DIGGERS".'

I've always loved a story Peter Coyote tells about hanging around (never say 'working') in the Haight-Ashbury Free Store one day: 'A customer might ask to see the manager and be told that they *were* the manager. Some people froze and waffled, unsure of how to respond.'[5] Just like at Marina DeBris's Inconvenience Store, 'some left, but some "got it".' Others 'accepted the invitation to re-do the store according to their own plan, which was the point. One's life was one's own, and if you could leap the hurdles of programmed expectations and self-imposed limits, the future promised boundless possibilities.' Anyways, this woman comes in and tries furtively to shoplift and Coyote tells her, 'You can't steal here,' and she gets indignant and denies it. So he says, 'But you thought you were stealing. You can't steal here because it's a Free Store. Read the sign, everything is free! You can have the whole fucking store if you feel like it. You can take over and tell me to get lost.' They spent the rest of the day 'shopping' together.

In broader society, shopping with money won the culture war, but the Diggers weren't the last radicals to imagine a different way. The futurist Jacque Fresco regarded the world's resources as the common heritage of all people, and, through his Venus Project in California made the case for a moneyless society. 'Whenever money is involved, there is elitism,' he writes in his 2002 book *The Best That Money Can't Buy*, proposing 'a resource-based economy [that] would use technology to overcome scarce resources and utilize renewable sources of energy.'[6] In Fresco's alternative future, intelligent machines will replace human labour and we all achieve higher standards of living. There will be no more planned obsolescence. Distribution centres will allow us to 'check out' whatever we need wherever we go, and since there's no value in selling these things, we'll be happy to give them back when we're done. If there were no money, there would be no wage slaves, and no one marginalised by low income. Yes, this would take a complete overhaul of society—we would need to develop a new incentive system (one based on sharing and equality, please), and surely those who benefit from the current system would fight, possibly to the death, to defend it—but until Fresco himself died aged 101 in 2017, he was convinced it was possible.

There is evidence that some of this moneyless malarkey is now happening in regular society. New tech-based, community-minded methods for free transactions are emerging as the share economy takes shape. Apps and social-networking sites make it easy to swap skills and material goods, while community swap meets for things like clothes and books are increasingly popular.

Free stores come and go (mostly go, as rents aren't as cheap as they used to be). In New York, an activist ran one from Ludlow Street on the Lower East Side for more than fifteen years, suspending her free wares on a fence after dark and inviting customers to take what they pleased. Her primary motive, she said, was to keep things out of landfill.[7] Close by, a couple of artists opened a pop-up free shop in 2015, but that was more of a pretentious statement than a true free-for-all. In Kamikatsu, our Japanese zero-waste village, there's a permanent kuru-kuru (circular) shop, where residents can donate unwanted items that are made available to others for free. In suburban Melbourne, the Really, Really Free Markets have become regular events where money, bartering and trading are banned, while online, Freecycle is thriving. Amanda Chapman sourced the kitchen cabinetry for her tiny house that way.

There is such a thing as a free lunch, actually

Initially, when Chapman offered me her dumpster cake, I was reluctant to partake—who wants to eat from a garbage can? Not me when I've just been researching bin juice—but when I heard her story, I changed my mind. Chapman's freezer was crammed with cakes from an upmarket grocery chain, individually wrapped and perfectly safe to eat. Whoever'd chucked them, because they had reached their display-by date, had used the compost rather than the landfill bin. 'You can't compost plastic,' Chapman rolled her eyes, 'unless it's PLA, maybe. That person was an idiot.'

There are those who know everything there is to know about the music of Miles Davis, or the history of Wales 400–1100, but Chapman's specialist subject is food waste. It began when she was still in high school and working a part-time job as a supermarket checkout chick. 'They had a plastic bag collection point, and one night they asked me to take it out the back. I said, "Where's the recycling bin?" and they said, "No, it goes in the skip."' That was bad enough, but seeing what else was in there made her blood boil. The bin contained edible, unspoiled food.

Food waste happens at the store level because of overstocking—customers like to browse packed shelves. When perishables reach their display-by date, they are removed. These dates refer to peak freshness; they don't mean that the food is 'off', and yet how many of us automatically throw away food because it has passed its sell-by date? It's nonsense; a tub of tzatziki hasn't turned rancid because it's twenty-four hours older than when it was 'fresh' the day before, nor has a packet of gourmet cake. We also, of course, waste food at home because, like the supermarkets, we overstock—we buy carelessly, seduced by our culture of convenience. If you'd had to grow that tomato, you'd be more likely to appreciate it.

OzHarvest claims that almost half of all the fruit and vegetables commercially grown go to waste. Most 'imperfect' fresh produce that doesn't reach supermarket standards (wrong size, wrong shape, wrong colour) gets wasted before it ever makes it to the shop floor, and there have been several high-profile campaigns and news stories about this; the outrageous sight of banana mountains and rivers of oranges helps inspire change. Nevertheless, much of the 'ugly' fruit that slips through still ends up in the bin. (In Australia, Woolworths and Harris Farm Markets are trying to solve this by selling it cheaper with cute marketing—'the odd bunch' etcetera. Alas, at Woolies, it's packed in plastic.) Supermarkets also turf damaged products, over some minor fault with the packaging. Chapman once found a crate of olive oil in a dumpster. 'One bottle had smashed or leaked or something so the rest were oily,' she says. 'We can't have oily oil, now can we?'

When the teenaged Chapman saw a story about dumpster diving freegans on the news, she had a strong urge to join them, 'But I was young and I still worked for the supermarket. I didn't dare.' It was several years later that she made her first freegan contact, via a subreddit feed. 'They'd been doing it for years. They were masters students, so hungry and poor, but also political. I just remember they had all these boxes of cereal lining their walls.' While Chapman didn't become a dedicated dumpster diver, she still does it occasionally to make a point.

Once, she went with two women who'd messaged her on Facebook. They got caught. 'We were three young girls with head torches on. Usually you wear dark colours, but I'd just been out so I was wearing florals. I guess we looked non-threatening.' The security guard left them to it, after asking them to please clean up after themselves. 'A couple of minutes later, a police car pulled down the alley. They asked us what we were doing, and we showed them about 40 packets of tortillas. We explained that we weren't trying to break in, and started talking to them about food waste and landfill. We pulled out some statistics, and I said to them, "Who is the criminal here?"'

True freegans, as opposed to casual divers, seek to reduce their participation in the conventional economy as much as possible, while taking the zero-waste ethos to the next level. By opting out of shopping completely, they live by choice on the margins and prioritise freedom over working for The Man. In general, they don't pay rent; they squat. They don't own cars; they walk, skate, bike, hitch or train-hop. They grow community gardens in abandoned lots. 'Urban foraging' challenges the injustice of allowing resources to go to waste when there are people in need.

The monumental fucked-up-ness of food waste in a hungry world

About a third of the food produced by the world each year is wasted. In the United States, it's more like 40 per cent. Yet forty-eight million Americans are food insecure, meaning at some point in the past twelve months they didn't have enough to eat.[8] Kids go to school hungry. Old people rely on Meals on Wheels. *National Geographic* reporter Tracie McMillan describes how the working poor might look like they're doing okay, with electronic goods and cars bought on credit, but many subsist on a minimum-wage diet of low-quality processed junk in a 'twilight zone where refrigerators are so frequently bare of all but mustard and ketchup that it provokes no remark, inspires no embarrassment. Here, dinners are cooked using macaroni-and-cheese mixes and other processed ingredients from food pantries.' Obesity and hunger are 'two sides of the same coin'.

Australians discard food worth $8 billion a year. One in five bags of groceries ends up in the bin, yet we are still hungry. The Australian Institute of Family Studies estimates food insecurity affects about 5 per cent of the population, but charities put that figure much higher. Perhaps as many as 3.6 million Australians experience it, and while refugees and Indigenous Australians are high risk groups, it can affect anyone. Could food rescue solve the problem? How realistic a solution is urban foraging? And what about community gardens and growing co-operatives? Could we not just grow our own vegetables like previous generations did?

Growing, foraging for and cooking nutritious food takes resources and know-how. If you're struggling to make the rent and hold down a job, planning dinner harvested from the garden is likely to be low on your to-do list. That's presuming you have access to a vegetable patch or allotment. One-fifth of Australians live in apartments, and the food-insecure are also more likely to be dealing with insecure housing. Gardening equipment costs money, plants take time to mature, and last time I looked, you couldn't grow bread and butter out the back.

Inevitably, dumpster diving and foraging tend to be white, middle-class dropout or back-to-the-land pursuits, led by the politically motivated with time to dedicate and the nous to learn where the wild mushrooms that won't kill you grow. Dumpster diving is illegal. Remember Kimberlé Crenshaw. Amanda Chapman might be let off by sympathetic security guards and get to deliver a speech about the travesty that is food waste, but will Black and brown kids be given the same opportunity?

This story of want, waste and unequal power has led to food activism in innovative forms. Today there are multiple groups making modern-day Digger stew. In America, Food Not Bombs began in 1980 when student protestors set up a soup kitchen outside a bank that was funding a local nuclear power station. They now make rescued dinners for protestors and strikers through hundreds of autonomous chapters across the world. In Amsterdam, dumpster divers started a free supermarket with their excess skip finds, which in 2015 morphed into a massive communal dinner party. Food Waste Feast was 'a pay-as-you-feel' three-course dinner held in a shared restaurant space. Two of the organisers went on to start a program to cook rescued food for refugees arriving in Greece via the Balkan route. Feeding the 5000 cooks giant, celebratory public dinners from waste food. The first one was held in London's Trafalgar Square in 2009, organised by Tristram Stuart, author of *Waste: Uncovering the global food scandal*.

Australia's first big food-rescue organisation was OzHarvest, launched in 2004. In 2016, they set up a free shop in Sydney; customers are asked to contribute what they can, and if that's nothing, fine. OzHarvest is by no means unique. FareShare works across 1300 towns in the United Kingdom to redistribute surplus food to charities that turn it into meals, and FoodCycle does a similar thing. In New Zealand, a Wellington woman, Robyn Langlands, started the country's first food-rescue service, Kaibosh, in 2008, inspired by wasted sandwiches. In Dunedin, Deborah Manning started FoodShare from the back of her car with day-old bread saved from supermarkets. I love the idea of New Zealand's Compost Collective, which connects people who have spare kitchen-scrap waste with those who need mulch.

Amanda Chapman is leading food-waste activism in Auckland. She was inspired by a project called the Solidarity Fridge, which began in a Spanish town near Bilbao where residents and restaurants drop their unwanted food at a public fridge, and anyone who wants it, takes it. There was some city grant money going in Auckland, so Chapman applied and won funds to set up a similar project there. And so it is that a once-vacant CBD lot on the corner of Wellesley Street and Mayoral Drive, already home to an urban bee-keeping collective, is the site of New Zealand's first Love Food Hate Waste Community Fridge. Volunteers check the temperatures and clean and stock the fridge, but like the Diggers they don't work there. Nobody owns the food. It is a fridge in common. A cold box of delights that anyone can partake of, and nobody pays.

Harvest festival

The kids outnumber the adults. They are running free in the field behind the homestead, clambering over hay bales and picking fruit from two prehistoric-looking Mediterranean fig trees. In the garden, the flowers are thickly spread with bumblebees and butterflies. A table has been set with trays of pots ready for seeding with broccoli, cabbage, cauliflower, spinach and kale. Summer, at the height of her powers today, is on notice. Autumn is coming to the Adelaide Hills.

A tiny girl with bits of grass tangled in her hair approaches. She looks me over in silence for a long while. 'Seeds,' she says eventually. Then very loud: '*I plant the seeds!*'

'Should I plant some?' I ask. She takes my arm and pulls me towards the table.

'Seeds!'

'Do you like vegetables?'

'No!' she says. 'I like jam.'

An older lady laughs and hands me an envelope of seeds.

'How many?' I need instructions, suddenly out of my comfort zone. They call me Geranium Killer. Once I even presided over the slow death of a desktop cactus.

'Four,' says Andrew Barker, tipping in six, then seven seeds into his pots. He clocks me count and says, 'It doesn't matter. It's not science; well maybe it is science, but it's—'

'Insurance,' says Jodie, one of a growing band of Grow Free-ers in these parts, where the idea to grow food with the express intention of giving it away was hatched by Barker in 2014, although don't tell him I told you that. He doesn't like to take ownership of Grow Free. 'I think of it as this idea that has come to life through all of us,' he says.[9]

I push my finger into the soil, then bed the seeds in, feeling the dirt beneath my nails (too long, should have cut them), and it dawns on me: I have never done this before. 'I plant the seeds!' I say, and everyone laughs.

Jodie's face flickers from amusement to pity and back. We should connect to the Earth and the soil at an early age, learn how green things grow and what it means to plant-whisper and to nurture Nature. Those are life skills, important as learning maths or French. As a kid, I did pick the food that others had grown; I remember it—the treat of the strawberry farm, the weight of the punnet in my sticky hand. Stealing the peas in their pods from a neighbour's garden and how juicy they were, and illicit.

'I maybe grew cress at school,' I say, and Jodie looks relieved. She has six grown-up children. They are country people, raised knowing milk comes from a cow, not a bottle.

Here, some of the young'uns have come back from fig picking and are giving their bounty away. The fruit tastes of sunshine. My tiny jam fan offers me a tiny flower. 'You should keep this,' I tell her, 'it's so pretty like you.'

'For *you*!' she shouts and runs off chasing butterflies.

In this idyllic garden among friends, sowing seeds and seeing the fruits of his community-building ripen, Andrew Barker should be happy but his eyes are sad. He hasn't been sleeping, he apologises; he's feeling low after the breakdown of a relationship. I mention this not to pry into his private life but because Grow Free is life—it's not about a quick joy fix, although it can and does provide that to the gardeners, givers and receivers involved. Grow Free is one of the biggest ideas I've come across writing this book, despite masquerading as a small, humble one. It aims to redraw the way we live in relation to the Earth and to each other. Not just on this golden afternoon when, to me at least, anything seems possible, but all the time, through ups and downs, sickness and health, scarcity and abundance.

'The idea of Grow Free is to change the way we look at ourselves and our communities, and the way we fit into the world, via the medium of food,' says Barker. 'It seems like Grow Free is about free healthy food, and yes, on one level, it is; but that food is also the medium through which we're trying to create a bigger change. We plant seeds, get together and grow good food and share it amongst neighbours, and if you want to leave it there, then that's okay, but it can also be about sowing the seeds for a new system. It can be about taking our power back, reinvigorating communities, localism, closing the inequality gap, environmentalism … '

'Just, everything then?'

A friend is taking her leave. She came from town to pick beetroots from the garden for a woman who has cancer, and reached out via the Grow Free Facebook page, explaining that she's feeling too rough to shop or plan meals but knows that she needs to eat healthy, organic vegetables. This project is about the real stuff. And it starts with a seed. Or four.

Barker insists his green revolution 'just happened, I guess'. He was bookish, studied geology and geophysics. In fact, he was halfway through a PhD on geothermal energy when he decided to live and work communally on an organic farm instead. His parents thought he was literally mad, and didn't speak to him for years, but Barker wanted a different kind of life.

Some friends were growing vegetables to sell at farmers' markets, and a chance meeting led them to a sort of Eden. 'We were dropping off some corn we'd grown in our backyard, and this woman said, "Who grew this corn? It looks great." Next thing we knew, she was offering us the run of this big farm she had. There were orchards under bird netting, and she wanted someone to take it in hand, and so we moved up there, about three or four of us full-time, although we had a lot of people visiting and helping, and we planted it with veggies and flowers, and with the existing fruit trees it became a paradise.'

I ask if there was a house on the property, imagining some *Stealing Beauty* scenario, and he laughs and says, 'We lived in tents.'

'For a year?'

'It was wonderful.' One of them was a French chef and they were totally self-sufficient eating food they'd grown themselves, feeding the land, bringing the butterflies, bees and worms back. 'It was my first experience on that kind of scale, having so many things planted and making my own compost and worm farms,' says Barker. 'It blew my mind.'

One day, he and the chef had cause to visit a supermarket to buy some ungrowable supplies. 'You know those moments in time that stick in your memory with an emotional charge? We were looking at these pale tomatoes packed in plastic; then we saw the spring onions and they should have dirt in their roots but they were immaculate, and it looked really strange and wrong. It's an aesthetic, convenience thing I know, but we were just horrified. I remember him saying, "Where is the dirt? How is this food?"'

When Barker left the farm, he packed his love of seeds with him. He was such an effective gardener, he soon had way too many and decided to give them way. 'I put up notices. I actually had to pay $20 a month to put them on boards to give away free seedlings.' Then something curious happened. 'People started coming to me saying they didn't need more seedlings but "How can we help? What can we do?"' They began organising working bees. 'We'd go to someone's house and help them with their garden and plant the seedlings we'd grown. It was just word of mouth at first.'

The carts followed. Upcycled. Parked in public places. The idea is to load them up with excess produce you've grown. 'There are nearly 170 sharing carts in Australia now,' says Barker. 'It has spread to New Zealand. It's about to go to the United States: there's going to be a Grow Free sharing cart in Chesapeake Bay, Maryland. There's no reciprocation, no acknowledgement. Mostly we don't get to see who takes the produce.' But when Barker holds his seedling days, he enjoys seeing the way people react. Especially when newcomers get involved and taste real food, some of them, clearly, for the very first time.

'Most of what we think of as food today is a poor representation,' he tells me. 'We store it for too long, we wrap it in plastic, we waste it. We grow it in soil that's been depleted. The big produce farms now run on hydroponic systems. They have to add all the nutrients in; the soil is just somewhere for the roots to go; there's no worms in there, no compost.

'The other day I took this family to a garden, and it was the first time any of them had picked an apple from a tree and eaten it. I watched them do it, and their little boy's face, he was like, "Ahhhhh." It's such a different experience.'

Seasonal eating may be a lifestyle buzz phrase, but it's not how the modern food system works. No, no. That's all about convenience, profit and demand (and we're to blame as much as the supermarkets). Apples are picked in Australia between February and May; when you buy one here in December, it's been 'asleep' for months. Apples, pears, onions, carrots, oranges, grapes, pumpkin and bananas are typically cold stored for up to a year. Many are picked too early on purpose, treated with a gas to slow ripening, then cold stored. All this is safe, and produce should retain its nutritional value, but taste suffers. It's just not the same, is it?

One Victorian restaurateur had this to say about peaches. 'As soon as there is a little bit of colour they take them off the tree. They put them in dark rooms. They ripen slowly there and when you get them to the table it's "oh yeah". This peach almost forgot that it's been a peach.'[10] What's more, fruit is increasingly genetically modified to taste sweeter, to satisfy palates warped by sugar-packed processed food. All this makes Barker shudder.

'But we can't all grow figs in our paddocks,' I say.

'I do realise that people living in flats in cities can't grow much food. They might have a pot of herbs somewhere, but then there are people like me, who will put a crate of veg on one of our carts every week, enough to feed four families. You don't need a heap of space to grow leafy greens that cost a lot to buy in the supermarket, but are easy and cheap to grow. Let's all grow what food we can, and share it.'

He tells me a story about a family with a big old lemon tree in their backyard, and how the daughter is sick and got in touch with Grow Free (a recurrent theme), and how they changed the way they eat as a result. The daughter sent Barker a picture of the tree. Realising how much fruit it bears, she wants to give some away.

Grow Free has been trying to persuade local councils to plant free fruit trees in parks, but so far there's been too much red tape. 'They always worry about vermin, but why? I think [the trees] would attract hungry people who feel like picking an apple. Imagine if councils planted fruit trees on city streets.'

'Avenues of apples!'

'Wouldn't that be lovely?'

Andrew Barker has a vision that is as grand as it is simple. 'If you could just loosen constraints on your mind and wander with me for a moment,' he says.[11] 'Imagine if the face of shopping were to change. Imagine that instead of walking up and down aisles, you get to walk round your neighbourhood and see what's on offer, see what your neighbours have grown, baked or preserved. Imaging if instead of writing out a large list of things that you need to buy from a supermarket, you instead walk around your block, see what your neighbours have left out for free, see what's in season, and decide a recipe based on that.' Imagine.

16
Consumerism gone mad

'The love of buying things can, by definition, provide only a transient sense of satisfaction.'
—Richard Denniss, from *Curing Affluenza*

'You of course must realise that if more people did what you are currently doing, the economy would take such a nosedive that there would be no recovery. American shopping is probably the most significant prop-up to our economy and during a recession, the last thing we need is a bunch of morons trying to stop want-based shopping.'
—Comment on *The Clean Bin Project* blog

But it's so cheap

On Boxing Day, while the city slept, shoppers queued outside a store waiting for a sale that wasn't on. When they discovered their mistake, did they turn home to do something less boring instead, pride bruised perhaps, but wallets full? No. Did they kick off a riot in protest? No. They kept on queuing. So brainwashed were they by the mad idea that the most fun you can have the day after Christmas is to bargain-hunt with strangers that even in full knowledge of the total absence of said bargains, they did it anyway. 'Bleary-eyed and clutching coffees, the people queueing outside one upmarket fashion store on Sydney's Pitt Street began arriving before dawn and formed a line stretching 200 metres,' reported the ABC. 'But when the doors finally opened at 8 am, the eager shoppers rushed in only to find there were no discounts. Not that it seems to have driven the crowds away, as people kept lining up just for the tradition of it.'[1] Since you're here, and up for changing the world, might I suggest we come up with some new traditions?

Having in my close circle precisely no one who needs anything money can buy, I decide not to shop for Christmas presents this year unless they can be eaten or drunk, but heading home to Yorkshire to see my stepdad who's been poorly, I succumb to the pressure. I don't want to be thought a Scrooge, and the window displays look so inviting. I choose a pair of garish socks, hoping that along with a decent bottle of plonk, they will cheer him up. 'Would you like three pairs?' says the sales assistant.

'I'm sorry?'

'Three pairs? Would you like three?' he repeats.

'I don't think … ' I falter. 'I mean, why?'

It is Black Friday, he explains, referring to the American sale-shopping frenzy that occurs the day after Thanksgiving, extending over the weekend. This year it will see 137 million Americans hit the shops. Competition for bargains is fierce; skirmishes, tramplings and even shootings have become the norm. In 2011, sale shoppers at a Target store in West Virginia stepped over the body of 61-year-old Walter Vance as he lay dying of heart failure. But never mind about all that; shopping is good for us, and good for the economy. As CBS News puts it, 'The biggest gift that the United States could get during the holiday season is robust shopping by the American consumer, who is now the primary engine powering economic performance.'[2]

Black Friday begins the holiday shopping period that accounts for 30 per cent of American retail sales annually. It is designed to shift stock, using the promise of deep discounts to coax customers into buying more than they came for. Like dressing up for Hallowe'en and shopping for Valentine's gifts, the trend has taken off across the pond as well as in Australia. Hence the special offer on the socks; three pairs cost just a couple of quid more than one. It would be rude not to.

My gift won't break the bank, but its purchase—unplanned, unnecessary—forms part of a broader trend that might. I am one of the millions who never pay off their credit card debts, although the interest is daylight robbery and accrued without good reason. The items I buy on tick are luxuries: velvet boots that make me feel like Anita Pallenberg in 1971, new beach towels, fashion books, a fancy juicing machine. No one I know calls me out on this or thinks it's bizarre. Pointless overspending is socially sanctioned behaviour.

Our culture has normalised debt so that we can justify living like kings and queens beyond our means. We are encouraged to put the accoutrements of an A-list life we've been told to aspire to on the tab, in order to feed 'the economy'. What's to stop us? Buy now, pay later! Or, pay never! Two out of three Americans in debt either expect to live that way for the rest of their lives, or have no idea when, or if, they'll pay it off.[3] In Australia, one-quarter of all home owner-occupiers with mortgages are only paying off the interest.[4] Banks are falling over themselves to give us personal loans for flash holidays and cars we cannot afford. We've been trained to live in the moment, to throw caution to the winds, like our governments do with climate change. To leave fretting about the future to someone else, while we get on with the important business of spoiling ourselves.

As observed by the 2017 Global Online Consumer Report, we 'no longer "go shopping"; but literally "are shopping"—at every moment and everywhere.'[5] Technology has seen to that, while the illusion of 'free' or 'cheap' credit is aspiration's great enabler. Everyone wants to keep up with someone.

As George Monbiot points out in one of his brilliant, system-knocking columns for *The Guardian*, 'If you have four Rolexes while another has five, you are a Rolex short of contentment.'[6] This problem is not confined to the wealthy. The poor, he writes, 'can be as susceptible to materialism as the rich. It is a general social affliction, visited upon us by government policy, corporate strategy, the collapse of communities and civic life, and our acquiescence in a system that is eating us from the inside out.' I love George Monbiot. He's unafraid to examine a thing in the bright light. Most of us don't care to. Or dare to, because we can't afford to bite the hand that feeds us, can we? Not with the credit card bill for the velvet boots.

Peak stuff

The most obvious solution is: if we cannot afford them, don't buy the boots in the first place. It shouldn't be so hard. We are creatures of free will, are we not? With the ability to act logically, given the facts, which are: that we have too much already, and that in privileged, post-industrial countries we have reached 'peak stuff'. As we run out of space in our wardrobes, cupboards, garages and car boots, the storage market booms. On the rare occasions when I visit the facility that charges me $150 a month to store our excess bedding, Christmas decorations and mystery boxes, I notice others like me, disconsolately pushing around metal trollies piled with junk. We avoid eye contact; we are ashamed.

When I speak at sustainable fashion events, I often mention the supposedly shocking truth that the average woman wears less than 40 per cent of what's in her wardrobe and, depending on which stat you prefer, wears an item of clothing just four, seven or ten times before giving it the heave-ho. That we are essentially buying clothes to throw away. But are we really shocked, or just pretending to be? Because after four years of campaigning on this issue, scores of eBay sales and multiple trips to Vinnie's, my own wardrobe still harbours Narnia-like secrets. There could be a goat living in the back of it for all I know.

For me, reducing and reusing is an endless seesaw—I sell and donate things but justify acquiring more party frocks or picture frames or table-cloths because they're vintage (no virgin resources, guilt free!) or beautifully made by an ethical designer I'm keen to support. Old habits linger. Culture is slow to change. When you've spent your whole life in acquisition mode, doing the opposite takes effort, and sometimes you can't summon the energy. Sometimes you buy three pairs of socks.

In 2017 I worked on a project for National Op Shop Week in Australia with the Salvos charity stores. Our mission was to prove that 'second-hand is not second best' by curating a pop-up shop in an art gallery in a hip 'hood. It was easy to find wonderful preloved things in Salvos' suburban branches: a genuine Prada handbag, a pair of Christian Louboutin platforms with lipstick-red soles, a 1950s paste jewellery set in its original box. I combed these places with their in-house stylist Faye de Lanty, who came up with the concept of in-store 'boutiques' so that less confident op-shoppers might be delivered from rummaging. She told me donations include loads of designer fashion in perfectly good nick. One woman read about our event and offered to donate some loot; de Lanty went to investigate and returned with a whole rail of top-end designer fashion, either barely worn or brand new with the tags still on. I don't know this woman's story, why she'd bought all this stuff and was passing it on (and it was very kind of her—she could have sold it for a tidy profit) but it seemed to me to illustrate a glaring truth: we are full to burst, like Mr Creosote in Monty Python's *The Meaning of Life*. Any more will destroy us, not to mention the planet.

Between 2000 and 2015, global clothing production approximately doubled,[7] driven by fast fashion in mature economies and rising middle-class affluence in growing ones. In Australia, Europe and North America, we're buying more clothes than ever before, and discarding them more quickly. The systems are not yet in place to capture most of this waste and turn it into a resource. Mechanical processes can shred pure cotton or wool fabrics and use that damaged fibre to make new yarn, but textiles woven from it tend to be of lower quality than the original. We're only at the beginning of refining processes that can chemically recycle mixed-fibre textiles. And of course all of this costs extra. According to the Swedish fast-fashion retailer H&M, which began introducing in-store recycling bins in 2013, only 0.1 per cent of all clothing collected by charities and take-back schemes around the world is recycled into new textiles.[8] Charity stores can and do feed used garments back into the system, but too much still goes to waste. Just 15 per cent of what's donated to Salvos is suitable for resale in their stores. Some of what's left ends up as industrial rags. Some gets baled and sent to Africa, where most second-hand shoppers haven't the means to be picky (and the flood of drossy used-clothing imports from the global north is decimating local textiles industries). In the United States, 84 per cent of discarded clothing ends up in landfill or the incinerator.

Fashion provides an interesting case study, but the problem of producing goods designed to be bought, used fleetingly then discarded goes way beyond a clothing. As part of the Anthropocene Working Group, scientists are trying to quantify the entirety of the 'stuff' produced by humankind, ever: all the plastic, all the broken Ikea furniture, dead computers and car parts that accumulate in rubbish tips; consumer goods great and small, right through to infrastructure like railroads and buildings. They call this system the 'technosphere' (as opposed to the biosphere), and estimate that the man-made stuff within it amounts to around thirty trillion tonnes. Sometimes it feels like most of it's in my office.

The lie that growth is always good

Conventional wisdom has it that a successful economy, and therefore society, is one that sees perpetual growth of GDP, but voices of dissent are beginning to be heard in the corridors of power. According to Joseph Stiglitz, a professor at Columbia University, it has long been recognised that GDP, which is supposed to measure the value of output of goods and services, 'may be a poor measure of well-being, or even market activity.'[9]

Its metrics are too narrow and easily distorted. 'If a few bankers get much richer,' he explains, 'average income can go up, even as most individuals' income is declining.'

Until recently, anyone suggesting that maybe we shouldn't be aiming for continuous growth, let alone that the current incarnation of the capitalist system might have run its useful course, was dismissed as a dangerous communist, freegan or flighty utopian crank. But a system that worked in 1945 faces a whole new set of circumstances today. Technology is fundamentally altering the scope and possibility of human interaction and transactions. The gap between haves and have-nots is widening. Populations are growing, resources dwindling, and the safety nets of the postwar welfare systems are buckling under the strain. In such a context, economists are compelled to consider how the old structure is holding up, even when governments don't care to. (There are exceptions: in October 2017, Jacinda Ardern, New Zealand's newly elected Prime Minister, was asked in a television interview, 'On a scale of one to ten, one being a complete disaster and ten being a rollicking success, where are we at with capitalism in New Zealand?' Ardern answered, 'Has it failed our people in recent times? Yes.'[10])

The system is out of whack; it's not benefitting the majority. 'There is no doubt that the cycle of production, consumption, disposal, recycling and production creates economic activity, jobs and, for some in the supply chain, wealth,' writes Australian economist Richard Denniss in *Curing Affluenza*.[11] 'But does this process in any way ensure the efficient allocation of scarce resources? Is throwing away functional goods really a good way to "make the economy strong"?' He thinks not. 'Modern capitalism relies on billions of people searching for new products that will fill the hole in their lives that was briefly plugged by the last purchase. The banks, the manufacturers, the advertisers and the retailers all make their fortune by selling us the dream that "there's happiness in them there hills".' Meanwhile the rich get richer and the poor slide further into debt.

Those in power tend to have a vested interest in maintaining the status quo, so they keep peddling the old Keynesian platitudes—that it's our duty to spend, that if we don't, the paradox of thrift will kick in causing spiralling recessions; that the market will do right by us; and that cutting taxes for the rich is good for everyone—but any fool can see there is something wrong when the way we do things promotes high levels of income inequality, traps those worst off in debt, encourages cronyism and fails to protect the environment.

While living standards keep rising in developing economies (despite all that food insecurity, since 1990 there has been a dramatic reduction in extreme poverty globally),[12] in established ones the gap between rich and poor keeps on widening. The World Bank—hardly a radical organisation—warns that income inequality 'is constraining national economies and destabilizing global collaboration in ways that put humanity's most critical achievements and aspirations at risk.'[13]

The richest 1 per cent own as much wealth as everyone else combined. In 2017, eight men (including Bill Gates, Mark Zuckerberg, Jeff Bezos and Amancio Ortega) owned the same wealth as the poorest half of humanity.[14] Gates, Microsoft's founder who at the time of writing is worth over US$90 billion according to *Forbes*, thinks people like him 'should pay significantly higher taxes'.[15]

'Left unchecked, growing inequality threatens to pull our societies apart,' writes Deborah Hardoon in the Oxfam briefing paper *An Economy for the 99%*:

> It increases crime and insecurity, and undermines the fight to end poverty. It leaves more people living in fear and fewer in hope. From Brexit to the success of Donald Trump's presidential campaign, a worrying rise in racism and the widespread disillusionment with mainstream politics, there are increasing signs that more and more people in rich countries are no longer willing to tolerate the status quo. Why would they, when experience suggests that what it delivers is wage stagnation, insecure jobs and a widening gap between the haves and the have-nots? The challenge is to build a positive alternative—not one that increases divisions.[16]

What might a new economic model look like? What if we introduced new measures of success? Health, for example, or happiness? Generosity? If we measured the success of our economy by how many people volunteered, or how many trees were planted? By how much time citizens got to spend with their families?

Tim Jackson, a British 'ecological economist', suggests we focus on wellbeing. 'What does it mean to be well? It means that we have our health, that we have a good level of nutrition—of course, very material demands—but beyond that it also means that we feel secure, that we enjoy the love of our families, that we are strong in our community, that we have a sense of meaning and purpose, that we have creative goals, that our energy in the world is useful to society,' he says.[17] 'When you think about these things, then it seems very clear that the wellbeing economy consists of care and craft and culture and creativity, and actually these tasks bring us into wellbeing and they also deliver wellbeing to other people.' He acknowledges there are 'still some practical things to solve'—what shape is such an economy?—but he says those should now be the focus of our economists, politicians and business leaders. 'In some ways that's a very nice place to be: we can see the means, we can see the end and we can develop, and we can begin to build it.'

Richard Denniss says we may have change if we want it. It's not as if we'd be breaking the rules:

> There is nothing in any economics textbook to tell us what our national goals should be. While talk of maximising growth, balancing the budget, increasing exports and improving national security all sound like answers to the question 'What should we do?', they aren't. They tell us nothing about what we think we need more of, what we think we can do with less of, and how the benefits of production should be distributed.[18]

As Joseph Stiglitz says, 'any good measure of how well we are doing must also take account of sustainability.'[19] It is not just that we humans are too greedy, consuming too much, but also that there are so very many of us. The planet isn't getting any bigger. In 2018 the global population is about 7.6 billion. There's a website called Worldometers that shows the number of births rise in real time. It's mesmerising to watch the numbers tick over. The deaths climb too, but in much lower numbers. According to UN projections, by 2050 there will be 9.8 billion of us competing for the Earth's finite resources.

Using UN data, the Global Footprint Network measures the yearly ecological resource use and resource capacity of nations and calculates the deficit. Every year, the service records the point at which the Earth went into the red. Currently humanity is using the equivalent of 1.7 Earths. In 2018, Earth Overshoot Day fell on 1 August. There's even an online tool you can use to measure your own footprint, as an individual, and find out 'How many planets do we need if everyone lives like you?' (visit footprintcalcuator.org). I found it sobering. While I barely drive, am energy efficient at home, shop local and am trying to reduce, reuse and go plastic-free, I fly a lot. Air-travel emissions are a major contributor to global warming (the International Civil Aviation Organisation warns that they could gobble up a quarter of the world's carbon budget by 2050) which is why *The New York Times* warns that for apartment dwellers who don't drive much, flying is likely your 'biggest carbon sin'.[20]

North Circular

Dame Ellen MacArthur knows what it's like to worry about resource use. 'The more I learned, the more I started to change my own life. I started travelling less, flying less, doing less. It felt like actually doing less was what we had to do,' she says in her TED talk about how she went from being the fastest person to sail around the world solo in 2005 to one of the foremost proponents of the circular economy today. Doing less, she says, didn't feel like the right solution. 'It felt like we were buying ourselves time, we were eking things out a bit longer. Even if everybody changed, it wouldn't solve the problem. It wouldn't fix the system. It was vital in the transition, but what fascinated me was: In the transition to what? What could actually work?'[21]

MacArthur started thinking this through at sea, because on her boat her supplies were finite. Back on dry land, she became convinced that she must grab her moment of fame and use it to try to change the world. The more she researched, the more obvious it became to MacArthur that we need to transition to a circular economy, whereby both biological and technical nutrients are fed back into the system in a continuous loop. Given finite materials, a 'take, make, dispose' system will eventually shut down. This was not politics; it was physics—and common sense.

I interviewed MacArthur in 2018 at the annual Copenhagen Fashion Summit, where the fashion industry comes together to try to figure out ways to be more sustainable. Our current linear model is unsustainably wasteful, she told me. 'It is a global problem which needs a global solution. This is not a part of a business that needs to change; it's the very nature of the entire economy. And it's a conversation for everyone. This isn't a conversation in a box about Nature and the environment; this is our global economy that can't function in the long term.'[22]

Like William McDonough and Michael Braungart, key thinkers behind the influential Cradle to Cradle concept, MacArthur advocates for changing the way products are made and systems operate to design out 'structural waste', thereby reducing environmental impacts and increasing wellbeing. 'Neither the health of natural systems, nor an awareness of their delicacy, complexity, and interconnectedness, have been part of the industrial design agenda,' say McDonough and Braungart. '[But] instead of presenting an inspiring and exciting vision of change, conventional environmental approaches focus on what *not* to do.'[23]

I also interviewed McDonough in Copenhagen. 'People don't realise the power of their own ability to create,'[24] he told me during a thrilling roller-coaster of a conversation that covers everything from Ralph Waldo Emerson's theories of Nature's 'ineffable essence' to how technology entrances us. 'Is Nature here for our use?' asked McDonough. 'That's a powerful concept that's been around forever; that's dominion. But stewardship is implicit in dominion, because you can't have dominion over something that's dead. I know. It's a sad fact. We're in the era of the Anthropocene [and] we're affecting the planet.' He describes climate change and environmental destruction as 'our de facto plan', not because we intend it, but because our actions cause these things unthinkingly. 'We need another plan.' Luckily, he's got one: 'Our goal is a delightfully diverse, safe, healthy, and just world, with clean air, water, soil and power—economically, equitably, ecologically and elegantly enjoyed.'

Another exciting thinker in this space is Jeremy Rifkin, an economist who advises the likes of Chinese Premier Li Keqiang and German Chancellor Angela Merkel. In his book and film *The Third Industrial Revolution*, Rifkin outlines his theories for reshaping the global economy for the future. He thinks millennials are uniquely placed 'to rethink the economic assumptions that govern how we live on this planet and find new approaches to innovation, business, and employment'.[25] He suggests we build a 'radical new sharing economy' out of the ashes of the clunky, old manufacturing-based one. He says we need a new, compelling economic vision for the world, we need to deploy it quick, and we need to get off carbon in four decades, everywhere. And he thinks we can:

> In the sharing economy, ownership gives way to access, sellers and buyers are replaced by providers and users, social capital becomes as important as market capital, consumerism is upended by sustainability, and quality-of-life indicators become more important than GDP. The sharing economy can become a circular economy in which goods and services are redistributed among multiple users, dramatically reducing society's ecological footprint.[26]

Could we really stop wasting and start sharing and caring about the environment, and not just between ourselves but on a mass, organised scale? Could we?

17
Meet the minimalists

'Most of the luxuries, and many of the so-called comforts of life, are not only not indispensable, but positive hindrances to the elevation of mankind.'
—Henry David Thoreau, *Walden: Or, Life in the Woods*

'If you're anything like how I used to be—miserable, constantly comparing yourself with others, or just believing your life sucks—I think you should try saying goodbye to some of your things.'
—Fumio Sasaki, *Goodbye, Things*

'You can keep the American dream: give us back our time, our freedom and our lives.'
—Joshua Millburn and Ryan Nicodemus, AKA The Minimalists

Less stuff, more meaning?

A classic suburban scene, set in a leafy Vermont street on a holiday weekend. A middle-class dad, Joshua Becker, is sorting out the junk in his garage while his wife Kim cleans the house inside and their five-year-old plays alone in the backyard. Ask me to pinpoint the problem with this scenario and I'd jump on the woman cleaning aspect: she's inside doing the housework while he tinkers about in his man cave. But when Becker's neighbour June sticks her head over the fence, she doesn't say, 'Hey Josh, is it not a bit 1985 to have her indoors scrubbing that bath, mate?' She says, 'Maybe you don't need to own all this stuff.' June's daughter has recently experienced the life-changing magic of becoming a person with less crap stored in the garage.

'The juxtaposition was striking,' recalls Becker on his popular website *Becoming Minimalist*, which launched in 2007 and attracts millions of monthly readers. 'My possessions piled up in the driveway ... my son in the backyard ... my day slipping away ... I immediately recognized something needed to change. My belongings were not adding value to my life. Instead, they were subtracting from it.'[1]

So he and the wife set about 'selling, giving and throwing away things they didn't need'. Within six months, they'd halved their possessions and increased their happiness, time, energy and bank balance. Rethinking their relationship with stuff gave them more freedom, explains Becker, to stop trying to keep up with the Joneses, for example, and to move—possessions 'weigh on the spirit and make us feel heavy'. Shedding belongings made them feel less stressed and more joyful by giving them space to focus on the more fulfilling, non-materialistic aspects of their lives: their relationships, community and passions.

Becker wrote a book, *The More of Less: Finding the life you want under everything you own*, and, along with 'simplicity blogger' Leo Babauta, became a leading American voice in the new-wave minimalist movement that's developed in response to hyper-consumerism and the deification of material wealth.

Babauta is the California-based, vegan, minimalist father of six behind the popular self-help blogs *Zen Habits* and *mnmlist*. These present practical ways to develop new habits around mindfulness, positive thinking and goal-setting to reduce stress and improve health and wellbeing, while shedding distractions and the negative vibes of obsessing over material possessions. Modern minimalism, according to Babauta, 'defines what's unnecessary as a luxury, and a waste.' But he resists the idea that it's all about decluttering. 'There's a misunderstanding about the minimalist movement, that you should somehow have almost nothing, fewer than 100 things, or a house that's empty and white,' he writes.[2] 'This can feel oppressive to some, and privileged to others. But that's not what minimalism is about, at least not to me. It's not about telling people they can't have clutter ... it's not even about possessions really. It's about asking a simple question: what is important to you?'

I ask the Australian economist and author of *Curing Affluenza* Richard Denniss about all this, and he tells me, 'For people who think buying stuff makes them happy, I say, "Look at the score board. Did it work? If you're on the right track, why would you change course?" But most people I've spoken to about this admit that they've wasted a lot of money on stuff that didn't make them [truly] happy. Transient happiness at the moment they bought it, maybe; but joy not so much.'[3]

There have always been those who live simply by choice, often for religious reasons. Becker is a former Christian pastor who views minimalism as a way to lessen his attachment to worldly things in order to strengthen his attachment to God. There's a great deal in the Bible about the perils of avarice and the corrupting influence of gold; it is easier for a camel to go through the eye of a needle than for a rich person to enter the kingdom of God. Jesus was always giving stuff away. Buddhism advises letting go of attachments. Monks and sadhus give up their worldly chattels to clear their path to enlightenment and free up their minds for prayer.

The ancient Greeks understood these urges. The philosopher Diogenes slept in an old wine barrel and lived off alms by choice, while Socrates believed that 'The secret of happiness is not found in seeking more, but in developing the capacity to enjoy less.' In China, legendary Tao philosopher Lao Tzu is said to have advised his followers to 'manifest plainness', while the idea of simplicity has floated tastemakers' boats from Seneca to Leonardo da Vinci, and from Leo Tolstoy to Coco Chanel. Chanel's first black evening dress, which she wore in the 1910s, was a response to the frou-frou pastel frills then fashionable. But by the time she decided 'elegance is refusal' in the 1920s, the modern consumerist society was on track to add another dimension to the quest for a simpler life.

Today minimalism is not just a framework for living; it's a trending topic and a big commercial business. Marketers are using minimalism's aesthetics to sell us more stuff to declutter, as sales of Marie Kondo books soar. Sustainable fashion brands sell pared-back chic in the form of fuss-free, clean-lined designs made from organic cotton in 50 shades of beige, while minimalist interiors are all the rage. Much of modern minimalism is all about the look.

The same year the Beckers began to reduce their accumulated junk, another Christian 'simplifier', Dave Bruno, devised what then seemed like an extreme method of shedding the downer that is possessions, which he detailed in *The 100 Thing Challenge: How I got rid of almost everything, remade my life, and regained my soul.* While continuing to live in his posh house and drive his smart car, he was also, shall we say, creative with his own rules, counting collections like his library of books as one thing, and excluding the stuff that's shared by him and the rest of his family—a cunning way to not have to count the kitchen table or crockery. For critics, Bruno didn't go far or deep enough, talking too much about his Christian faith and not enough about the origins and effects of America's consumerist culture. We needed more. We needed two former salesmen from Ohio calling themselves the Minimalists.

Rock-star declutterers
Ordinarily, this is where the music lives. I've seen PJ Harvey play this stage in lilac fake fur that matched the circles under her eyes, and Nick Cave, electric, like a man possessed, scissor-kicking in front of the red velvet curtains to 'Red Right Hand', but tonight's act has no guitars, no backing singers or stage costumes. There's a bit of me, I don't mind admitting, that yearns for sequins, or at least a Bryan Ferry hip swivel, but Joshua Millburn and Ryan Nicodemus are anti-distraction; they are here, in their plain black shirts and jeans, to spread the gospel according to the Minimalists. Indeed, there is something of the Billy Graham about their delivery. Or Anthony Robbins.

'Where do you want to be a year from now?' calls Nicodemus, and the full house cheers. 'Two years from now?' More cheers. '*Five years* from now?' There's a collective gasp from the fans; some have come from as far as Western Australia, a four-hour flight. 'Imagine a life with less!' I can imagine it; I'm living it—my wallet is lighter than before I booked this ticket, which cost me nearly eighty bucks. With practised rhythm, Nicodemus delivers his lines: 'Less stuff, less clutter, less stress, and debt and discontent. A life with fewer distractions.'

'That's what I'm talking about!' The woman behind me is putting on her own show, the restaurant scene in *When Harry Met Sally*. 'Yes!' she shouts. 'Yes!'

'Now imagine a life with more: more time, more meaningful relationships.'
'Yes, *yes!*' shouts Meg Ryan.

'More growth and contribution and contentment, a life of passion unencumbered by the trappings of the chaotic world around you. What you're imagining is an intentional life. I'm not talking about an easy life,

I'm not talking about a perfect life, but a simple one, and to get there, you might have to let go of some stuff that's in the way. So, who here wants to talk about letting go?' The audience whoops and claps. Meg groans in appreciation so loudly my chair shakes. This doesn't sit well with my English reserve. I can tell it's only going to get worse. I'm recording it so I get the quotes right, and a man in an expensive suit swivels around in his seat and hisses about the light on my phone.

The young woman sitting next to me is paying intense attention to the performance; no Meg Ryan antics, but it's clearly working for her. For me, however, these two seem to represent a culture of individualism that feels old-fashioned. I think about Jeremy Rifkin's theory, explained in *The Third Industrial Revolution*, that the next generation is focused on community, connectivity, networks and inclusivity, as well as the understanding that our actions have impacts not just on ourselves and the people around us but on the biosphere as a whole; and I keep hoping for Millburn and Nicodemus to tap into that. I'm willing them to say something about the broader societal or environmental benefits of downsizing and reducing consumption. About how the popularity of minimalism might point to a bigger shift in thinking about how we should structure the economy and the ways in which we relate to one another within it, but overwhelmingly their message is: this will make you feel good.

'"Taking out the trash" is an appropriate metaphor for this journey since minimalism is fundamentally about getting rid of life's excess,' they explain on their blog.[4] 'And the reason we must jettison what's unnecessary is so we can focus on what's important: we want to live a meaningful life, one that is filled with happiness, passion, and freedom.' In the meantime—this post being for Day 11 of their '21-Day Journey into Minimalism' program— 'Ryan actually *is* taking out the trash today: he is taking dozens (yes, dozens) of large trash bags to the curb for the trash collector to collect ... Trash. Donate. Sell.'

Why is 'trash' first on that list? Where is sustainability in this conversation? I felt similar frustration when I read Marie Kondo's best-selling book *The Life-changing Magic of Tidying Up: The Japanese art of decluttering and organizing*. I found nothing in there to indicate that Kondo grasps the idea that there is no away. It's all: chuck it in the bin, change your life! 'Start by discarding, all at once, intensely and completely,' she writes. 'I have worked with clients who have thrown out two hundred 45-litre garbage bags in one go.'[5]

What I see here is the same sweaty-palmed urgency for instant gratification that motivates the shopaholic. Whether you are *getting* or *getting rid of* the stuff in question, the drivers are the same. It's about the power buzz, not the value—and certainly not the true cost—of the possessions in question.

Nicodemus turned to minimalism because, as he explains on stage, 'I had this gaping void in my life, so I tried to fill that void the same way many people do: with stuff, lots of stuff ... I bought new cars and electronics and closets full of expensive clothes.' Unhealthy, unlucky in love, overworked, depressed, drinking too much and doing drugs, he felt 'stagnant' and like his life lacked purpose. He was attempting to buy his way to happiness. And now?

Cutting the clutter obviously helped him, and the idea sparks with the cheering crowd in this theatre tonight. Okay. We can all relate to the search for more happiness and meaning, but let's not dress it up as activism.

18
What's the alternative?

'To me it seems archaic to be delivering power to millions of houses when each house is touching the power of the sun.'
—Michael Reynolds, architect and inventor of Earthship Biotecture

'We desire to liberate ourselves from the cruder forms of exploitation; the plunder of the planet, the slavery of man and beast, the slaughter of men in war, and animals for food.'
—Helen and Scott Nearing, *The Good Life*

'Happiness then, is found to be something perfect and self-sufficient.'
—Aristotle, *The Nicomachean Ethics*

Choose life

Kate Hall is tipping the ends of green beans and the insides of a capsicum into the biscuit tin she keeps on her kitchen bench. 'It's for the compost,'[1] she explains, brutally dispatching broccoli stalks to the same end.

'You could eat those, you know,' I say, just to push her buttons. I am not one to talk—we do not compost (about a third of Australians do; another third are 'compost aspirers'[2]). Admitting that in these pages feels shameful, like confessing to a McDonald's habit or voting for Tony Abbott. I do not tell Kate Hall. She is twenty-one and newly married, her whole life ahead of her to be disappointed. She still thinks the world is a good place.

'We tried,' she says. 'It was ruining all our meals. I hate broccoli stalks.' Compost loves green veggies, grass clippings, leaf matter. 'You can put old newspapers in there, not too many, but a few is fine.' Vegetable matter is broken down by aerobic bacteria using oxygen, so a healthy, airy compost heap doesn't smell bad. Not unless you contaminate it with the wrong sort of rubbish. Meat, for example, produces a different sort of bacteria: anaerobic. Those bacteria heat up and stink as they do their rotting work, attracting rats and other scavengers, and breeding flies along the way. The healthiest compost is basically vegan.

Hall, a sustainable-lifestyle blogger, spreads it on her rose garden and tomato plants, but it's her musician husband Tim (she sings, they met while playing a gig) who really gets excited about the compost. 'He's into growing competitive pumpkins. He got the seeds from this guy who grows the biggest pumpkins in New Zealand.'

I'm visiting the Halls to try to figure out how young sustainably minded folks live in cities, integrating the green lifestyle movement into their ordinary lives, without making the sorts of drastic changes (building THOWs, giving up takeaway) that the mainstream finds alienating. From what I can see, it's entirely possible to 'be the change' by increments, and to be pragmatic about it too. Hall admits she's still learning and often changes her eco routines and ideas.

The couple shares a house in a beachside suburb of Auckland with two flatmates. It's a challenge getting the flatties to fully commit to Kate's war-on-waste kitchen rules, she says, but she keeps trying. One of them has a plastic bag habit. 'She's awesome,' says Hall, 'but I just, I mean … ' She flings open the pantry door and shows me a fabric tube, the likes of which I haven't seen for sale in twenty years, designed to store plastic bags. It's full. Her expression says: how hard is it to take a cloth bag? It can't be as hard as being the enforcer.

'We've given up bin liners,' she says, inviting me to inspect her kitchen waste baskets. There are three, in addition to her compost tub. The smallest, the sin bin, is marked 'Landfill'. All that's in it is a clump of dust from the vacuum cleaner and one of those bewildering juice-absorbing cushions from a packet of organic chicken breasts. The bin marked 'recycling' contains a wine bottle, a milk carton and a few bits of cardboard.

'Soft Plastics' is for the plastic packaging she hasn't yet managed to edit out of her life: post satchels, cheese wrappers. Tim likes sliced bread and the odd bar of commercially produced chocolate. The plastic packets go in here, and when the bin is full, Hall takes it to the Love NZ Soft Plastics Scheme bin at the mall. As in Australia, where REDcycle runs a similar initiative, this plastic is used to manufacture playground furniture, bollards and speed humps.

'I haven't worked out how to make candy for Tim,' says Hall, 'yet.' She is trying to tackle one thing at a time to avoid the overwhelm. An early win came from making her own muesli from nuts and grains from the bulk-goods store; she toasts it at home with honey and oil. I have eaten this muesli—it's fantastic, much nicer than the overly sugared junk you can buy in the supermarket.

The Halls are not technically zero-waste, but they aspire to it. They've switched to bamboo toothbrushes and use shampoo bars wrapped in recyclable paper. Hall has given up tampons in favour of a menstrual cup, which she insists is 'convenient and not gross at all' and something called Hannahpads. (When I get home, I look this up and discover it's a weird brand of floral cloth sanitary napkin made in Korea and designed to be washed and reused. I seriously consider buying a packet. Could I become Hannahpad Woman?)

Hall makes waxed food wraps out of old pillowcases (Tim's has a Star Wars logo print). They've carried reusable water bottles 'since forever' and think people who don't have a KeepCup are 'super old-fashioned'. Tim works in events marketing for a hipster burger joint that is big on healthy ingredients and uses eco-friendly packaging but has yet to solve the straws problem. When the Halls go out for drinks, they both happily lecture the bar staff on the evils of plastic. 'You have to say why,' says Kate. 'Otherwise they just think you're a freak who hates straws.'

'But you are a freak who hates straws.'

'Ha ha, but we hate them for environmental reasons. You have to explain yourself to change minds.'

'Does it work?'

'Sometimes.'

She feels confident holding forth on plastic, less so on meat. 'People do ask, "How can you be sustainable if you're not vegan?" but I'm not perfect,' says Hall. 'I'm just learning about all this. I'm doing my best. For now, I feel like, I grew up eating meat and I think I'm okay with it as long as the animals have been treated right.' She has coeliac disease; there are enough foods she can't eat, and New Zealand, she points out, is a farming country. Her father is a vet.

Her cockatiel Zugda whistles as if to agree. He hops on the workbench and starts to peck at a stray bean stalk. Zugda?

'It means policeman in Mongolian. I've had him for ten years.'

Hall acquired Zugda when she moved back to Auckland from Ulaanbaatar, where her father worked for two years as a vet. Hall was ten when she arrived in the Mongolian capital, with her older brother, younger sister and their mother, who is a speech therapist. 'I didn't even know it was a country until Dad was like, "Right family, we're moving to Mongolia." He went off for a month to check it out then came back, and was all, "Let's do this." Mum hates flying; she is so scared of it, I'm surprised she agreed.' It was the best thing they ever did, says Hall. 'I don't think my brother and sister felt that way, but I loved it. I still miss it.' Life in Ulaanbaatar taught her at a young, impressionable age that 'after a certain point, when you don't have to worry about food and shelter, money has nothing to do with happiness.'

When I ask her to describe the happiest day of her life, she describes the time she spent with a Mongolian girl of her own age who couldn't speak English, while their parents tended to some sick goats. 'We had to entertain each other. I don't know for how long—it felt like hours—and we communicated through sign language and play, pointing and having fun. It stuck with me. I think that was when I felt most alive.' Then she laughs, and says, 'Oh and my wedding day, obviously. That was pretty cool. Dad grew the sunflowers for my bouquet, and as I was walking down the aisle I saw there was a caterpillar hanging out on one of them.' It was a makeshift aisle, not a flouncy, flower-decked church one; really more of a path. The Halls got married in a park and ran their own ceremony, only allowing the celebrant to step in for the bit required by law.

Hall says her Mongolian years 'were the exact opposite to our life in New Zealand in so many ways. Even going to the shop or for a walk was a challenge and maybe an adventure. I remember a bus trip to the Russian border sleeping in tents, and Dad doing surgery on a reindeer. [In the city] from our kitchen window, we could see a ger district—you know, yurts? And people were still living so traditionally in their tents; there was still horse-and-cart transport. We had this friend who was a homeless man with one leg. We would hang out with him. It made me assess all the ways I live my life because there are so many other ways you can do it.'

'But you were only a kid,' I say. 'Isn't it possible that you didn't think that then? That you only put that spin on it in hindsight?'

'It's possible, but I don't think it matters really, do you?'

The next time Hall had a 'What the?' moment was on her honeymoon. They'd been travelling in South-East Asia then took a South Pacific cruise.

It was meant to be a luxury treat, and while Hall is quick to say that it was and that Tim was being so sweet and they had fun drinking cocktails and watching shows and swimming in all three of the on-deck pool options, the excess of the set-up freaked her out. 'It was ten storeys of people taking advantage of the all-you-can-eat buffet.' Watching the ship staff clear the plates, she realised 'this is not a compost situation. I've heard sometimes waste from ships gets offloaded into the ocean; I don't know if it does or not, but it made me question everything. Even carbon emissions. I tried to think, Would it be worse if all those thousands of people took separate holidays? Maybe it wouldn't. Maybe the ship is more efficient. I'm not an expert; I just knew the waste made me feel uncomfortable, and the greed. The whole thing was so greedy.'

Hall was raised to get two cups out of every tea bag. '[On the cruise] there were people piling everything on their plates at breakfast: pancakes, cream and yoghurt and berries and fruit and bacon and eggs and pastries. And it was 24/7 pizza land! All the cocktails came with straws. There was no off-switch.' Nothing the humans could not consume—they only had to ask, any time of day or night. Hall came home determined to live as sustainably as possible, and to talk about it to anyone who'd listen. She says most of her friends either feel the same or are getting there. 'My generation doesn't look at waste and resources the way yours does,' she says. 'Sorry.'

'Don't be. You're right,' I tell her.

Hall is optimistic that the world is changing, and she's busy doing her bit. She shares her hints, tips and discoveries on social media, and blogs as *Ethically Kate*. 'If I want to make a difference, I have to share my experiences, even when I get it wrong,' she says. 'It's a process.'

We're moving into a Mongolian tent, LOL

Yurts (or gers—the words describe tents with slightly different roof shapes, but have become interchangeable) are traditional Mongolian tent dwellings with domed roofs, made from wooden poles and lattice, with a wool-insulated canvas outer. Typically, they're about 2 metres high, have a hole in the top for a chimney and are home to between five and fifteen people. The bigger ones are usually divided into smaller spaces inside, sometimes with a loft platform, and the circular shape is practical—it helps them withstand the strong winds that blow on the Central Asian grasslands and mountain slopes, where for thousands of years Mongolia's nomads have regularly packed up their homes and transported them by horse, yak or camel to graze their herds and follow trade routes. There is something romantic about these tents. Kings and warriors lived in yurts—Genghis Khan ruled from one—and the crafts of carving and sewing them have been passed down through generations. In a modern city, however, yurts spell hardship.

The ger district Kate Hall could see from her kitchen window is an informal settlement on the edges of Mongolia's capital. After the revolution of 1990 started the process of ending Communist rule, shepherds began to migrate there in large numbers, lured by the empty promise of economic empowerment; unemployment in Ulaanbaatar's ger district is around ten times the national average. Most tent dwellings are not connected to the municipal water, sewerage or power supplies, which is a problem when they're crammed into small spaces. They burn coal or whatever else they can find to keep warm, contributing to the city's chronic pollution problem.

Tenting it on a secluded New Zealand hillside with its own wells, solar panels and back-up generator couldn't be more different. Lucy Aitken Read lives the good yurt life with her husband Tim, their daughters Ramona, seven, and Juno, four, and dog Zoe. I found them on the internet, where Aitken Read shares video diaries on her YouTube channel, Lulastic and the Hippyshake. These have titles like 'How to eat a stinging nettle', and 'Are we a feral family?' and show her kids joyfully playing in their mud kitchen or harvesting pumpkins they've grown themselves. The videos make you yearn for a simpler life, until Aitken Read comes out with something that stops you short—that she collects her menstrual blood in a vintage teapot and uses it to fertilise her flowers, for example—and you think, Hang on a minute; these people are completely bananas. Their kids don't go to school. Aitken Read hasn't washed her hair with shampoo since 2012. She didn't flinch when a strange woman (me) emailed out of the blue and asked to visit. 'We have the river, hiking, waterfalls all just at our fence line.' I was welcome to stay the night, she replied (there's a second, smaller yurt on the property for guests).

I'm approaching the mountain, and the green gets louder until the tarmac, now a thin grey vibration, is all but drowned out. The forest rises steeply to my left while, down the hill, the river (which in the late nineteenth century was so polluted from goldmining that the government declared it a 'sludge channel') runs clear. Serenity, finally. It's been a white-knuckle ride; I've spent the last hour being bullied by speeding trucks on the freeway. I unstick my palms from the steering wheel and, for the first time, give some proper thought to what I'm doing ... which is? I'm not even sure. I don't know these people from Adam, and my experience of self-sufficient living stops with watching 1970s sitcom *The Good Life*.

In the first episode, 'Plough Your Own Furrow', Tom (Richard Briers) turns forty, flips out that he's 'a grotty little cog in a whacking great machine' and quits his job designing plastic toys. 'It's quality of life, that's what I'm after,' he tells his wife Barbara (Felicity Kendal), so they surrender their telephone, buy a goat, cry off the acquisition of 'things' in general, and turn their suburban garden into an allotment—much to the horror of their snooty neighbours. I seem to remember an episode about generating power from poop.

The concept of obtaining 'the good life' via a green thumb, embracing voluntary simplicity and unshackling oneself from reliance on corporations or government-run utilities was popular in the '70s. The back-to-the-land movement was growing in response to the pressures of consumerism and the feeling that the '60s revolution hadn't quite delivered on its promise. Young renegades were picking up dusty old copies of Scott and Helen Nearing's 1954 book *Living the Good Life: How to live simply and sanely in a troubled world* and retreating in search of rural idylls.

In 1970 another American couple, John and Jane Shuttleworth, founded *Mother Earth News* out of Ohio, providing much-referenced DIY info on off-grid living and alternative energy, while in the United Kingdom, John Seymour's *The Complete Book of Self-Sufficiency* did a similar job. (*The Good Life* writers were inspired by Seymour.) On the fringes, there were the communes where everything was shared, including, perhaps, lovers; but mostly the self-sufficient '70s were more Tom and Barbara than anything else. Part-time practitioners stayed put and dabbled. They grew a few tomato plants and swore by the vegetarian recipes in *The Moosewood Cookbook*.

Today in America, the off-grid scene is thriving among doomsday preppers, but in New Zealand, as in Australia and the United Kingdom, the resurgent movement is gentler. It's mostly tree changers—families and couples looking to reconnect with Nature. Escape to the country. Keep chickens.

Nevertheless, it crosses my mind that Lulastic might be a cult, that on arrival I will be asked to surrender my possessions and prepare lentils in the nud. They had a camp here the other day, where scores of off-grid, homeschooled families from across New Zealand came together. Perhaps they formed sacred feminine moon circles and chanted (Aitken Read has written a book about this: 'By meeting together on a New Moon we are reclaiming our power as women.') I haven't been able to find out much about her husband. They're not vegetarian, that I know. They might boil me in a pot over their Bunsen burner or whatever it is they cook dinner on.

Nah. They would have an oven. 'Off-grid' simply means you're not connected to a utility power source and instead generate your own electricity. Create more than you need, and you can feed it back into 'the grid' to make a profit. Plenty of people do just that by installing solar panels on their roofs in Australia. But the 2014 Canadian documentary *Life Off Grid* shows how those who are self-sufficient with their energy may ditch other grids too: municipal water, sewerage, garbage collection, phone lines, even wi-fi. If you live in a remote place, it is sometimes the only way, but others are motivated by their values. Rediscovering practical domestic skills like sewing and mending is common, and off-gridders become 'handy' by necessity, learning to fix and tinker with machines and systems. Many rear animals and grow at least part of what they eat. Some build their own houses, like Amanda Chapman with her THOW, or those inspired by cult hero Michael Reynolds to build an Earthship.

In 1972, Reynolds used bricks made from old beer cans wired together to build his first house made from recycled materials in Taos, New Mexico. He went on to pioneer the use of other reclaimed materials, notably earth-rammed tyres, to design houses that act more like machines than simple shelters, to maximise natural heating and cooling, and capture and recycle water. His architecture recasts waste as a resource, not just by material use, but through the functionality of the buildings themselves—with grey water systems, for example, that collect rain, pipe it to showers, then reuse it to water plants. Reynolds compares *on*-grid living to a human being linked up to life support in a hospital. He is the off-grid philosopher, encouraging all of us to change, even if we've no intention of moving house. 'The way we've been living is over,' he says.[3] 'Our rules and regulations are about things that aren't pertinent any more—stick frame houses that you pump heat into, endless amounts of energy and water, wasteful methods of living.' That first house he built? The one with the cans. It was round. He was inspired by the traditional Navajo hogan, which bears an uncanny resemblance to a yurt.

I get lost of course—dead ends, dirt roads, no phone signal. Then I spy a painted sign nailed to the fence: 'TRIBE OFFGRID.' Bump past a few other properties—each house in this valley is off-grid—and an arrow leads me to the yurts. I gladly ditch my wheels and hike up the hill. A gang of surprisingly vocal chickens comes to greet me, followed by Aitkin Read. Her hair looks fantastic. So that's what no 'poo can do, if you've the stamina to get through the greasy weeks while your sebum rebalances.

I'm mid prattle when she smiles and says, 'How about a swim in the river? It will change your energy. Cold though. Can you handle cold?'⁴ I tell her I'm from Leeds. I was born cold.

'I'll go again!' calls Ramona, appearing in her togs.

They wait while I duck into the composting toilet to get changed (for the record, it's not smelly; a diverter captures the urine and sends it off to water the fruit trees), then we stroll through a field of English weeds: clovers, buttercups, cow parsley. Déjà vu. It's just like the fields I grew up with. Aitken Read thinks the early settlers might have brought their own weeds with them 'to give their cows a rounded diet. Probably there were beautiful native grasses that would have done that, but they didn't want to give them a chance.' She sounds like a Kiwi, less English than she does on her YouTube channel. 'I pick up accents. I might pick up yours talking to you,' she says. 'I grew up in Yorkshire. My accent was so thick no one could understand me.'

Lucy's parents worked for the Salvation Army and moved around a lot, but lived in south London when she was a teenager. When she was eighteen, they left for New Zealand and she went with them, then yo-yoed back a forth for a few years. She met Tim in Wellington. 'I don't have a Yorkshire accent,' I say.

'You do a bit.'

'Come on!' says Ramona.

We pass through a thicket with a gap hacked into it. A carved staircase leads down to the swimming hole. The water is absurdly clear and cool, like someone filled a pond with Evian from the fridge. Along the shores, the orange flowers of a tree whose name I don't remember lean down to gaze at their own reflection.

Ramona and I talk about how much she loves to swim in the river, and I say I bet she wishes she could do it all day, and Aitken Read says, 'Sometimes she does, if she wants.' The kids are as free-range as the chooks. I ask about the homeschooling and she tells me, 'Look, it's more unschooling to be honest. It's just that we don't tend to use that phrase upfront because it alarms people and then they bring their prejudices. Once you see how this works, and you see how the children are learning, it all makes sense, I promise you.'

She says both terms—unschooling and homeschooling—feel inadequate to her: 'I'm trying to call it "life-learning" because school just isn't on our radar; we exist outside of the school paradigm. We believe that children are made to learn; they cannot not learn. From the moment they wake up, they're driven by curiosity, so we want to foster this environment where their learning continues to be completely autonomous and completely joyful, and no one ever tells them how they have to learn or what they need to learn now, or how fast they need to learn it. They will just do it at their own pace, and we will trust them to do so.' She won't teach them to read until they ask her to.

'But what if they don't?'

'They will, when they're ready.'

She has a master's degree, but when I ask, where from? she can't remember, even though it's the London School of Economics, one of the most prestigious educational establishments in Britain. 'Oh, who cares? I mean, what does any of it mean, really?' Hmm. Tim trained as a teacher, so while they may reject traditional schooling now, they are both formally educated to a high level, which obviously has an effect on the kids, even with the lack of structure, so I do find it all slightly, what's the word? Bewildering? Unique? Then again, I don't have kids of my own, and in truth I don't feel strongly about how other people choose to raise their families. Who am I to judge? When Aitken Read says, 'We are parenting on the edge. There's not many people doing it.' I think, fair enough; it appears to be working for them, in this moment, rather as this river swim is working for me. 'Did you know that a study found more kids could identify a Dalek than an owl?' she says.

Back at camp she shows me around. They grow veggies and fruit, collect eggs from their chickens, farm cattle and ducks for meat and keep bees, but they aren't entirely self-sufficient. Aitken Read says she tried that but something had to give; to make time for content-creation for Lulastic, she happily buys some vegetables. The family is plastic-free; they compost, and farm organically, using no synthetic chemicals on the land or in the home.

Power comes mostly from solar panels, although they have gas bottles for their stovetop.

'Off-grid isn't this thrifty hack,' she says. 'The solar system was thousands to pay upfront. It is quite a privileged thing to do because of the money required at the start. If you're doing it in community, you can avoid some of that. We lived for fifteen months on somebody else's land with no costs, working for our rent.' That afforded them valuable experience, a sort of apprenticeship, but it wasn't a trial. They already knew they'd enjoy it.

The Aitken Reads used to live a 'normal' life in London, in that they owned a house in a street. She was working as a climate-change campaigner for Oxfam, biked her commute, and loved her job. 'I know it's common in the NGO world to come away feeling disillusioned, but I felt the opposite,' she tells me. 'I worked there for five years, and I saw some significant change happen as a result of this continuous working away at little things every day, as well as some of the big projects we ran. I really believed in it, and still do now. It's hugely affected my life, knowing that the small things can make a difference.'

In the summer of 2013, when Juno was a newborn, they moved out of Camberwell and into 'Betty', a VW campervan, taking off around Europe for three months before returning to New Zealand. They didn't know where they would settle, only that they wanted to make a life off-grid and 'find their people'. They had money from selling their house to buy a parcel of land. Aitken Read describes finding it as 'a Heavens-opening moment: Taa-daaa! We just absolutely knew that this land, way farther away than we'd wanted to be, was right.' Soon she was sharing a blog post titled, 'We're moving into a Mongolian tent, LOL.'

They sourced the big yurt on Trade Me, still in its box. It went up in a day-and-a-half with the help of twelve friends on a working bee. 'The little one goes up in three hours,' she says. It's like a hip hotel room, complete with carefully selected vintage furniture and a proper, comfy bed. Lie down, look up and the ceiling is a storybook circus tent. 'You can close that,' she says, pointing to the hole in the roof, 'but it's nice to see the stars.'

Aitken Read defines herself as an activist who wants to make the world fairer for everyone. 'In our rational brain, when we were living in the city, we believed that was where the most change would happen,' she says, 'pushed forward by pioneers who were taking sustainability and making it work amongst the high rises. We were really disparaging of the hippies who just took off to remote corners of the world.'

211

'Like they were opting out of society? Giving up, somehow?'

'Exactly.'

I tell her about my interview with the economist Richard Denniss, and how he insists that individual piety won't change the world, and she nods. 'Yes, I see that, and we did worry about that. But we had this really strong urge and now I feel like it was the call of the wild … calling us to this place, this mountain and this river, to live this life here. It was like a mystical calling, and we did it; we yielded to this heart sense. But look, I do remember that we were really disparaging of this sort of thing.'

'So how did you reconcile it?'

'We were wrong! If you look through history, there are always outliers in any social movement who are pushing, pushing, pushing, and they are called the weirdos, and people hate them, people get angry about them, and we need these people.'

'People like you?'

'Yes, because when you push these things forward, society moves a little bit towards that. In any movement, you have people who are on the extreme edge of it (that's why we have the phrase "the cutting edge") and they are making the first inroads. It takes time for mainstream society to catch up, or to care, but in just nudging them a little bit, we're doing a useful job.'

She tells me a story about a 'nature playgroup' she started last year. 'We have all these kids come to our farm and play in nature,' she says. 'The first session was getting the kids building a fire. I was explaining about kindling and I said, "What are some of the things you can use?" One said, "Cardboard!" Another chose a magazine. A tiny girl said, "Oh you could get some sticks," and then this little boy said, "Or you could light a candle under the curtains." There are lots of ways to start a fire. You don't have to send the whole house up in smoke.' I frown and she says, 'You can go off-grid in smaller ways, in spirit if you like. You can switch to a good green energy supplier.'

'Lucy, that's hardly the same, is it? That's not redesigning society.'

Truth is, I feel a bit disappointed.

'Off-grid,' she says, 'is a mindset.'

19
On mindfulness

'The solution is that we need to build a kinder and braver world.'
—Lady Gaga, in conversation with the Dalai Lama at
the US Conference of Mayors, Indianapolis, 2016

'Whether we can wake up or not depends on whether we can walk mindfully on our Mother Earth. The future of all life, including our own, depends on our mindful steps. We have to hear the bells of mindfulness that are sounding all across our planet.'
—Thich Nhat Hanh, *The World We Have*

Start within

How to join the dots between all the issues raised in this book? The women's movement, equal rights and social justice in general, and the pressing need to create fairer systems for everyone, but also in specific cases: in the fashion and food supply chains, and in workplaces where discrimination and harassment occur? Where to begin to spur change when it comes to intimidating issues like modern slavery and climate change? How to engage different generations, and grassroots communities? Make positive change in our own lives and the lives of those around us, then send these good vibrations rippling outward to reach governments and important decision-makers? How to *not* decide it's all too damn hard, give up and go home?

I don't mind telling you, I've thought that myself a few times. Really, can I make a difference beyond giving up plastic bags? Where is the key, the mythical silver bullet, when you need it, eh? Of course, it's nowhere, because there is no silver bullet. Change is as hard as it is valuable. The quick fix is a lie. But … there is this one thing.

According to Christine Wamsler, professor of sustainability science at Lund University, mindfulness can help. She defines it as 'more than just moment-to-moment awareness. It is a kind, curious and non-judgemental awareness that helps us relate to ourselves, others, and our environment with compassion.'

We can access it by meditation and yoga, those well-known chill-out tools that can make us feel more grounded, more content, but Wamsler's research suggests deeper powers. In an article for *The Conversation*, she writes that 'mindfulness can not only change how we think about the social and environmental crises that affect our world, but can also help us to take the actions needed to build a more sustainable society.'[1] Through it, we might increase our sensitivity to context, and access greater empathy for people and planet. It can't hurt that meditation helps reduce stress and boost focus too.

I always roll my eyes at those fairy stories where the one thing the questing heroine is searching for turns out to have been right in front of her nose the whole time. I mean, surely the answer to the 'How to change the world' question is: get rid of Trump and his ilk from the corridors of power, banish all Weinstein-like bosses and defeat the NRA. Or it's mass divestment from the fossil fuel industry. It's smash the capitalist system and rebuild the economy, as Tim Jackson suggests, based on care, craft, culture and creativity. Surely?

Bah-bow. The answer is both simpler and infinitely more complex. The answer is us. That is the one grand, overarching thing I've learned during the collecting and telling of the stories shared in this book, and it's also what connects them all. You can't see or touch it. It's hard to even describe it, but it is there.

You might call it the power of the human spirit, or talk in terms of internality, or just plain humanity. Some bring God into it. Personally, I think of it more as a spark, but do feel free to give it your own name, shape and description. Lucy Aitken Read calls it 'the liveness'. STRAWkler Harriet Spark saw it in Great Barrier Reef; Tim Silverwood in the magnitude of the oceans. It is plain to see in Indigenous Australians' connection to their land, and it's there in a subtler way through every one of these stories of collaboration. It was present on the first Earth Day, when Gaylord Nelson described his vision for 'an environment of decency, quality and mutual respect for all other human beings and all other living creatures'.

It's in the coral polyps and the zooxanthellae and the polar bears and the vulnerable speckled warblers, and the butterflies dancing above Andrew Barker's seedlings. Surely you saw it on his Grow Free tables. It's in the giving. It's also in the tears over species loss and the passion to do something about it, and it flows through the rivers, even the ones choked by garbage, in fact more so there. It is the trees of course. I have felt it there myself most strongly, when I put my hands on their trunks in the park when no one is looking, and whisper my apologies for the graffiti some kid carved on the bark and the pissing dogs and the paper this is printed on.

It is in recognising that we are part of Nature, not above it; and that as the protest signs say, there is no Planet B.

The Gaia hypothesis proposes that all living and non-living elements on Earth are connected and synergise together to keep life in balance. While much of the scientific community rejects the theory (which was popularised by British scientist James Lovelock in the 1970s), still more the suggestion that the Earth is somehow 'alive', the idea is echoed through history and religion across cultures, from Plato and Buddhism to all the poets, painters, artists and writers who have personified Nature in their work, including me.

The Dalai Lama reminds us that it is accessible and universal. 'My call for a spiritual revolution is not a call for a religious revolution. Nor is it a reference to a way of life that is somehow otherworldly, still less to something magical or mysterious. Rather, it is a call for a radical reorientation away from our habitual preoccupation with self. It is a call to turn toward the wider community of beings with whom we are connected, and for conduct which recognizes others' interests alongside our own.'

The spark in my mind's eye ignites from a combination of our connectivity and innate creativity, compassion and empathy. It's the meeting of mind and heart, and it understands its place in the greater whole. Do you see it now? No need to try to catch it. You have your own. Enough talk. Now go, do.

Notes

Author's note

1 Definition adapted from *The New Collins Concise Dictionary of the English Language*, Collins, London, 1987.

2 Erica Chenoweth & Jeremy Pressman, 'Last month, 83% of US protests were against Trump', *Washington Post*, 28 September 2017.

3 Hernán Cortés Saenz, Isabel Ortiz, Sara Burke & Mohamed Berrada, *World Protests 2006–2013: Executive Summary*, Initiative for Policy Dialogue working paper #275, Colombia University, New York.

4 Successive polls have revealed this. In September 2017, an online poll conducted by Research Now for the Australia Institute found only 30 per cent supported the mine, while 68 per cent opposed government subsidising a loan to Adani. In October, a Roy Morgan Snap SMS Survey found that 53.5 per cent of respondents thought the mine 'should not go ahead', while only 16 per cent thought it should; the rest either hadn't heard of it or didn't have a preference. A January 2018 ReachTEL poll found 65.1 per cent of Australians opposed or strongly opposed the building of the mine.

5 Gerardo Ceballos, Paul Ehrlich, Anthony Barnosky, Andrés García, Robert Pringle & Todd Palmer, 'Accelerated modern human-induced species losses: Entering the sixth mass extinction', *Science Advances*, vol. 1, no. 5, 19 June 2015, e1400253 DOI: 10.1126/sciadv.1400253.

6 In January 2018. Tracey Crouch is actually Minister for Sport and Civil Society, but loneliness issues are now officially part of her portfolio.

7 Maria Alejandra Rodriguez Acha, 'How young feminists are tackling climate justice in 2016', *Huffington Post*, 3 July 2016.

8 Heidi Przybyla, 'Women's march an entry point for new activist wave', *USA Today*, 5.

1: The Pussyhat Project

1   Quoted in Carmen Fishwick & Caroline Bannock, 'Why we protested in solidarity with the Women's March on Washington', *The Guardian*, 23 January 2017.

2   Kaveh Waddell, 'The exhausting work of tallying America's largest protest', *Atlantic*, 23 January 2017. Spreadsheet accessed here: docs.google.com/ spreadsheets/d/1xa0iLqYKz8x9Yc_rfhtmSOJQ2EGgeUVjvV4A8LsIaxY/html view?sle=true#gid=0.

3   Jayna Zweiman, Skype interview with author, December 2017.

4   Quoted in Emily Crockett, '9 prominent feminists on what Hillary Clinton's historic candidacy really means', *Vox*, 22 August 2016.

5   Susan Bordo, *The Destruction of Hillary Clinton*, Text Publishing, Melbourne, 2017, extract accessed via *The Guardian* here: www.theguardian.com/us-news/ commentisfree/2017/apr/03/the-destruction-of-hillary-clinton-sexism-sanders- and-the-millennial-feminists.

6   William A. Galston & Clara Hendrickson, 'How millennials voted in this election,' Brookings, 21 November 2016, accessed here: https://www.brookings.edu/blog/ fixgov/2016/11/21/how-millennials-voted/.

7   Michelle Goldberg, 'The empire strikes back', *Slate*, 27 December 2016.

8   Krista Suh, Skype interview with author, December 2017.

9   Quoted in Emanuella Grinberg, 'Hillary Clinton's Pantsuit Nation suits up for election day', CNN, 8 November 2016.

10   Erin Gloria Ryan, 'Pantsuit Nation is the worst: Why a book of uplifting Facebook posts won't heal America', *Daily Beast*, 21 December 2016.

11   Naomi Wolf, *The Beauty Myth*, Vintage, London, 1991, pp. 15–16.

12   Quoted in Anne L. Macdonald, *No Idle Hands: The social history of American knitting*, Random House, New York, 2010.

13   Paul Hawken, *Blessed Unrest: How the largest social movement in history is restoring grace, justice, and beauty to the world*, Kindle edition, Penguin Publishing Group, New York, 2007, p. 175.

14   Quoted in Tanya Klich, 'What entrepreneurs can learn from the founders of the Pussyhat Project', *Forbes*, 29 January 2017.

15   Holly Derr, 'Pink flag: What message do 'pussy hats' really send?', *Bitch Media*, 17 January 2017.

16   *Blavity*, 22 January 2018, accessed here: blavity.com/protesters-put-a-puy-hat- on-a-statue-of-harriet-tubman-black-twitter-asks-what-are-you-doing.

17   In Samhita Mukhopadhyay & Kate Harding (eds), *Nasty Women: Feminism, resistance, and revolution in Trump's America*, Kindle edition, Picador, New York, p. 119.

18   Anne Summers, telephone interview with author, December 2017.

19   Anne Summers, 'Beware Donald Trump: The pussyhat will be the protest symbol of our times', *The Sydney Morning Herald*, 3 February 2017.

20   Sylvia Pankhurst, *The Suffragette: The History of the Women's Militant Suffrage Movement, 1905–1910*, Sturgis & Walton Co., London, 1911, accessed here: archive. org/stream/suffragettehisto00pankuoft/suffragettehisto00pankuoft_djvu.txt.

2: On craftivism

1   Yoko Ono, 'What is the relationship between the world and the artist?', artist's statement published in *This Is Not Here*, exhibition catalogue, Everson Museum of Art, Syracuse, 1971, accessed here: imaginepeace.com/archives/2622.

2   Betsy Greer, Skype interview with author, January 2018.

3   Betsy Greer, *Knitting For Good*, Trumpeter Books, Boston, 2008, p. 4.

4   Patrick Barkham, 'Iraq War 10 years on: A mass protest that defined a generation', *The Guardian*, 15 February 2013.

5   Kathleen Hanna on Noisey, October 2016, accessed here: www.youtube.com/watch?v=mLNCCvZ71m4.

6   Quoted in Patrick J. McDonnell, 'Argentines remember a mother who joined the "disappeared"', *Los Angeles Times*, 24 March 2006.

7   Quoted in Josephine Fisher, *Mothers of the Disappeared*, South End Press, Boston, 1989, p. 54.

8   Quoted in Uki Goni, '40 years later, the mothers of Argentina's "disappeared" refuse to be silent', *The Guardian*, 28 April 2017.

9   Margaret Snook, 'Chilean Arpilleras: A chapter of history written on cloth', *Cachando Chile*, 11 September 2010.

10 Magda Sayeg, 'How yarn bombing grew into a worldwide movement', TEDYouth, November 2015.

11 Sayraphim Lothian, telephone interview with author, January 2018.

12 Clive Hamilton, 'What do we want? Charting the rise and fall of protest in Australia', *The Conversation*, 17 November 2016.

13 Casey Jenkins, telephone interview with author, January 2018.

14 Emma Rees, 'Casting off shame through vaginal knitting', *The Conversation*, 5 December 2013.

15 Germaine Greer on *Balderdash and Piffle*, BBC TV, January 2006.

16 Adam Weinstein, 'Vaginal knitting is the new thing in performance art', *Gawker*, 27 November 2013.

3: Make the change you wish to see

1   Gene Sharp, *198 Methods of Nonviolent Action*, Porter Sargent, Boston, 1973.

2   Mark Engler & Paul Engler, *This Is an Uprising*, Nation Books, New York, 2017, p. 14.

3   Sarah Corbett, Skype interview with author, March 2018.

4   Sarah Corbett, *How to Be a Craftivist: The art of gentle protest*, Kindle edn, Random House, London, 2017, Kindle locations 2602–95.

5   Tony Abbott, 'Tony Abbott on why same sex marriage would fundamentally change society', *The Sydney Morning Herald*, 13 September 2007.

6   Adam Gartrell, 'Mental health groups sound alarm over dramatic same-sex marriage spike', *The Sydney Morning Herald*, 17 September 2017.

7   Sherele Moody, 'I'm spiralling into marriage equality depression', *The Courier Mail*, 15 September 2017.

4: Fashion revolution

1   Amy Kazmin, 'How Benetton faced up to the aftermath of Rana Plaza', *Financial Times*, 21 April 2015.

2   Quoted in Lizzie Rivera, 'Fashion Revolution: Behind the scenes of a £2 trillion industry', *Independent*, 24 April 2017.

3   Quoted in 'Bangladesh factory collapse toll passes 1,000', BBC, 10 May 2013.

4   Quoted in Laura Kuenssberg, 'Western companies "should share blame" for Bangladesh factory conditions', ITV, 30 April 2013, accessed here: www.itv.com/news/2013-04-30/western-companies-should-share-blame-for-bangladesh-factory-conditions/.

5   Carry Somers, by email, April 2018.

6   Carry Somers, interview with author, London, September 2014.

7   Orsola de Castro, Skype interview with author, January 2018.

8   Erin Mazursky, 'The rules have changed: How to build a "movement of movements" in the US', *Medium*, 22 November 2016.

9   Fashion Revolution mission statement, fashionrevolution.org.

10 Death toll estimates vary wildly, from half a million to eight million. See Yongyi Song, 'Chronology of mass killings during the Chinese Cultural Revolution (1966–1976)', *Online Encyclopedia of Mass Violence*, Center for International Studies and Research, Paris, 25 August 2011.

11 'Sweep away all monsters', *Peking Review*, vol. 9, no. 23, 3 June 1966.

12 Lucy Siegle, 'Fashion still doesn't give a damn about the deaths of garment workers', *The Guardian*, 5 May 2013.

13 Quoted in ibid.

14 Livia Firth, 'The Oscars 2010', *Eco-age.com* (blog).

15 Sarah Ditty et. al., *Fashion Transparency Index 2017*, Fashion Revolution, UK, 2017, p. 4.

16 'Statement from Kalpona Akter on the collapse of a building in Bangladesh,' *Jobs for Justice*, 24 April 2013.

17 Kalpona Akter, interview with author, Sydney, April 2017.

18 Ibid.

5: Three ways to be an activist

1   Cathy Otten, *With Ash on their Faces: Yezidi women and the Islamic State*, OR Books, New York, 2017, extract accessed here: www.theguardian.com/world/2017/jul/25/slaves-of-isis-the-long-walk-of-the-yazidi-women.

2   Amanda Foreman, phone interview with author, January 2018.

3   Kimberlé Crenshaw, 'The Urgency of Intersectionality', TEDWomen, October 2016.

4   Kimberlé Crenshaw, 'Demarginalizing the intersection of race and sex: A Black feminist critique of antidiscrimination doctrine, feminist theory and antiracist politics', *The University of Chicago Legal Forum*, no. 140, 1989, pp. 139–67.

5   Reni Eddo-Lodge in a video interview with Foyles booksellers, 30 May 2007, accessed here: www.youtube.com/watch?v=2vJZdeSqfFY.

6   Accessed here: resistanceschoolberkeley.org/session-1/.
7   Saru Jayaraman, *Behind the Kitchen Door*, ILR Press, Ithaca, NY, p. 2.
8   Saru Jayaraman, interview with KCET, 5 March 2013, accessed here: www.kcet
    .org/food/an-interview-with-saru-jayaraman.
9   Ibid.
10 Jayaraman, *Behind the Kitchen Door*, Foreword, p. x.
11 Tarana Burke on *7.30*, ABC TV, 19 October 2017.

6: We stand with you

1   Cara Buckley, 'Powerful women in Hollywood unveil anti-harassment action plan', *New York Times*, 1 January 2018.
2   Ashley Judd on *HARDtalk*, BBC TV, 15 January 2018.
3   Rashida Jones, during a Time's Up panel discussion at the Makers 2018 conference, 5 February 2018, accessed here: www.theroot.com/watch-rashida-jones-says-metoo-and-time-s-up-must-be-1822777066.
4   Rose McGowan, *Brave*, HQ, New York, 2018, p. 224.
5   According to Tina Tchen, the lawyer heading up the Times Up Legal Defense Fund, which is housed at the National Women's Law Center, in an interview with CNN, 1 March 2018.
6   Quoted in Emma Brockes, 'Me too founder, Tarana Burke: "You have to use your privilege to serve other people"', *Observer*, 15 January 2018.
7   Statement accessed here: amysmartgirls.com/advocates-activists-for-gender-racial-justice-join-actresses-at-tonights-goldenglobes-e98c926865b3.
8   *Access Hollywood* red carpet interview, accessed here: www.youtube.com/watch?v=7DdSSjp4Z8k.
9   Quoted in Kayla Kumari Upadhyaya, 'Amy Poehler advocated for restaurant workers' rights at Midtown rally', *Eater New York*, 21 February 2018.
10 Ai-jen Poo, 'I was Meryl Streep's "plus one" at the Golden Globes', *Cosmopolitan*, 10 January 2018.
11 Ai-jen Poo, interview on the *Business of Giving* podcast, 22 January 2018.
12 Rosa Parks, interviewed April 1956 on Pacifica radio station KPFA, accessed here: www.democracynow.org/2005/10/25/rosa_parks_1913_2005_we_air.
13 Rosa Parks with Jim Haskins, *Rosa Parks: My story*, Dial Books, New York, 1992, p. 116.
14 Doreen St Félix, 'The Fever Dream of Oprah for President', *The New Yorker*, 9 January 2018.
15 Eva Peyser, 'I can't believe I have to explain why Oprah shouldn't be president', *Vice*, 9 January 2018.
16 Winfrey dismissed this idea in an interview; see Laura Brown, 'O That's Good', *InStyle*, March 2018.
17 Alyssa Milano, 'My comment on the Harvey Weinstein scandal', *Patriot Not Partisan*, 9 October 2017.
18 Tarana Burke on *The Call* podcast, January 2018.

19 Tarana Burke, 'The Inception', *Just Be Inc*, accessed here: justbeinc.wixsite.com/justbeinc/the-me-too-movement-cmml.
20 Quoted in Sandra E. Garcia, 'The woman who created #metoo long before hashtags', *The New York Times*, 20 October 2017.
21 Edward Felsenthal, 'Behind the scenes of *TIME*'s Person of the Year 2017', *TIME*, 6 December 2017.
22 Stephanie Zacharek, Eliana Dockterman & Haley Sweetland Edwards, 'The Silence Breakers', *TIME*, December 2017.
23 Chris Hemmings, 'Not all men are guilty of violence and sexism, but all men have a responsibility to stop those crimes', *The Telegraph* (UK), 4 September 2017.
24 Rose McGowan in her five-part documentary series, *Citizen Rose*.
25 Donald Trump tweet, 15 October 2016, accessed here: twitter.com/realdonaldtrump/status/787244543003467776?lang=en.
26 Tara Moss, email interview with author, January 2018.
27 Zachary Cohen, 'From fellow solder to monster in uniform: #metoo in the military', CNN, 7 February 2018.
28 Leta Hong Fincher, 'China is attempting to muzzle #MeToo', NPR, 1 February 2018, accessed here: www.npr.org/sections/parallels/2018/02/01/582167268/china-is-attempting-to-muzzle-metoo.

7: Green piece

1 Monica Rhor, 'Me Too founder Tarana Burke on how the movement began', *Houston Chronicle*, 8 December 2017.
2 Cameron Russell, Skype interview with author, January 2018.
3 According to the World Bank, 40 per cent of productive land is projected to be lost in the southern region of Bangladesh as a result of a 65-centimetre sea-level rise by the 2080s. About twenty million people in the coastal areas of Bangladesh are already affected by salinity in drinking water. Rising sea levels and more intense cyclones and storm surges could intensify the contamination of groundwater and surface water, causing more diarrhoea outbreaks.
4 Quoted in Becky Chung, 'From supermodel to managing editor: How Cameron Russell's TED Talk inspired her to start a magazine', *TED* blog, 12 August 2014.
5 Doug Struck, 'Burning river reborn—how Cleveland saved the Cuyahoga—and itself', *Christian Science Monitor*, 8 August 2017.
6 Gaylord Nelson, interview with Dr Randy Champeau, Director of the Wisconsin Center for Environmental Education, 1990, accessed here: eeinwisconsin.org/resource/about.aspx?s=96170.0.0.2209.
7 The proposal was from Fred Dutton, one of JFK's assistant secretaries of state, who suggested bringing in famous people like Jacques Cousteau and Jesse Jackson to add legitimacy. Memo accessed here: www.nelsonearthday.net/collection/earthday-draft.php.
8 Denis Hayes, first Earth Day national co-ordinator, speaking in Washington at the 40th event in 2010.

9   Gaylord Nelson, speech to Earth Day rally, 22 April 1970, accessed here: www.youtube.com/watch?v=y3RCPAtmpv8&list=PL3480E41AA956A42B& index=2.

10 Joseph Lelyveld, 'Millions join Earth Day observances across the nation', *The New York Times*, 23 April 1970.

11 Walter Cronkite on CBS News, accessed here: www.earthday.org/about/ the-history-of-earth-day/.

12 Brentin Mock, 'Are there two different versions of environmentalist, one "white", one "black"?' *Grist*, 31 July 2014.

13 Nicole Smith Dahmen et al., 'The overwhelming whiteness of US environmentalism is hobbling the fight against climate change', *Quartz*, 4 January 2017.

14 Quoted in Jason Mark, 'Naomi Klein: Big green groups are more damaging than climate deniers', *The Guardian*, 11 September 2013.

15 Lornett Vestal, 'The unbearable whiteness of hiking and how to solve it', *Sierra Club* blog, 7 December 2016.

16 David George Haskell, *The Songs of Trees: Stories from nature's great connectors*, Black Inc., Melbourne, 2017, pp. 172–3.

17 Quoted in Mele-Ane Havea, 'Amelia Telford is protecting country', *Dumbo Feather*, third quarter 2017, no. 52.

8: The rise of the climate movement

1   Naomi Klein, *This Changes Everything*, Simon & Schuster, New York, 2014.

2   John McQuaid, 'Mining the mountains', *Smithsonian*, January 2009.

3   Matthew R.V. Ross, Brian L. McGlynn & Emily S. Bernhardt, 'Deep impact: Effects of mountaintop mining on surface topography, bedrock structure, and downstream waters', *Environmental Science and Technology*, 22 January 2016.

4   Tim Flannery, *The Weather Makers*, Text, Melbourne, 2005, p. 177.

5   Laurent C.M. Lebreton, *Stochastic analysis of deep sea oil spill trajectories in the Great Australian Bight*, Wilderness Society South Australia, Adelaide, 2015.

6   Dominic C. DiGiulio & Robert B. Jackson, 'Impact to underground sources of drinking water and domestic wells from production well stimulation and completion practices in the Pavillion, Wyoming, Field', *Environmental Science and Technology*, vol. 50, no. 8, 2016, pp. 4524–36.

7   Chris Burn, 'Theresa May: Fracking across Yorkshire will be financially beneficial for communities', *The Yorkshire Post*, 23 February 2018.

8   Klein, *This Changes Everything*, p. 143.

9   Based on global emissions for 2010; see IPCC, *Climate Change 2014: Impacts, adaption and vulnerability*, Working Group II Contribution to the Fifth Assessment Report of the Intergovernmental Panel on Climate Change, Cambridge University Press, New York, 2014.

10 Flannery, *The Weather Makers*, p. 5.

11 James Hansen et al., 'Target atmospheric CO2: Where should humanity aim?', *The Open Atmosphere Science Journal*, vol. 2, 2008, pp. 217–31.

12 International Energy Agency, *World Energy Outlook Executive Summary*, 2011.

13 Parag Khanna, 'The world 4 degrees warmer,' *New Scientist*, 5 September 2009.

14 Australian IPCC scientist Joëlle Gergis points out that Khanna is not a scientist, and that CISRO cites projections that are much less dramatic.

15 IPCC, *Climate Change 2014*.

16 Tim Flannery, *Atmosphere of Hope*, Text, Melbourne, 2015, p. 156.

17 David George Haskell, *The Songs of Trees: Stories from nature's great connectors*, Penguin Random House, New York, 2017, p. 56.

18 Hansen, 'Target Atmospheric CO_2', p. 1.

19 Matt Lodder, 'I protested at Tate Britain because we can't ignore the gallery's controversial relationship with BP any longer', *Independent*, 29 November 2015.

20 'NASA study finds carbon emissions could dramatically increase risk of US mega-droughts', NASA press release, 13 February 2015.

21 Z. Leviston, M. Greenhill & I. Walker, *Australian Attitudes to Climate Change and Adaptation: 2010–2014*, CSIRO, Australia, 2015.

22 Lesley Hughes on *7.30*, November 2014.

23 Lesley Head, 'Grief will be our companion in climate change', *lesleyhead.com* blog, 21 August 2016.

24 Clive Hamilton, *Earthmasters: Playing God with the climate*, Allen & Unwin, Sydney, 2013, p. 162.

25 Joe Duggan, telephone interview with author, December 2017.

26 Leviston, Greenhill & Walker, *Australian attitudes to climate change and adaptation*.

27 May Boeve, interview with author, Sydney, December 2017.

28 Jeremy Hodges, 'Electric cars might be cheaper than gas guzzlers in 7 years', *Bloomberg*, 22 March 2018.

29 International Energy Agency, *World Energy Outlook 2017*, IEA, Paris, 2017.

30 Peter Erickson et al., 'Effect of subsidies to fossil fuel companies on United States crude oil production', *Nature Energy*, vol. 2, 2017, pp. 891–8.

31 Quoted from the Complaint for Public Nuisance filed on behalf of the People of the State of California, 19 September 2017, accessed here: www.sfcityattorney .org/wp-content/uploads/2017/09/2017-09-19-File-Stamped-Complaint-for-Public-Nuisance.pdf.

32 Bill McKibben, 'Global warming's terrifying new math', *Rolling Stone*, 19 July 2012.

33 Bill McKibben in *Do The Math* (documentary), written and directed by Kelly Nyks & Jared P. Scott, PF Pictures, New York, 2013.

34 Bill McKibben, *The End of Nature*, 2nd edition, Random House, New York, 2006, p. 20.

35 McKibben in *Do The Math*.

36 Boeve, interview with author, Sydney, November, 2017.

37 May Boeve, 'Trump has declared war on our climate—we won't let him win', *The Hill*, 6 February 2018.

38 Grant Jacobsen, 'The Al Gore effect: *An Inconvenient Truth* and voluntary carbon offsets', *Journal of Environmental Economics and Management*, vol. 61, no. 1, January 2011, pp. 67–78.

39 Quoted in Robert Collier, 'Global warming activists try to stir Americans to change', *San Francisco Chronicle*, 22 March 2007.

40 Bill McKibben, 'The power of the click', *Los Angeles Times*, 16 October 2007.

41 Brady Dennis, 'How is this weekend's climate march different from its predecessor?', *The Washington Post*, 27 April 2017.

9: Fight Club

1   Breana Macpherson-Rice, interview with author, Sydney, December 2017.

2   @realDonaldTrump tweet accessed here: twitter.com/realdonaldtrump/status/266259787405225984.

3   Elizabeth Morley, interview with author, Sydney, December 2017.

4   Breana Macpherson-Rice, 'I stood up for real action on climate change and now I'm going to court', *Junkee*, 8 September 2016.

5   Aiofe Nicklason, 'Why I disrobed for divestment,' *fossilfreemu.org*, 26 April 2016.

6   Bob Brown, 'The Adani mine is this generation's Franklin River. People power can stop it', *The Guardian*, 24 March 2017.

7   Lise Mellor, *Brown, Robert James*, Sydney Medical School Online Museum and Archive, University of Sydney, Sydney, 2008.

8   Bob Brown in the film *The Wild Franklin River*, directed by Chris Noone, Stacey Gavrily and Michael Cordell, Wombat Films, 1980.

9   Bob Brown, interview with Martin Clark, Melbourne Law School, 24 July 2013, accessed here: cpb-ap-se2.wpmucdn.com/blogs.unimelb.edu.au/dist/2/77/files/2013/07/Remembering-Tasmanian-Dams-Interview-Transcripts3.pdf.

10 Quoted in Bill Griffiths, 'How archaeology helped save the Franklin River', *The Conversation*, 2 March 2018.

11 Brown, 'The Adani mine'.

12 Several 2017 polls confirm this, including a ReachTEL survey commissioned by the Stop Adani Alliance, and a Roy Morgan SMS survey, both conducted in October 2017. Three-quarters of those polled by another ReachTEL survey commissioned by GetUp! in January 2017 did not think lending government money to Adani was a good idea.

13 In Charlie Peel, 'Prospect of vigilante action against Adani protestors has Bowen police worried', *The Australian*, 23 January 2018.

14 Adani Mining CEO Jeyakumar Janakaraj, interviewed by *Mining Global* magazine, April 2015.

15 Quoted in Rod Campbell, 'Fact check: Will Adani's coal mine really boost employment by 10,000 jobs?', *The Australian*, 31 August 2015.

16 The council's statement on the proposed mine, 'Stop Adani destroying our land and culture', can be accessed here: wanganjagalingou.com.au/our-fight/.

17 See the NSW Minerals Council website, accessed here : www.nswmining.com.au/environment/rehabilitation-mine-closure.

18 Adam Walters, *The Hole Truth: The mess coal companies plan to leave in NSW*, commissioned by Hunter Communities Network, Energy & Resources Insights, Sydney, 2016, p. 10.

19 Ibid., p. 6.
20 AnneMaree McLoughlin, speech outside Newcastle EPA, 20 February 2017, quoted in Scott Bevan, 'Hunter mine noise protest clamours to be heard', *Newcastle Herald*, 20 February 2017.
21 George Tlaskal, personal submission regarding Warkworth Coal Mine and Mount Thorley Coal Mines Continuation Project, 4 August 2014, accessed here: www.huntervalleyprotectionalliance.com/pdf/WARKW_Continuation_GT20140804.pdf.
22 Ibid.
23 George Tlaskal, Submission to PAC regarding Warkworth Coal Mine and Mount Thorley Coal Mines Continuation Project, 10 December 2014, accessed via www.pac.nsw.gov.au.
24 Quoted in Shannon Dan, 'Aboriginal elders acquitted of criminal charges', *Singleton Argus*, 2 June 2017.
25 Catherine Clifford, 'Broke's powerless protectors', *Newcastle Herald*, 29 May 2015.
26 Alan Jones, speech to the Lockyer Valley Ratepayers Association, 9 November 2014.
27 Drew Hutton, in 'Lock me away', *Australian Story*, ABC TV, 4 August 2014.
28 Ibid.
29 Quoted in Joanne McCarthy, 'Wollar resident Bev Smiles faces jail as one of the first to be charged under new anti-coal-protest laws', *Newcastle Herald*, 14 April 2017.

10: Youthquake

1 Joel Stein, 'Millennials: The Me Me Me Generation', *TIME*, May 2013.
2 Logan Casey, 'Minding the generation gap: Investigating media portrayal of millennials and Gen Z', *The New York Times*, 31 October 2016.
3 Derrick Feldmann, Amy Thayer & Melissa Wall, *The 2017 Millennial Impact Report: Phase 1: Millennial dialogue on the landscape of cause engagement and social issues*, Achieve, West Palm Beach, FL, 2017, p. ii.
4 Jeff Fromm, 'Gen Z is on the rise, here is what you need to know', *Forbes*, 4 January 2017.
5 Morgan O' Donnell, 'Millennials: The new face of activism', *Odyssey*, 12 October 2015.
6 Jeremy Heimans & Henry Timms, 'Understanding "New Power"', *Harvard Business Review*, December 2014.
7 Xiuhtezcatl Martinez in *Kid Warrior: The Xiuhtezcatl Martinez story*, accessed here: www.youtube.com/watch?v=M_EK_9m1H88.
8 Xiuhtezcatl Martinez, 'Hip-hop environmental activism', TEDxYouth, May 2014.
9 Itzcuauhtli Martinez, quoted in *From Silence into Action*, accessed here: www.climatesilencenow.org/about.html.
10 Mark Ruffalo, '11-year-old demands climate action with vow of silence pledge', *Eco Watch*, 10 December 2014.

11 Organisers expected 500,000 and claim 800,000 turned up. CBS news reports 202,796 (with a margin of error of 15 per cent) on the advice of Digital Design & Imaging Service, a company that specialises in aerial photography and visual impact studies; however, this company underestimates the numbers at the Women's Marches by almost half. *Bustle* reports there were roughly half the number of Metro rides in Washington, DC on the day of March for Our Lives compared with the day of the Women's Marches.

12 Eric Levitz, 'There is no epidemic of mass shootings', *New York* magazine, 1 March 2018.

13 Jugal Patel, 'After Sandy Hook more than 400 people have been shot in over 200 school shootings', *The New York Times*, 15 February 2018.

14 Ali Watkins, John Ismay, Thomas Gibbons-Neff, 'Once banned, now loved and loathed: How the AR-15 became "America's Rifle"', *The New York Times*, 3 March 2018.

15 Quoted in Emily Witt, 'How the survivors of Parkland founded the Never Again movement', *The New Yorker*, 19 February 2018.

16 Jaclyn Corin, 'I helped organise the March for Our Lives because there is strength in numbers', *Seventeen*, 21 March 2018.

17 Dave Cullen, 'Inside the secret meme lab designed to propel #NeverAgain beyond the march', *Vanity Fair*, 22 March 2018.

18 Corin, 'I helped organise the March for Our Lives'.

19 David Hogg, on CNN, 18 February 2018.

20 Quoted in Charlotte Atler, 'The school shooting generation has had enough', *TIME*, 22 March 2018.

21 Cullen, 'Inside the secret meme lab'.

22 *Generation Nation: Redefining America's Boomers, X-ers, Millennials and Gen Z in Post-Obama America*, Collaborata study, 2017.

23 Cameron Kasky on MSNBC, 14 March 2018.

24 Giuliana Matamoros and Lyliah Skinner, interviewed in 'Why they march: Four best friends from Parkland explain why the march matters to them', *New York* magazine video interview, accessed here: www.youtube.com/watch?list=PL4B448958847DA6FB&time_continue=1&v=0Eenp9fkf-k.

25 ibid.

26 Cameron Kasky, speech at March for Our Lives rally, Washington, DC, 24 March 2018.

27 Anna Rose, interview with author, Sydney, January 2018.

28 Amanda McKenzie, interview with author, Heron Island, September 2017.

11: SOS—Save Our Seas

1 Lucy Cormack, 'Climate-driven migration of tropical fish linked to underwater deforestation', *Sydney Morning Herald*, 9 July 2014.

2 C. Le Quéré et al., 'The global carbon budget 1959–2011', *Earth System Science Data*, vol. 5, , 2013, pp. 165–85.

3 Tim Flannery, *Atmosphere of Hope: Searching for solutions to the climate crisis*, Text Melbourne, 2015, pp. 35–6.

4   Kirsten Isensee & Louis Valdes, *Ocean Acidification*, Global Sustainable Development Report 2015 Brief, UNESCO, Paris, 2015.
5   Sophie Dove, presentation to group, Heron Island, September 2017.
6   David Helvarg, 'A wave of ocean activism to hit D.C.', *National Geographic* blog, 8 April 2017.
7   Quoted in Medhavi Arora, 'From filthy to fabulous: Mumbai beach undergoes dramatic makeover', CNN, 22 May 2017.
8   Afroz Shah, in a UN video interview recorded to celebrate his Champion of the Earth 2016 award, 2 February 2017, accessed here: www.youtube.com/watch?v=FnALkpJ89zo.
9   Ibid.
10 Tim Silverwood, interview with author, Sydney, January 2018.
11 Chris Tyree & Dan Morrison, 'Invisibles, the plastic inside us', *Orb Media*, September 2017.

12: The anti-plastics movement

1   David de Rothschild, speech at the Pop Tech 2010 conference, May 2011, accessed here: www.youtube.com/watch?v=ae3ka4Ze7zI.
2   Charles Moore, 'Trash revisited: Across the Pacific Ocean, plastics, plastics everywhere', *Natural History*, November 2003.
3   Charles Moore et al., 'A comparison of plastic and plankton in the North Pacific Central Gyre', *Marine Pollution Bulletin*, vol. 42, no. 12, December 2001, pp. 1297–300.
4   Quoted in Richard Grant, 'David de Rothschild interview: Adventure capital', *Telegraph* (UK), 7 April 2014.
5   David de Rothschild, 'The *Plastiki*', *The Wall Street Journal*, 23 January 2013.
6   Richard Grant, 'David de Rothschild interview: Adventure capital', *Telegraph* (UK), 7 April 2014.
7   Matthew Taylor, '$180bn investment in plastic factories feeds global packaging binge', *The Guardian*, 26 December 2017.
8   'ExxonMobil begins production on new polyethylene line at Mont Belvieu plastics plant', ExxonMobil press release, 17 October 2017, accessed here: news.exxonmobil.com/press-release/exxonmobil-begins-production-new-polyethylene-line-mont-belvieu-plastics-plant.
9   World Economic Forum, Ellen MacArthur Foundation and McKinsey & Company, *The New Plastics Economy: Rethinking the future of plastics*, 2016, accessed here: www.ellenmacarthurfoundation.org/publications.
10 Tim Silverwood, interview with author, Sydney, January 2018.
11 Tim Silverwood, 'Beach of shame', *Plastic Soup News*, 30 June 2011.
12 Tim Silverwood, 'Plastic Beach', *Coastalwatch.com*, 14 October 2011.
13 Rebecca Prinze-Ruiz, telephone interview with author, July 2017.

13: Zero waste

1   Erin Rhoads, interview with author, Melbourne, February 2018.

2   Vidhi Doshi, 'Burn it, dissolve it, eat it: Is the solution to India's waste problem in the bag?', *The Guardian*, 2 March 2016.
3   Paromita Shastri, 'Storm in a kulhar', *Outlook India*, 2 August 2004.
4   Akira Sakano, 'Zero waste: A way to enrich your life and the society', TEDxAPU, February 2017.
5   Quoted in Doroti Kiss, 'Life in a zero waste city: An interview with Akira Sakano', *Better World International* blog, 4 May 2016.
6   Quoted in Cherise Fong, 'Kamikatsu: The Japanese village of almost zero waste', *Makery*, 13 June 2017.
7   Ariana Schwartz, 'Zero waste FAQs', *Paris to Go* blog.
8   Béa Johnson on CNN, April 2012.
9   Isabelle Chapman, 'Zero waste isn't just for hippies anymore', CNN, 7 December 2017.
10 'Where are all the male zero wasters?' *Reddit*, accessed here: www.reddit.com/r/ZeroWaste/comments/6fve1d/where_are_all_the_male_zero_wasters/.
11 Bridget Brennan, 'Top 10 things everyone should know about women consumers', *Forbes*, 12 January 2015.
12 Kate Weiner, 'Low-waste living as activism', *Loam*, 7 December 2017.
13 Leilani Clark, 'Zero-waste bloggers: The millennials who can fit a year's worth of trash in a jar', *The Guardian*, 22 April 2016.
14 Adam Minter, *Junkyard Planet: Travels in the billion-dollar trash trade*, Kindle edition, Bloomsbury, New York, 2013, Kindle locations 220–1.
15 Ibid. Kindle locations 227–8.
16 Ibid. Kindle locations 132–4.

14: Let's build a tiny house!
1   Amanda Chapman, interview with author, Auckland, January 2018.
2   From 'Blasting through the past with architect and tiny house grandfather Lester Walker', *The Tiny House Podcast*, series 1, episode 26, no date.
3   Julie Lasky, 'The surprising origins of the tiny house phenomenon', *Curbed*, 13 July 2016.
4   Quotes from Henry D. Thoreau, *Walden*, accessed via the Thoreau Institute website, walden.org.
5   Adam Verwymeren, 'Interview with Jay Shafer', *Networx*, 2 January 2012.

15: Rejecting money
1   Quoted in Luke Cooper, 'Australians throw away nearly $10 billion in food waste each year', *Huffpost Australia*, 24 October 2017.
2   Luke Leitch, 'Anarchy in the UK: Vivienne Westwood's son Joe Corre burns $6 million of his punk archive in London', Vogue.com, 28 November 2016.
3   Gerrard Winstanley, *The True Levellers Standard Advanced*, 1649, accessed here: www.rogerlovejoy.co.uk/philosophy/diggers/diggers2.htm.
4   Excerpt from the film *Les Diggers des San Francisco*, accessed here: www.diggers.org/rap_on_free_store.htm.

5 Peter Coyote, 'Free frame of reference', petercoyote.com.
6 Jacques Fresco, *The Best that Money Can't Buy: Beyond politics, poverty and war*, Global Cyber-Visions, Venus, FL, 2002, p. 34.
7 Elie, 'Vicki Rovere's free store still a late night attraction on Ludlow after 15 years', *Bowery Boogie*, 21 May 2015.
8 Tracie McMillan, 'The new face of hunger', *National Geographic*, no date.
9 Andew Barker, interview with author, Adelaide, March 2018.
10 Quoted in Melissa Fyfe & Royce Miller, 'What they do to food', *The Age*, 9 June 2012.
11 Andrew Barker, 'Free food for all: Give what you can, take what you need', TEDxAdelaide, October 2017.

16: Consumerism gone mad
1 'Boxing Day shoppers queue from before dawn—only to find no sales', *ABC News Breakfast*, 26 December 2017, ABC TV, accessed here: www.abc.net.au/news/2017-12-26/boxing-day-sales-shoppers-find-no-discounts-after-queueing/9285680.
2 Larry Knight, 'Why holiday shopping is so important for the US economy', *CBS News*, 28 November 2016.
3 According to a 2018 creditcards.com survey, accessed here: www.creditcards.com/credit-card-news/debt-free-living-survey.php.
4 Australian Prudential Regulation Authority, *Quarterly Authorised Deposit-Taking Institution Property Exposures: September 2017*, APRA, Sydney, 2017.
5 KPMG, *The Truth about Online Consumers*, 2017 Global Online Consumer Report, KPMG, 2017, p .2.
6 George Monbiot, 'Materialism: a system that eats us from the inside out', *The Guardian*, 10 December 2013.
7 Ellen MacArthur Foundation, *A New Textiles Economy: Redesigning fashion's future*, Ellen MacArthur Foundation, 2017, p. 18.
8 Alden Wicker, 'Fast fashion is creating an environmental crisis', *Newsweek*, 1 September 2016.
9 Joseph Stiglitz, 'The great GDP swindle', *The Guardian*, 13 September 2009.
10 Jacinda Ardern speaking to *The Nation*, Three (NZ), 21 October 2017.
11 Richard Denniss, *Curing Affluenza*, Kindle edition, Black Inc., Melbourne, 2017, Kindle locations 679–81.
12 World Bank, *Poverty and Shared Prosperity 2016: Taking on inequality*, World Bank, Washington, DC, 2016, p. 1.
13 Ibid.
14 Deborah Hardoon, *An Economy for the 99%: It's time to build a human economy that benefits everyone, not just the privileged few*, Oxfam Briefing Paper, Oxford, January 2017.
15 Bill Gates, speaking to CNN, 18 February 2018.
16 Hardoon, *An Economy for the 99%*, p. 2.

17 Tim Jackson, speaking to Network of Wellbeing, accessed here: www.networkof wellbeing.org/index.php/videos/post/tim-jackson-a-wellbeing-economy-could-give-government-renewed-sense-of-purp.
18 Denniss, *Curing Affluenza*, Kindle locations 238–40.
19 Stiglitz, 'The great GDP swindle'.
20 Elisabeth Rosenthal, 'Your biggest carbon sin may be air travel', *The New York Times*, 26 January 2013.
21 Ellen MacArthur, 'The surprising thing I learned sailing solo around the world', TED2015, 29 June 2015.
22 Ellen MacArthur, interview with author, Copenhagen, May 2018.
23 Michael Braungart & William McDonough, *Cradle to Cradle: Remaking the way we make things*, Vintage, London, 2009, p. 26.
24 William McDonough, interview with author, Copenhagen, May 2018.
25 In April 2017, *The Third Industrial Revolution: A Radical New Sharing Economy* debuted as both a book and a film, produced by *Vice* and accessed here: /impact.vice.com/en_us/article/bj5zaq/watch-vices-new-documentary-the-third-industrial-revolution-a-radical-new-sharing-economy.
26 Ibid.

17: Meet the minimalists

1 Joshua Becker, becomingminimalist.com.
2 Leo Babauta, 'The minimalist question is the important thing', accessed here: mnmlist.com/question.
3 Richard Denniss, interview with author, Sydney, November 2017.
4 Joshua Fields Millburn & Ryan Nicodemus, 'Day 11: Trash', *Our 21-Day Journey into Minimalism*, accessed here: theminimalists.com.
5 Marie Kondo, *The Life-changing Magic of Tidying Up: The Japanese art of de-cluttering*, Ten Speed Press, Berkeley, Calif., 2014, pp. 1–2.

18: What's the alternative?

1 Kate Hall, interview with author, Auckland, January 2018.
2 According to 'Australian Attitudes to Composting and Recycling', a 2013 Closed Loop recycling survey.
3 Michael Reynolds quote from an interview with *The Good Stuff*, accessed here: www.youtube.com/watch?v=Xj5NO32ahB0&t=141s.
4 Lucy Aitken Read, interview with author, New Zealand, January 2018.

19: On mindfulness

1 Christine Wamsler, 'How mindfulness can help the shift towards a more sustainable society', *The Conversation*, 29 June 2017.

Acknowledgements

The idea for this book sparked at the Women's Marches but I wrote the first lines (with a little help from Laura Wells and a bottle of champagne) several months later on Heron Island. It was here, thanks to Clare Ainsworth Herschell, that I found my eco tribe and learned, from Tim Flannery and Sophie Dove, how climate change is impacting our oceans. I take ongoing inspiration from everyone in our group, especially Clare, Laura, Anna Rose, Julia Wheeler, Heidi Leffner, Jess Miller, Jess Scully, Jodi Pettersen, Tory Loudon and Jo and Joshua Yeldham.

The wonderful Emma Rusher at Melbourne University Press immediately understood what I had set out to achieve, and backed this book from the get-go. Her unfailing enthusiasm helped me beyond measure. Emma, you are the bee's knees. (Also, world, can we please save the bees?)

I am grateful to the team at MUP, and in particular to Sally Heath for her carefully considered and kindly delivered editorial guidance.

Thank you, my beloved husband for never complaining about a wife who spends weeks on end locked in her office, emerging only to ask what's for dinner, then scuttling back to eat and type alone. To all my friends who lent their ears and offered encouragement.

I am endlessly inspired by the ethical and sustainable fashion community, and to the Wardrobe Crisis podcast listeners for your stories, comments and support.

Last but by no means least, thank you to the change-makers who agreed to be interviewed or have your brains tapped for this book, some of you at very short notice over the Christmas holidays. Heartfelt thanks to: Lucy Aitken Read, Elena Antoniou, Andrew Barker, Kristian Barron, May Boeve, Orsola de Castro, Amanda Chapman, Sarah Corbett, Katherine Davis, Marina DeBris, Sarah Ditty, Joe Duggan, Betsy Greer, Kate Hall, Natalie Isaacs, Casey Jenkins, Kirsten Lee, Daisy Little, Sayraphim Lothian, Amanda McKenzie, Breanna Macpherson-Rice, Ellen McMahon, Elizabeth Morley, Tara Moss, Blair Palese, Kim Pearce, Rebecca Prince-Ruiz, Erin Rhoads, Timo Rissanen, Anna Rose, Cameron Russell, Harriet Spark, Tim Silverwood, Krista Suh, Carry Somers, Anne Summers, Amanda Tattersall, Valentina Zarew and Jayna Zweiman. This book is for you.

Index